ANDY CHRISTOPHER MILLER is a poet, author and psychologist. A winner of the Yeovil Poetry Prize, he has published book chapters, magazine and journal articles on topics as diverse as relationships, travel and mountaineering. His book, *The Naples of England* (2015), is a memoir of family, truth and secrets and what it was like to grow up in seaside Britain in the years following the Second World War. *The Ragged Weave of Yesterday* (2017) examines the psychology and practice of personal diary writing. *Never: A Word* (2021) is a novel looking at the impact of family secrets across three generations of women and *Way To The West* (2023), combines original watercolours of the west of Cornwall by Vally Miller with matching poetry from Andy.

He has served as an Honorary Professor at the Universities of both Nottingham and Warwick and published ten books in this capacity. He was also the first recipient of the British Psychological Society's award for Distinguished Contribution to Educational and Child Psychology.

Praise for Andy Christopher Miller's writing

'... the best writing I've read for ages ... climbs through the important things in life' Prof Terry Gifford, Director, International Festival of Mountaineering Literature

'... may already be a collector's item ... for there is a breath of humanity in this book' Ed Drummond, Poet, activist and legendary British rock climber

'... a wonderful book ... anyone yet to read it has a real treat in store' John Lindley, Poet Laureate for Cheshire & Manchester Cathedral Poet

'...a distinctive voice' Daisy Goodwin, Poet, television writer ('Victoria') and Yeovil Literary Prize judge

'... can shift from lovingly recalled detail to moments of powerful experience' Tony Jones, Winner for best radio drama, Writers Guild of Great Britain

'... the writing is lovely; lyrical, subtle, original and surprising' Chris Thompson, Radio and television writer ('The Archers', 'Heartbeat', 'Emmerdale')

'... moving, funny and compelling' Megan Taylor, Author, 'The Lives Of Ghosts'

'... vivid and touching' Frances Thimann, Author, 'November Wedding'

'... an honest author' Judi Moore, Author, 'Little Mouse'

'... pulses with life and energy' Aly Stoneman, Left Lion, Nottingham

'... an intimate and immensely readable book' Dr Phil Stringer, University College London

'... self-effacing, honest and with a gentle humour' Prof Tim Crook, Goldsmiths, University of London

'... powerfully moving' Dr Nathan Lambert, University of Nottingham

A YEAR ON THE ETHELS
A LIFE IN THE HILLS

A Life in the Hills (Contents).	5
Ethels Introduction (Day 1).	9
Ethels Early Days (Days 2 – 3)	19
Autumn Ethels (Days 4 – 11)	37
Winter Ethels (Days 12 – 33)	99
Spring Ethels (Days 34 – 44)	161
Summer Ethels (Days 45 – 54)	235
Final Stretch (Day 55)	317
Ethels Index	330
Acknowledgements	332

Independently Published
68 The Dale
Wirksworth
Derbyshire
DE4 4EJ

All rights reserved. No part of this book may be reproduced in any form without the written permission of the publisher

Andy Christopher Miller 2025

ALL PROFITS FROM THE SALE OF THIS BOOK WILL BE DONATED TO THE COUNCIL FOR THE PROTECTION OF RURAL ENGLAND, PEAK DISTRICT AND SOUTH YORKSHIRE

www.andycmiller.co.uk

A LIFE ON THE HILLS

CONTENTS

Introduction 1963 Dartmoor, *13*
1963 Lulworth Cove, *22*
1964 Lessons from Lliwedd, *28*

1960s 1967 Froggatt Edge, *57*
1967 How Hard is Mild Severe? *62*
1967 Williams' Barn, *64*
1967 Shadrack, *68*
1967 A Firm Constitution, *73*
1967 Glencoe, *77*
1967 Saturday Night & Sunday Morning, *82*
1968 West Penwith, *87*
1969 The Word on the Cliff, *91*
1969 Carnedd Llewelyn, *95*

1970s 1971 First Alp, *139*
1972 Skye, *142*
1971 The Cairngorm Tragedy, *145*
1974 Reassembled in Iran, *148*
1977 Friends Like These, *151*
1978 Yarncliffe Quarry, *154*
1979 Renaissance in the Lakes, *157*

1980s 1980 Buxton, *181*
1982 Abbey Brook, *186*
1985 Hanging in the Balance, *191*
1986 Eldorado Canyon, *196*
1986 Longs Peak, *200*
1988 Christmas on the Rocks, *208*

              1988 The Annapurna Circuit, *212*
              1988 Jomsom, *218*
              1989 Tour de Mont Blanc, *220*
              1989 A Taste of Life, *230*

1990s &   1990 Dovedale, *259*
Beyond   1990 Mount Whitney, *262*
              1990 Tuolomne Meadows, *268*
              1992 Grand Combin, *273*
              1992 High Tor, *279*
              1997 Dinas Mot, *284*
              2000 Tour de Monte Rosa, *288*
              2012 Over the Moors, *299*
              2012 Tall Ship, *293*
              2016 Visited upon the Sons, *301*

Finishing 2016 Refresher Session, *311*
stretch

Addendum (1946 – 2017) Andy Handford, *323*
              (1944 – 2018) Mark Vallance, *326*

INTRODUCTION

Ethels Day 1 – 31st August

West Nab, Black Hill & White Low

We're away from home early. It's an adventure.
A café in Holmfirth and we're their first customers. Then, the road, a long steep pull out of town, up onto the high ground where I don't know exactly what to expect.
Moorland, yes. Open, empty ground, yes.
Heather and cotton grass, probably. Bilberry.
Sphagnum moss, a possibility.
So, I do know almost exactly what to expect.
Except, I do not know these different skylines with their unanticipated dips and rises, their shadows, this new complexity of distances. There are dwellings in the valleys, whole villages and sombre towns down below. Self-contained, isolated buildings perched on scarps or sunk deep in defiles.
The draw of the unfamiliar, miles and miles of it, quickens the blood.
The map indicates that West Nab is only a short climb from the road but the track, or any feasible route, takes a bit of finding as we are straight away floundering among tall tussocks and rough boggy ground. Already the prospect of completing ninety-five such tops, the 'Ethels', within one year seems like a ridiculously vainglorious ambition.
After a few false starts, better sense prevails. We give the map more attention, focus on its details – wall ends, contours – and are soon at the summit. But 'summit', 'prominence', even 'top', are fluid terms here and can slide around in interpretation.
In 2021, the Council for the Protection of Rural England designated ninety-five hills in the Peak District as 'Ethels', in tribute to the pioneering environmentalist, Ethel Haythornthwaite who founded the charity in 1924

at the age of twenty-two and after the death of her husband in the First World War.

Apart from the trig point, West Nab has no dramatically significant distinguishing features. Just rounded gritstone boulders and patches of sand ground down by wind and the unending persistence of millennia. And the occasional attentions of sheep.

This is the first of my ninety-five and yet how fitting. The Pennine anonymity invites reflection, its understated nature suits perfectly the steady plod. Past and present can disappear into each other across extended but muted vistas.

A brief trek along the road and we are then on the Pennine Way. It is new terrain for me, solidly constructed gates, fresh timber worked with pride. Beneath us, substantial slabs to aid the walking. Once, I had railed against this interference with the landscape, this intrusion into an 'unspoilt' vastness. Now, with erosion mainly contained, the benefits are obvious. The rectangular stones are cut with their striations, their grain, prominent and echoing the lay of the region.

What youthful pomposity I had shown. Much older now, I have less energy for taking stances, 'principled' or otherwise. One step in front of the other, drop the pace for the inclines, use the stick and increased concentration on the descents. Let the thoughts do as they may.

At Black Hill, we have pulled ourselves up to one of the highest points in the Peak District, Derbyshire's lonely northern outpost. When travelling the Pennine Way from Edale, its starting point in the south, the walker must cross Kinder Scout, Bleaklow and then Black Hill. These three massifs demonstrate the top heavy, serious character of Derbyshire in its furthest territories. Far away are the picturesque villages with their duck ponds and tea shops, their stately homes and tourist hordes.

The mist blows wet. Away to the south and west the rain can be seen, progressing. We attempt to judge its course, rearrange our rucksacks while seated on the ground eating lunch, make decisions about extra layers and waterproofs. A few other walkers arrive at the trig point expressing satisfaction, relief, accomplishment, unsure about ceremonies.

From here, we leave the Way for what feels like a long, liberating walk to the south, one eye on the map and compass, one eye on the ground beneath our feet, and our third eye on the weather. The exact location of White Moss requires outdoor detective work over spongey terrain, a combination of the exact coordinates and the altitude. A little to the left, two steps to the right, one more and that's as near as dammit. Has anybody else ever visited this precise spot, felt this very same sense of silly, springy satisfaction?

The way back is known, the long trek requires no thought, only movement. The conversation requires no response, only acknowledgement. The minutes becomes hours, the afternoon stretches to its limit.

And then, nearing the road, we see the people. Youngsters spread out on the opposite hillside, beating. Birds clattering into the sky. A keeper, red-faced and ruddy, thrashing through the heather.

'You lot ought to have more sense', spittle flecking during his self-important hectoring.

'And you lot – 'we begin to shout back, as the heads pop up from behind the bunkers. The sky is filled with whirring birds, the birds are filled with panic. The afternoon is filled with urgency, death and feathers.

'Pass by, my gun is broken!' barks a young man in tweed and cap seated behind a butt. His lady companion, in headscarf and sunglasses, stares out, disdainful and silent.

'You should be ashamed of yourselves!' I later think to shout back. Instead, there and then, my plodding meditation shattered, I manage only the gruffly surly and inarticulate.

I am an old-age pensioner, in my mid-seventies, with a respectable career behind me.

How have I come to be hurling insults, inchoate rage, at a pillar – a bean pole – of the British establishment?

How has it come to this?

1964. Dartmoor

We had hitched in pairs and successfully met up again in Buckfastleigh without major delays to our planned schedule. Of the four of us, I was perhaps the most apprehensive about the long, uphill haul ahead. We were to follow the lane for more than a mile before striking out on our first taste of this open country. The borrowed army boots, firmly laced, welded my toes into a solid unit and, as I swung the rucksack up onto my back, the attached billy cans jangled.

Dick consulted his map and remained tight-lipped in response to my queries.

'It's looks as if ...' he said at last, before frowning and then turning the map through ninety degrees.

'We should be able to .... yes ... yes, that's okay ... now, keep together!'

And away he strode, his long legs stretching out and his chin raised and set for the top.

'Follow my pace!'

At my grammar school the notion of 'being officer material' was much discussed and speculated upon. Its definition seemed elusive but it could, I learned, be readily identified and with a high degree of certainly. Some possessed it and others did not. It was clearly closely related to the concept of 'leadership potential'. And, although never formally stated, I knew that these were alien to me, to my nature, to my type even, whatever all those notions really meant.

I knew that I was never destined to be an 'officer' and was more than content with that. But, at the same time, I was equally unwilling and unprepared to be one of 'the men'.

We were all red-faced and breathing more heavily by the top of the hill as that early September afternoon began to shed its summer shift and reach for the cloak of autumn.

My first steps across the moor, after all the weeks of lurid anticipation, were remarkably mundane. The ground was solid and passable. There was no quicksand or bog. Adders, intertwined and pulsing in their dozens, were nowhere to seen. The huge horizon refrained from crushing all hope with its distance and absence. The empty, cooling sky looked down without hostility.

We walked for a couple of hours, up to a lofty tor, down into tiny valleys where small streams mingled playfully. My awkward load pulled at my shoulders, unsteadying my gait at times, and my calves and thighs registered unfamiliar aches in response to the clambering over rough, undulating terrain.

At our first chosen camping spot, a flattened, riverside patch big enough for our two tents, Dick instructed us in the basics of camp management. Boiling water to drink. Yes. Keeping mud and damp outside sleeping quarters. Check. Digging a hole for ablutions and the subsequent careful burying. Hmm. I wondered whether I could possibly hold on for three whole days?

But the food tasted wonderful, fried and burnt and scraped though it was. And the mysterious atmosphere inside the tent, the strangely filtered light as the day died away and the musty smell familiar from childhood games, electrified me. And I lay awake for a long time listening to the conspiratorial babbling of the stream, half imagining that Hunt's Everest expedition had included me after all, half terrified of what might be moving about, unhindered and undetected, in that darkest of wildernesses outside.

The next day passed in similar fashion, fresh views of new stretches of moor, the long, slow rise up to tors, those solitary fortresses guarding yet more new perspectives. Our loads, blisters and the uncertain footings threatened to take away some of the pleasure.

The recurring sense of our distance from the ordinary and everyday then replenished it.

And on our third and final day, as tiredness was dampening down the wonder of it all, our plodding silence was shattered by a startling occurrence. Up from the heather, absurdly but effectively camouflaged, a solider, a young man as if from a comic or a film. A young man, little older than us, with a rifle.

'Halt! Stay where you are! Where have you come from?

'Where have we – ?'

'Have you seen anybody, any other soldiers?'

I spluttered, both surprised and indignant. And I watched the rifle.

Dick was more articulate, more compliant, lifting up his map and offering the precise location of our previous night's camp.

'You'd better come with me', he said. Or did he order?

He gestured with his rifle butt for us to follow him up the next hillside and walked beside us, half guiding us and half implying that we should consider ourselves somehow arrested.

At the top, among rocks piled like giant loaves and lopsided pancakes, was a small group of equally young soldiers squatting down out of a wind that blew about the tor. A wind that must also be bringing down the body temperature of the young man stripped to his underpants and with arms wide apart strapped to the highest of the boulders.

'Don't mind him,' said the slightly older and presumably senior member of the squad. 'He'll talk sooner or later'.

Somehow the prisoner did not seem too anguished. Somehow this embodiment of officer material did not seem too authoritative. Out here, far from habitation, were the games of my childhood being re-enacted on a grander scale. With uniforms. And with real guns.

15

We played our parts with varying degrees of seriousness and commitment. Dick colluded with factual answers to their questions while I struggled to find clever and convincing terms in which to convey my disdain. Struggled and failed.

We were released, allowed on our way, unsure whether to say 'thank you' or not, but persuaded that a parting protest would be unwise.

And so, my first experience of Dartmoor, of trudging across empty land and camping in the deep, dark folds of night, came to an end.

There were tales to tell, ones that would grow in the telling.

A hankering for bigger, bolder adventures.

EARLY DAYS

Ethels Day 2 – 8th September

Ramshaw Rocks, The Roaches & Hen Cloud

I am almost giddy with excitement, parking on the lane alongside Ramshaw Rocks. It's September. The sky is intensely blue and the sun fierce and determined. I can see the rough land falling away and then rising up towards the haphazard ridge of Hen Cloud and, further west, the Roaches.

The spikes and other contortions of Ramshaw are only steps away, five minutes at the most, but in my eagerness, I forget one thing after another – lunch, walking pole – and have to retrace the first thirty or so yards back to the car a number of times. And then once more to check that I have indeed locked it.

Ah these rocks! Among all the weathered gritstone creations across the Peak District, these still stand out as special. They belong not just to a different, pre-human age but to epochs before life, before consciousness, before the something that we once were struggled out from the sea. They must have terrified and enticed our earliest ancestors in equal measure and they do so still. Despite our speeding cars, our lofty aeroplanes and our shiny, desperate superficiality.

'Look on my works, ye mighty, and despair!'

A little care is needed. Time to steady up and stop tripping over myself. I must calm down before peering over this black, scaley ridge onto the main road below. I am chattering away, singing even, and telling myself that I am still here, still as in love with this place as ever, having first sensed the awe that hovers here when I lived in Buxton in the early 1980s.

My walk of seven miles or so is spread beneath and around me, Nature's cartography open to view and devoid of any shady respite from the sun. Some of the paths, tracks and lanes will be new to my tread but the circuit overall is familiar.

Trudging up the lane towards Roache End, slowed by the heavy heat, I meet a man of about my age weaving an idle course on an electric bike.

We both seem to welcome the opportunity for conversation, and he tells me that he and his wife have lived on a narrow boat since 1981.

'It was Thatcher and all that, finally did it'.

He has just popped out to do some shopping in Leek but has somehow found himself taking a turn up around the Roaches. Over the hills and far away. As oft times before.

This is no idle ramble and by the crest of the Roaches, I have aches in my calves and thighs. The magnificent spread of Cheshire that now appears is restorative though, a natural anaesthetic. The mighty ramparts of these Staffordshire edges stand defiantly above the cultivation below, rich and nourishing in their own way. From these tops, in my climbing heyday, I have surrendered to fiery sunsets and marvelled at this huge western sky, framed by rock towers and encyclopaedic in scope.

But today it is the risk of dehydrated mirage, of shimmering perspectives and misplaced feet. On across the sloping slabs, past pools where spirits dance when we are all at bed. Hen Cloud is ahead proudly asserting its independence, its solid constitution, its subservience to none.

From its magnificent top, I can see my car, a tiny red dot between the bracken and the sky. But the map shows a tangle of ill-defined paths, a lack of definition at crucial points, a sense that not everywhere has yet been finely and finally pinned down, brought fully to order.

Or maybe, in my tiredness, my focus has slipped.

I decide to plunge down through the heather into the trees, hoping the feint path just visible on the map will materialise or that others will have trodden a way. But neither happen. Still working my way downwards, I wade through nettles making for the stream in the valley bottom. Again, my hunches let me down and the water is too wide and too deep to cross, and I return to the nettles and stumble along the course of the stream until I reach barbed wire. I surmount this carefully and then a bridge across the water.

My car is no longer visible from this small sunken valley and there is much rough ground still to navigate. Brambles, nettles, long grass, steep dips, water. Walls and more barbed wire. I fall from a style when my knee gives way and lie winded on the ground, the nettles stings now at full volume as a sense of futility threatens to scoop me up and carry me away.

The car reappears, now no more than half a mile away, but attainable only by means of an unrelenting uphill trudge through heather that is growing over deadly, invisible rocks.

In a state of growing weariness, I try to remind myself of my love for this place. I try to rekindle that affection, feel it more intensely despite the sunburn, cuts and stings. Despite the seeming impossibility of ever reaching the car.

Love hurts.

I have been here before.

I have always returned.

1963. Lulworth Cove

Hanging around with a clergyman.

My parents heartily approved.

Such a positive change from hanging around the pinball tables down at the fair. And such a change in role models, from motorbike heroes who were idolised by the girls lined up around the jukebox alcove where the music and the big dipper overhead shook the walls and boards beneath their feet. From these leather-clad, exploding stars to a man of the cloth.

I trusted Bob. Or, at least, I tried to as he attempted to assure me that the climb down from the top of the cliff was nothing to worry about if taken carefully. My school friend, Martin, had summoned the requisite confidence and begun to pick his way down but I stood frozen with fear some forty or fifty sickening feet above a murmuring, predatory sea.

'We'll put a rope on you and you'll be alright,' said Bob. 'Just watch where you are placing your feet and take your time'.

And somehow, with the firm anchor of the rope around my waist barely allowing me to step down at all, I managed to work my way to the small ledge just above the water where Martin was waiting. Bob joined us with swift, fluent movements as if on some vertical obstacle course that had long since become second nature, requiring only the minimum of his attention. Here we roped up for our first proper rock climb. And here, with a sea of unknown depth just beneath our feet, Bob instructed us in matters of the waist belay and bowline, the three points of contact, the careful footwork and the superiority of balance over brute strength.

I had joined the church youth club not to find God but to meet girls when it had become clear that those at the fair would forever be beyond my reach. At around half past eight on Saturday evenings, Bob, the young curate who ran the club, began scraping the wooden chairs back into rows, barring the clanking, heavy exit door with no more than a keen eye and a chilling charm. The tap and cluck from the table tennis room died away and we sat, avoiding his glance, beneath the buzz of a yellow strip light while Bob dispensed spiritual guidance for the regulation fifteen minutes.

Wearingly familiar Bible stories gained some lift from Bob's dispensation. Frank had been coming to know the Lord, he told us, he really had, in the days before his powerful Norton roared from the road, splintering a row of fence posts before its fatal impact with the telegraph pole.

And on the evening when the snooker tables crashed onto their sides and the billiard balls ricocheted and whined against the tiled walls and flagstone floors, Bob strode between them parting the sea of missiles. He halted hostilities by dragging out a large, dusty gymnasium mat, as brown and bristly as a fox.

'Queensberry rules chaps. No punching or biting, no knees and no hitting below the belt'.

First, he took on one ringleader, circling in an almost polite fashion until the first engagement, before the assault on balance, the thud of bodies against the floor. The assertion of strength and the weakening in one shoulder and then the other. Afterwards, blood, sweat, spittle and torn clothes, with Bob extending a handshake, wiping his mouth and then turning to repeat his challenge to the leader of the opposite gang.

No milk and water respectability this. No Holy Joe, genteel and practiced among his catechisms.

Bob's curriculum vitae was transcribed directly from the adventure stories of my childhood – public school, Cambridge, the Marines, with whom he had crossed the Sahara and become a rock climber and mountaineer.

Divinity college. Not one glimpse of any such experiences in my years growing up on the Westham estate.

He sparred, to my delight, in the correspondence columns of the local paper with Mr Plant, the local coast guard:

> *sheer irresponsibility, treacherous terrain, endangering others*

versus

> *the spiritual need for unimpeded adventure, the full exploration of one's limits*

The thrill of debate, the ripostes and the counterarguments

> *over-stretched rescue services, the duty to set an example*

clashing directly with

> *teamwork, skills acquired during disciplined apprenticeships, the testing of character*

I had always avoided clubs and organisations designed to deliver a disciplined experience of adventure to young people. The enthusiasts for the Scouts I had known in my younger years seemed most often to be the boys with a profligate strength, the fighters. The later enthusiasts for the Duke of Edinburgh award, on the other hand, were the supporters of order and leadership, of Queen, country and the responsibly constructed outdoor latrine. But whatever it was that made me wary and suspicious did not apply out here on the cliffs. Standing with Martin on that small ledge above a sullen sea, with no escape but upwards, I could hear Bob above us hammering in a piton that would provide a secure anchor for the three of us, his voice booming in full song and the blows of metal on metal providing cold chinks of accompaniment.

'For – those – in – *thwack* – per – il – *thwack* – on – the – *thwack* – sea'.

Here was adventure devoid of the smothering oversight

of institutions.
No packs, no troops, no gangs.
High stakes on walls of untouched, sea-scoured limestone.
No hierarchies, no accrediting bodies.
The only disciplinary forces, God and gravity.

Ethels Day 3 – 14th September

The Cloud, Croker Hill & Gun

The forecast is for heavy rain all day and we are scheduled for the most westerly of the Ethels. With waterproofs, a car, and easy recourse to the coffee shops of Congleton or Leek if absolutely necessary (and if not necessary at all), we decide to keep our commitment. This outing is very different in scale and scope from the previous two 'bigger' days. Instead of long walks, rough terrain, isolated tops, there is a pattern of drive, park, climb, repeat.

There is a much-used path from a council car park up through trees to the top of The Cloud, from where we can look down onto Congleton and beyond to flatter land setting a course for border country, for Wales, Snowdon. The Gritstone Way and the Staffordshire Way both cross here, a meeting of the Ways and when two women walkers also arrive, we have a meeting of minds as well. The rain is holding off, but the sky's serious countenance suggests that we should not linger for too long.

Careful map work is required but not for the hills. For the tight roads and lanes as we attempt to find a pull off place for the car. Our next destination is Croker Hill, just above the Sutton Common telecommunications tower, which dominates this area. The mast, encrusted with satellite dishes and laced with metal ledges and ladders, scoffs at the natural world. Bland buildings, exuding the creepy control of officialdom, are surrounded by security fencing topped with barbed wire. If not destruction, this is certainly construction and with an intercontinental reach.

We find a farm track where we can leave the car out of the way and cross a few fields that have been halfheartedly given over to farming, to stand beneath the tower and to search around behind for the hill's very highest point.

Then, once again, we are navigating new lanes and roads to find the public car park up on Gun Moor. From here, and with the minimum of ascent, we follow a track through the heather for only a few minutes to arrive at the trig point. Hardly a hill climb, more a dog walker's stroll but the reward is immense – a full panorama of the Peak District's western rim!

I have never realised that so many areas could be viewed from one place. There, that must be the Roaches way over there but from a totally new angle. With Hen Cloud even further back. Sweeping northwards, there's Shining Tor, joining the pantheon. But that still accounts for only half of this unique spread. Way, way further north there is the bulk of Kinder with its many facets, barely distinguishable from each other now from this perspective. And, further still, that cannot possibly be the edge of Bleaklow, can it, muscling into this montage, this never-before-seen amalgamation of so many separate days' outings and journeys?

Not insignificant, Gun, not at all. Instead, it is a mighty viewpoint masked and anonymous by virtue of its very modesty.

1964. Lessons from Lliwedd

I only climbed one more time at Lulworth Cove with Bob but, when he turned his explorations to nearby Portland instead, it became far easier to grab a few routes there of a Saturday afternoon or even a weekday evening after school.

Although my parents continued to approve of my spending time with a pillar of the establishment, they baulked a little when Bob, waiting for me once, jokily began to climb the lamp post just across the road from our house. Somehow, behaviour that would be frowned upon if carried out by one of the ne'er-do-wells from our estate, had to be tolerated as an eccentricity on this occasion. Another time, my friends and I watched Joe Brown making a televised rock-climbing ascent from Bob's bedsit while we waited for him to return from officiating at a wedding. He rushed into the room and vaulted over the sofa in his cassock only to reappear in seconds in old shirt and track suit bottoms, ready for the limestone. This juxtaposition of the conventional and respectable with the daring and iconoclastic, absurdist almost in nature, suited well my adolescent self, searching for a way to be in the world.

Still does, really.

Hospital visiting, weddings and a subsidiary role at evening service were, however, insufficient to keep Bob in Weymouth and he was away within a year or so to the new challenge of running a Boys Club in Bermondsey. A year later, aged seventeen, my friend and I hitched there during our Easter holiday. In an empty light early the next morning, the city already in motion along its streets and river, we each requisitioned a best fit set of equipment from the club's storeroom – boots, anorak, sleeping bag and inflatable mattress – and set the compass for the North up the recently opened M1, the furthest in that direction ever for me.

Running in his new yellow Ford Anglia at speeds never more than forty miles an hour, we were heading into thinly sketched mountain marvels. The fourth member of our party was Eric, a young man probably no more than ten years our senior, whom Bob had first met as a regular inmate on his rounds of visiting at Dorchester prison.

After a whole day, we arrived in Snowdonia. Driving through the Nant Ffrancon Pass, looking for the track down to our barn, massive hillsides rose in slides of scree above the road. Buttresses of the deepest Celtic green, rough ground tumbling out of the mist and down to the valley floor, these were landscapes beyond anything I had ever imagined. Our base – our lives – for the next week.

Eric's eyes followed another waterfall upwards, its source hidden in the sky.

'Thuck-in nell, Bob. Look at those bath-tuds'.

Silence from the driver. Mortification from the other passengers.

'Caw, thuck me!'

'Eric!'

'Nnn?'

'The ears, Eric. Getting a little red'.

'What? Oh! Oh, thuckin nell, Bob. Thorry'.

All week heavy mist, cloud and rain dominated the valley. Each morning this weather paraded insolently between the isolated farm dwellings and the bluffs of inhospitable ground. In the barn, we attempted to prepare meals over primus stoves, the smell of the meths never completely absent, the pans never fully free from the burned-on remnants of our previous efforts. Bob modelled orderly living among the privations. Each evening, after soakings and exhaustion on the hills, he led a brief session of prayers accompanied by mugs of cocoa. Nobody dared raise the possibility of a lift to the village pub.

On our final day, we attempted a route on Lliwedd, a mountain composed of north-facing cliffs and buttresses. Some years later, when I met a wider circle of contemporary climbers, I learned that this colossal arena had been all but abandoned by modern climbers because of its lonely, inhospitable aspect and its loose rock. Because all my previous climbing had been on new, unexplored cliffs, I had not realised that cliffs had a history, that their many routes had usually been pioneered in earlier days, described, graded and committed to the pages of guidebooks. This, the earliest stage of my mountaineering education, comprised of Bob supplementing our daily experiences out on those inhospitable cliffs with stirring tales of the generation of pioneers from the 1920s and 1930s. Men with an almost vanished ethic of privation and hardship.

So, on that final day on Lliwedd, we were two or three rope lengths up the route, about two hundred and fifty feet, and I was standing alone in snow left over from the winter on a tiny ledge, when the exposure took its grip on me. To either side, un-climbable walls thinning out into nothingness. The line by which we had just ascended disappeared quickly into cloud beneath our feet. Improbably steep rock above looked just passable, at least for the few feet into which visibility extended. As soon as somebody climbed into the mist, their voice was snatched away by the sideways buffeting of the wind. Out of contact, except for the wet rope around my back and wrists, the void in front and beneath, the hopeless features of the rock walls all around, I was trapped on this tiny, snowbound stance.

As my turn to climb again arrived, my resolution dissolved into the icy indifference of the landscape, the dripping rock pillars, the patches of stale snow, the grey tumult above, below and to my sides. There was the best part of another thousand feet of this, of continuing upwards, further and further from safe, solid ground. I was already shaking, with the needles of cold probing every point of entry into my clothing, shivering at the lost hope of ever feeling safe again. Part of me wanted to jump, to untie my waist belay and cast free, to end the accumulating sense of hopelessness. Part wanted to blame Bob or kick at the rock and withered heather. I could only just bite back the adolescent howl that said I wanted to end it all, a howl that nobody would hear.

When I reached Bob he was hunched up against the weather, bringing in the rope, and still smiling.

'I'm sorry, Bob. I can't .... I just don't think I can ...'

'Don't worry, Andy,' he shouted against the wind, although he was only a couple of feet from me on our tiny belay ledge.

'You can do it. God loves you'.

But we did then retreat, when Bob had had a little more time in which to gauge the depth of my despair. I was held on a tight rope as I tried to climb down the way we had come. The day had ended in failure and not that long after it had begun. My hopes of a possible future as a rugged mountaineer had fallen and been dashed on the ground below.

*

It was the day after my humbling on Lliwedd, and uncertainty and misery were not yet finished with me.

A combination of luck and, well, more luck had gifted me lifts all the way down through the border counties on an exciting tour of these unfamiliar areas. But with evening drawing in, the empty road on the south side of Shepton Mallet was indifferent to my plight.

I had always enjoyed the unpredictability of throwing myself onto the chance generosity of strangers, in what I took to be the Zen-like practice of surrendering to fate, and this had served me well enough. However, pitifully few cars were passing, and those that were seemed decidedly averse to picking up wet, dishevelled individuals on a rapidly darkening country road.

I tried to marshal my thoughts, weigh my options, but instead the waves of self-pity that I thought had been left high on the north face of Lliwedd, swamped my attempts at rationality. The hedgerow still retained patches of snow and I knew that my inadequate clothes and the absence of any remaining sense of adventure made me very ill-suited to a rainy night spent shivering and frightened in the corner of some field. My parents, some fifty country miles or so away, did not possess a telephone and knew nobody who did. They did not possess a car and knew nobody etcetera. Anyway, I believed myself ferociously independent of them in my Kerouac-like lonesome travelling. With only pennies in my pocket, I did wonder whether Shepton Mallet had a Salvation Army hostel, of the sort I had read about in George Orwell's book but somehow doubted it. There was nobody around to ask. Hitchhiker mythology, of which I was an ardent imbiber, had it that police stations might allow a

stranded traveller to sleep in an empty cell. I went seeking the kindly arm of the law. A lone person back in the deserted town gave me directions but the police station was closed with a notice directing anybody in an emergency to contact Wells on a provided number.

I knew that my emergency could not count as one of theirs.

I also knew that any slim chance of a lift had now been fully snuffed out by the cold, black night weaving its way through the streets of the town, holding me in its fiercest grip. A lone church bell tolling somewhere and breaking the otherwise silent night, added to the weight of despair pressing down on me.

A church bell!

Churches were left open at nights. I could follow the sound, feel sanctuary and reassurance drawing closer with each step. A pew, a cassock for a pillow, shelter from an ill-intentioned night.

The heavy door creaked open. Instead of silence though, a service with a small congregation was in progress. Muted voices, soothing incantations rising into the high arches above. I lowered my rucksack onto the nearest bench, eased myself down, tightly cloaked in supplication, and waited for the ceremony to finish so that I could seek permission to sleep there.

When the congregation did disperse, I shuffled towards the vicar and the request I had been formulating, words suffused with extreme humility and gratitude, tumbled incoherently instead from my lips. An older couple caught some of what I said and must have read my intention, because they turned back up the aisle.

'What's the matter, Father? Can we be of help?'

I explained my predicament again, still at an excited gabble, and expressed the profound appreciation that would accompany any permission to sleep in the church that night.

'He can come with us. It's no trouble. Both boys are away. We have a spare bed for him'.

And so, I sank into the leather upholstery of the back seat of their car, giddy with the odour of luxury, as we drove silently and smoothly through streets that had seemed so inhospitable, had cared so little for me, only a short while before. Their house was a long single-storey building, entered through a sturdy front door that was illuminated by a porch light. Mats covered an uneven stone floor in the hallway and I noticed some of the framed photographs on the walls - productions of Gilbert and Sullivan, young men in rugby kit, another in an army officer's uniform. They showed me into a large and comfortable dining room, the like of which I had occasionally seen on television and in films.

'I'll get you some pyjamas. Gavin's should just about fit you and I'll bet you would like a bath wouldn't you?' said the woman, this woman who was easily the kindest I had ever met. I mumbled my agreement and then she offered to wash my clothes while I was submerged in the suds.

'I can pop them in the dryer afterwards and they will be ready for you in the morning. Have you got anything else there in that knapsack of yours needing washing?'

And so began an evening dressed in over-sized and heavily laundered pyjamas and swaddled in an enveloping dressing gown. We ate at the large table, comfortably conversing about Iolanthe and The Gondoliers, mountains and adventure, and their sons, one at university and one in the army. I kept my insistent atheism well in check but, despite the manner of our meeting, religion never surfaced. I could not decide whether I had been hopelessly ill-prepared or tailored precisely for such an evening by my grammar school, or my father's values or by life on our council estate. But I could recognize without question the security, the kindness and the generosity that had come my way that evening.

I slept soundly, for the first time since before my week on the freezing, concrete floor of the barn. I could wish to stay beneath the starched sheets, weighted down beneath that heavy stack of blankets, stay for as long as possible. But a new sun full of optimism was above the horizon, the Spring had arrived unexpectedly with full flourish and there was the smell of a breakfast frying. My clothes, no longer tattered and somehow no longer threadbare, had been ironed and were folded on a chair outside my door. The breakfast on a patterned plate completed the whole experience.

The unbelievable experience of acceptance, shelter and nurture. The contrast with Llewedd and the barn's chastening challenges to character. Life lessons that could never be bettered, that would never leave me.

I was driven the short distance to my hitch-hiking spot from the evening before. The road was no longer hostile and dismal. I extended my thumb joyously. The sun's warmth penetrated my clothes.

The first car stopped, and a quick succession of lifts had me deposited home on Weymouth sea front before the early brilliance of the morning had fully burned away from the surface of the sea.

THE ETHELS – AUTUMN

Ethels Day 4 – 19th September

Harborough Rocks

It is a beautiful late summer's day and we have a desire to be mobile.

We walk the High Peak Trail with crunchy cinders underfoot. Along cuttings blasted by navigators, through Hopton Tunnel where the darkness becomes almost absolute before the light from the further arch grows larger and more warming. Up the incline with its steady, perfectly proportioned rise. And all the while alert to the sound of approaching bikes, sharing the pleasure of being here with others through surreptitious smiles and brief exchanges.

Once wagons full of rock and ore, provisions, or farm produce clanked along this line. The rough mechanics of chain, track and winch engineered huge loads across these heights. A whole supply line driven by steam across the mighty bulk of the Southern Pennines.

Today, instead of industrial and commercial loads, it carries people released from labour, the casual and the determined. At our destination and on one side of the track, a cement works that hums with activity day and night. Screening off its activities behind windowless green walls feels like an admission of its intrusiveness, of its still ravenous industrial appetite. On the other side, however, a landscape seeking peace, the dolomitic limestone towers and pinnacles of Harborough Rocks.

Miniscule compared to their Italian namesakes, these rocks nonetheless present a striking contrast in form and aspect to the White Peak's other carboniferous limestone cliffs, both the natural and the quarried. Satisfyingly steep, if short in stature, they offer easier rock-climbing routes and I have made occasional visits here of a summer's evening in decades past for a bit of solitary muscle stretching after a desk-bound day. Now, youngsters can be seen, helmeted, roped up, listening with laser-focus to an instructor's explanations. All so much ahead of them.

Today, the sky has a gloriously filmic quality. Clouds, small or wispy, are fanning out as if from some vanishing point in the sky, as if a canopy for some impending spectacle. We scramble up a bank to the side to reach the trig point and from here cast our view to the distant south. The Midlands. And is that Cannock Chase? Could that be the Wrekin? Or that, perhaps?

I have never before thought of Harborough Rocks as a 'summit' or even as an especially high place. But the views are extensive. The atmosphere has an ancient quality and the lead mine ruins and the once-inhabited cave all attest to it being a location through the ages for human existence, toil and reverence.

To live among such heights!

Ethels Day 5 – 20th September

Grindslow Knoll

We are away from the Edale car park by 9.30, walking in an ideal temperature. Sunlight is taking every opportunity to flicker through the foliage along the narrow road up through the village. The last time I walked this way, four years or so ago, I was with my eldest son and his eldest son, three generations of us repeating a pattern from the past. But today, we all three of us are of an age and wonder whether our legs, lungs and sense of levity, are still attuned to an undertaking such as this.

Over the footbridge and out from the shadow of trees and the panorama of a moorland amphitheatre opens above us. To our right, the high fortress of Ringing Roger standing dominant above the valley. Sweeping round, the southern edge of the Kinder plateau, its buttresses and towers dwarfed by the distance. Across the water-smoothed ledges where Grindsbrook itself begins its downward tumble, and then on to the west and the final rise to Grindslow Knoll, one of only four of the Ethels to rise above six hundred metres.

The track up to Ringing Roger zig zags, kindly levelling out the climb where it can. We still stop for rests, for sweat to be wiped from our eyes, for adjustments to be made to head gear. Good humour, jokes and chat push us on, upwards.

We pass one or two other walkers and the exchanges are cordial, ribald even at times, all of us united in shared endeavour. Here are wonderful formations, stacks of lopsided gritstone pancakes, rounded boulders hunched like armadillos, cliffs split by those vertical and horizontal cracks that climbers cannot keep their jammed fists from.

If we must have images of our country that would justify killing or dying in war, then for me it could be the Edale Valley seen from above. A sleepy contentment spreads along its entire length, across a spectrum that includes villages, through to individual beasts and humans, right down to the very bugs and insects. *Above the deep and dreamless sleep.*

But this is fantasy, so easily induced by the colours and proportions of these hills. So hopelessly beguiling to those of us who merely look on in quiet admiration. In addition to our coffee and a sense of wonderment, we add a nip of whiskey.

On round the edge of the plateau now to reach the slabs at the head of Grindsbrook, level plates of rock, ochre and red, and finely polished by wind and weather, but mainly water, over millennia. A gentle rise now, our walk trailing out behind us. Thus, we reach our highest point.

Why do people pose with their arms outstretched before magnificent views? I have done it myself. Perhaps it is an attempt to embrace beauty, to hold on to its elusiveness, to take some of the deep contentment witnessed in the land into our own core? To keep ourselves anchored, tethered to simple truths, before we descend into the world again with all its hectic urgencies?

Such speculations are taken on the air.

Satisfied and with sun-roughened skin, we descend.

Ethels Day 6 – 22nd September

Minninglow

I am cycling along the High Peak Trail, pushing the pedals round and whizzing through the late afternoon. Is it safe to leave my bike locked to a gatepost? If it were stolen or vandalised, how many hours would it take me to retrace my journey back home on foot?

Cattle watch me tuck my bike as far from sight as possible, chewing nonchalantly and perhaps approving of my attempts. I pass through the gate, and they retreat a step or two but continue their ruminations. I follow the path upwards through their field towards the circular clump of trees that have dominated my experience of this area for half a century or so. And for all our myriad predecessors. Over millennia.

The leggy beech trees are contained and protected behind a beautifully constructed circular fence. Inside, these lofty guardians with their tombs and barrows, outside the cows free to wander and graze.

Inside the fence, within the ring, the light beats about between the branches, rattling my composure. Those sleeping beneath have weathered ages, geology and shifts of culture. Excavations even.

The clouds register displeasure, the treetops blow about erratically using whatever means to ring out warning. The ground stays steady, but I am unsettled and talk in a quiet, reassuring voice to myself.

Back outside the enclosure, the land for miles around speaks permanence, solidity, predictability, and I am grateful for its response.

I pedal home furiously, singing discordantly and free.

Ethels Day 7 – 23rd September

Pilsbury Hill & Carder Low

Cycling to Ethels is feasible, I've discovered, and the weather is holding. It's time to push on into the autumn and the lovely hills north of Hartington.

Along the High Peak Trail and it is tempting to yield to the urging from the cinders and the gravel beneath my wheels:

'Gorge on the speed, devour these miles!'

'Be alive, defy the shortening of the day, disdain the cooling and the dark!'

But I resist. It's familiar territory, but I must chunk it up differently in my mind, take my time, keep a bit back for the hills and the extra miles.

The gates do not irritate, they slow me but are part of the procedure. I have no energy to fritter away on frustration and I come in time to Parsley Hay and refreshment. The comings and goings are a delight – cycle hire, the water dish for the dogs, shouts of 'Number thirty-three!' and 'Two sausage rolls!' Around me but not of me. I am in a different world, one of loosely shifting schedules, of new ambitions, dreams and old affections.

Leaving the trail, onto the quiet lanes, freewheeling down into the dips. I have the countryside to myself, the cars are rare, the occasional tractor is as it should be. This terrain, these lanes, are truly a balm for any sore and harried nerves. Cars should be excluded from them all, silence should carry only the gentle and the lost and needy, powered by the engines of hope and optimism.

Up a gentle incline and a whole landscape opens to the west. The land seems content, rippling away into the distance, untroubled and untroubling. There is little habitation. Days may pass here unnoticed. The seasons may turn unobserved. An old, barred gate stands open, half hinged and falling but secure enough as an anchor for my bike. A large dew pond reflects back the sunlight and a wooden stile gives me access to the hillside up to the summit barrows of Pilsbury Hill.

Everywhere the ancients populate these Ethels, sleeping through the ages, steady through the turmoil.

My legs are springy from the bike, almost out of control. Ten minutes is all it takes. I survey the hills in all directions and focus on Carder Low, the next on my list. Back past the bike and then on down across fields, trying to spot stiles and gates that allow me access to this neighbouring top. The fields here are managed, walls are built high, well maintained. The barbed wire has been methodically arranged.

I walk the lengths of fields, return across their widths, unable to find crossing points. I resort to climbing, balancing on tops, finding the energy to pick up my ankles, jumping even higher to clear the wire, fighting to ignore the consequences of a snag or trip. Once I could land like an acrobat, knees bend, touch the ground and up. Once. Years ago. Now I crumple, feel the unyielding ground, the blunt force of contact.

I am veering towards the rocky top of Carder Low but the exertions are taking their toll. The scattered limestone blocks are particularly appealing and I sit in no hurry to begin my descent. I resolve to pay more attention to the map, to work out the least restricted way back to predictable passage before leaving this agreeable eyrie.

Eventually back at Parsley Hay, I make free with the menu - cake, ice cream, tea – excusing all excess in the name of restoration and fuelling the last hour home.

It will have been thirty-four miles on the bike, a few more on foot, plus the anxious high jumps, and I finally allow my composure to be shredded by furious pedalling and a headset pounding out rock and roll.

Ethels Day 8 – 23rd September

Harland Edge

A second attempt is needed, having been defeated by this most unlikely of Ethels a few days earlier.
Harland Edge seems, from a distance, an unprepossessing line of grit and heather on the most eastern edge of the collection. Little more than a mile or so from our parking spot, I was sure we could comfortably reach its highest point and be back in time for an appointment at home. There was little by way of ascent involved and no route-finding complications.
We picked our way up past Hob Hurst's House, where Bronze Age human remains were once entombed. Neither elf nor giant was abroad beneath a September sun that sprawled, lazy and indulgent, across the open moorland. Surmounting the edge, our map was directing us through half a mile of rough ground, heather in tangles that tripped us and scratched our ankles. Progress was surprisingly, and painfully, slow and we were reduced to surveying the next few yards, looking for the easiest passage and realising that I had grossly underestimated the time required.
I took lessons from this rebuff. That these undertakings cannot necessarily play supporting roles to everyday commitments. They demand the spotlight, the prime position, these petulant characters, and they can be spiteful and sulky if so denied.
Three days pass and I am invited to make another attempt, this time from the south. We can see the trig point from the road but this is not the highest point. The boundary wall is solid and high, built to repel, and we drive up and back a few times searching for any breach. Finally, crossing barbed wire with care, we are amongst the vegetation again, thigh high and antagonistic. The

few yards to the trig point take time, the sky is heavy with threat and the slog to the highest point is the least appealing feature of any of the Ethels so far.

We debate ethics, strategies, interpretations – pull at the purpose of the whole enterprise in such a way that it could rapidly unravel and become as nothing. Quickly, we decide that by climbing the trig point itself and then reaching high, I can touch the necessary altitude. I am helped to scrabble onto the plinth, to stretch towards the clouds with my balance steadied by anchors of bravado.

There is a moral here. Somewhere.

A logic from a shared absurdity.

A lesson from a 'lesser' Ethel.

Ethels Day 9 – 28th September

Musden Low

Last week we were struggling to make the highest point of the easternmost Ethel. Today, the route to the top of the one that is furthest south is clear and obvious. It is a straightforward ascent – and it is on private land.

Leaving the car in a layby, we are on a footpath across a farmer's fields. There is dampness in the air and we are wearing waterproofs in anticipation of a further deterioration in the weather.

Ahead of us, decorated with grazing sheep, a gradually ascending hillside that the map reveals to be our intended objective, the highest point. We leave the path and make satisfactory progress up the skyline ridge. The climb is gentle and we have enough breathe to maintain a rambling conversation with ease.

Summits, even the less sensational such as this, whisper a levity, hint at a grounded joy. Among the ancestors once again, within the orbit of their burials, we take our photographs, aware of the juxtaposition of prehistory with the contemporary. The churn of the seasons, the subjugation of the land, now as ever.

We descend, taking in a wider sweep of the hillside, and the rain arrives. Keeping our hoods secure about our heads and our faces turned from the squall eliminates convivial exchange, and we fall into silent progress.

But back through the fields, in the shelter of the trees, we resume our talk, distracted from the fading reach of summer.

Ethels Day 10 – 3rd October

Whetstone Ridge

The weekend storms ease at last, so I slip out mid-afternoon to try two hills from the Buxton-Congleton Road. The rain is holding off and there are bursts of brilliant, boisterous sunshine in the spaces between dark, malevolent clouds.

Steeply down from the road and I am soon among ruins. Broken, blackened gritstone walls. Energy and industry spent, long gone, the remains of these buildings idling away the decades, resigned to further collapse.

The tracks once carrying heavy loads are overgrown and do not always match those on my map. Or, at least, my cursory examination fails to match the paper to the land, so I strike off up a steep bank hoping to find a shorter route to the top of Cheeks Hill. The shortening days, the nip in the air, my lengthening shadow, all advise against tarrying, and I thrash around on the open hillside trying to decide where exactly its highest point may be. Satisfied at being near enough and realising that Axe Edge Moor is far further away than I had first thought, I decide this must suffice for today.

Back at the car, I know something is not right. It's a matter of scale. There is higher ground, miles of it, behind where I have just been. That cannot have been Cheeks Hill. I have not paid enough attention to the map. To salvage something, I decide to take in Whetstone Ride on the other side of the main road. The track should be straightforward, the walking easy, and the warm colours of late afternoon are cradling the landscape, holding me, the sheep, the walls, fields and hills, all within a golden embrace. But, again, something is not right. Again, it is a matter of scale. The track has suddenly finished. A scarp rises where it should not. I have somehow turned towards the south. I tell myself – again – that I must concentrate, I really must pay attention. Especially to wall boundaries!

I am now forced to make another steep ascent over scruffy land and then, on a compass bearing, traverse a stretch of lonely, boggy ground. I tell myself it's an inconvenience, nothing more. That and the barbed wire are the price of my inattention. The evening meanwhile continues its determined course, and I meet a Peak and Northern Footpaths Society sign. With beautiful metalwork in municipal green, it stands here alone across the seasons, long out of its own time, holding up but listing now.

The map shows the fine contours of a distinctive ridge but, after more barbed wire, I am again unsure about the exact location of the highest point. I trample around the most probable ground then pick up the definite track back to the road. The last of the afternoon light tingles on the air, and I walk the final mile back to the car surrounded by furious orchestration, by happiness blasting all around.

Ethels Day 11 – 6th October

Higgar Tor, White Path Moss, High Neb, Stanedge Pole & Sir William Hill

This road, up from Hathersage towards the Surprise View, I first travelled at Easter 1968 when hitch hiking from North Wales to Sheffield. On that day, the tops up by Burbage Brook and the Toad's Mouth were covered by deep and sullen snow. Through the mist, a road sign declared, with no hint of mockery, that we had entered the City of Sheffield. The only figure to be seen, manifesting from out of the gloom, was an old shepherd with a collie dog and his coat tied round with twine. Hardy's line – *'only a man harrowing clods in a slow, silent walk'* - sprung to mind and reappears to this day every time I travel this road.

Today there is no sign of snow. Instead, the piercing light from a strong sun in a brilliant blue sky is picking out every feature of the land. Almost, seemingly, each individual blade of grass. The fields are stretching upwards, scratching at the bracken and acid soil of the moors. And I am rising also, in anticipation, in hope and in joy.

Higgar Tor is a short hop, skip and jump from the car and I am among its boulders, at its fortress wall, in only a few minutes. Other walkers bustle about in winter gear. In autumn's aura. This is only the warm-up and Sir William Hill, likewise, will be a brief, concluding excursion later.

There is no time to linger before the day's main act, the mighty Stanage Edge, monarch of the high ground and acres by the thousands that it commands. Famously four miles long, the Edge has always held some menace for me, has never allowed an over-familiarity. With all my main climbing partners over half a century and more, I have approached it with respect, knowing full well who was boss. One friend, more ambitious in his climbing than me, arrived back at college on crutches in the late 1960s. He had been pushing up his grade on a climb called Elllis' Eliminate and had run out of strength at the end of a long sideways traverse where an awkward move still required some calm, collected problem solving. He was fortunate to have landed as he did and that his injuries were not more catastrophic.

In a beautiful essay about one of its most famous routes, Right Unconquerable, Jim Perrin evokes the rules of engagement with gritstone climbs, its unforgiving nature and its unmatched rewards. '*Torn hands, scraped knees, strained arms and a dry throat are all in a gritstoner's day*'. He also, however, captured with great eloquence the rare delight that resulted from such efforts – '*A time past, when the rocks stood about unknown to us, and eager and lustful we explored their every intimacy, climbed until the failing light veiled the crags with shadow and widowed them into night*'.

There are two slight prominences along the edge, a couple of miles apart, designated as Ethels. Flattened slabs of weathered grit provide an engaging and constantly changing route between them. It is possible to walk swiftly but only with the mind on constant alert. Full attention is required for the twists and turns, for steps to one side and then the other, for small hops and leaps between rocks.

From High Neb, the furthest Ethel, I return via a deviation to Stanedge Pole where a marker has stood to aid travellers since medieval times.

Two friends from my earliest trips to the Peak District return to me today. They move about in my imaginings, full of life and bravado. I am walking through the past, alone and fully engaged with them.

They are back with us, young again, laughing, adventurous and determined.
The day is perfect and complete.

THE 1960s

1967. Froggatt Edge

'The Peak District?'
'It's Derbyshire. Up the M1. Sign up if you're interested. But you'd better be quick. It's first come, first served, and the minibus only holds twelve'.

And served I was. A journey up the gleaming, night-time motorway to the furthest north I had ever been. I heard songs about Joe Brown and other mythical figures, braggarts' accounts of adventures, stories of near misses. My early experiences of climbing at Lulworth and Portland held little interest for the others, they were too peripheral to a mountaineering world full of its traditions, legends and anecdotes. I was content to submit instead to a mesmerising induction, to a bagful of tales, as big and as full as a world.

When, nearing midnight on that Friday evening in February, we turned off the motorway and passed through the quiet streets of Chesterfield, I peered through the window at houses that somehow felt different from those in the south of the country. But what was it about their apparent solidity, the red brick, lamp posts, road signs or pavements? All, in one sense, so familiar yet at the same to time so alien – and exciting! Was it, in fact, just a sense of mounting trepidation, smothered and denied, casting these otherwise mundane features in such an alluring but unsettling light?

Beyond the town, the outside dissolved into dark. Steep banks seemed to rise above the road, in other places we were flanked by empty moorland or surrounded by trees. A dozen or so miles further and the minibus pulled off the narrow road and lumbered down a rough track to arrive at our destination, the Bob Downes Memorial Hut. Here, those members of the Goldsmiths College Mountaineering Club who knew the ropes swung into action, unlocking the door, opening shutters, supervising the unloading of food, and indicating where sleeping bags should be placed along the lower and upper mattresses. Amongst this practised efficiency, I struggled as a newcomer to find a role or, failing that, a place where I could stand without blocking the flow of business-like activity.

The next morning continued in a similar fashion as two people set about preparing a fried breakfast for the whole group, which had swelled in number following the arrival in the night of two more cars. Again, unable to find a way to be helpful, I kept a low profile browsing the framed black and white photographs on the wall. Some were of climbers on nearby crags, others were of Bob Downes himself, a skilled and bold young climber who had died a few years earlier, only in his mid-twenties, high in the Himalayas. This sobering reminder of what we were engaged in, to whatever degree, formed a strange juxtaposition to the energetic camaraderie all around, to the minibus, the songs, the snoring ranks of bodies, the breakfasts, and the big plans for the day.

Birchens Edge. Not far away, we were to go there as a group in cars and the minibus. It was traditional starting ground for 'beginners' and I was unsure whether that designation applied to me or not. We had been the only climbers on Portland and at Lulworth and I thought of myself as some sort of pioneer. Not a 'beginner'. But my humbling on Lliwedd three years earlier, my last attempt at climbing, had taught me to be very cautious about claiming any superior knowledge or experience. I allowed myself to be shown knots, informed about belaying technique, advised to place my instep and not toes on small holds, all the while biting back the desire to say 'I know, I know'.

The climbs were short, only about thirty feet in height. But they were difficult, even the ones graded the easiest. The moves required thought, the holds were not obvious, and having to rely so much on the frictional properties of the gritstone was a strange and disconcerting experience. We had sung with gusto about 'old, long gone, hand jam Joe', but now in all urgency we were forced to rely on this very improbable and unnatural technique. On a fist placed into a crack with its dimensions then increased by folding the thumb across the palm. Locking flesh in this manner into the grip of roughened rock was meant to secure our position.

We climbed all day, hungry and eager to take it all in. Mark, who I recognised from my hall of residence, assumed an easy authority and recommended climbing pairings and routes that should, all being well, be within our capabilities. On the top of the cliff was a monument to Admiral Nelson and the names of many of the climbs chimed with this - Trafalgar Crack, Sail Chimney, Victory Crack. I climbed second on some these, secured by a tight rope from above. But I was also keen to demonstrate some proficiency and volunteered to lead a few easy routes as well. And one particular horror, Kiss Me Hardy, a ferocious little chimney, I even struggled up solo.

The adrenalin surges, the natural world, the impossibility of youth, the everlasting moment.

That night in the pub in Bakewell, we were all full of stories from the day, raucous and uncontainable, immediate and bonded, flushed with accomplishment. And after all this, back at the hut, I sat in an old, battered armchair in front of the fire talking with one of the two girls who were on the trip, a chirpy, blonde-haired adventurer from Manchester. The freest spirit I had ever encountered. Exhaustion was pulling me into sleep, taking away my words. As the fire dwindled and died so too did any semblance of conversation on my part. If only the moment could be sustained, if only my ability to engage, to respond, was not deserting me, turning instead into something that would be lifeless and cold by the morning.

After a deep, sound sleep, the breakfast routine again burst into action and we were soon ascending steeply and directly from the hut up through twinkly woods, up to Frogatt Edge. Here were bigger walls and slabs than Birchens, their sense of seriousness, the majesty of cliffs standing like open books, high and proud above the River Derwent valley. Climbing history was all around – Joe Brown, Don Whillans, Valkyrie, Three Pebble Slab.

We climbed all day and I swelled with satisfaction at having the nerve and the technical ability to lead a couple of the easier routes. Belayed at the top, bringing up my second, I was buffeted by a wind that tasted of very early spring. The shivers going through me derived partly from the bite of this breeze but also from an outrageous sense of being fully alive, in new company, and in a landscape towards which I was already feeling a compelling attraction.

At the end of the day we would coil these ropes, stuff our equipment into bags and rucksacks, walk back down the track in fading daylight. Euphoria would be coursing through my body. Muscles would be stretched and swollen. Even among the intemperate laughter and frantic camaraderie, I would experience a silent, steely streak of satisfaction. We would begin the drive south. We would arrive weary and late at night, back in New Cross and Lewisham, hemmed in by the city all around us.

But, for now, only the present, its immediacy, could occupy me. I looked down at the sparse habitation below, the dwellings scattered along the river. I was convinced that such contentment could never be mine but did swear, solemnly and sincerely, that if, somehow, I could actually end up living among such magnificence, then, no matter what, I would rise every morning in deep reverence and acknowledge my good fortune.

1967. How Hard is Mild Severe?

And how mild is Hard Severe?

There was a lot to learn. But, oh, how we suck in that information when it matters the most. When it's a question of life and death. Or, of endorphins, adrenaline and that elusive spot between terror and the delectable.

My early lessons included those in poise. Don't cling on for dear life. Place the feet carefully, let them do the work, take the weight. And always attempt to stand in balance if at all possible. Ideally, we should be light, strong and graceful. The ballet dancer was our role model, not the weightlifter. Take time. Look around and weigh each option. Make small moves, don't attempt to raise both a foot and a hand at the same time and do not, whatever else, do not lunge. Three points of contact, however insistently the terror is telling you to get away from this precise spot, to get higher, to the safety of some ledge or other, somewhere currently out of reach. Address the panic. Become its master. Move only when the body's trembling and its rapid descent into violent shaking have been conquered.

These disciplines are learned, although not in so many words, in the early stages. By climbing second and by being held on a very tight rope by the leader above.

Although guidebooks gave descriptions of routes and even graded their difficulty, I certainly needed to hear those judgements verbally confirmed or contradicted by a real person, one whom I could explicitly trust.

There was a well-polished art to the descriptions of climbs. So, for instance, when a guidebook used a phrase such as '*surmount the block with some difficulty...*', a desperate grapple with the rock, perhaps with an absence of obvious hand or footholds, could be expected. '*Step delicately ...*' almost certainly predicted a severe shortage of footholds with only friction or improbable ripples or rugosities for one's feet.

An airy stance ...' might well be a tiny fleck of rock serving as the only resting platform on an otherwise sheer and blank face. And so on.

Climbing guidebooks were works of art and absorbing fireside reading when away from the crags and planning a next trip. And no piece of information was more essential than the grading of a particular climb's difficulty, by means of a gloriously idiosyncratic adjectival system. Whereas in the U.S.A a straightforward and unambiguous scale was employed - 5.5, 5.6, 5.7, 5.8 and so on towards impossibility - and in the Alps the equally pragmatic I, II, III, IV, V and VI, we British had invented a sequence of descriptors possessing an echoing oddness similar to the shipping forecast regions –

Moderate, Difficult, Hard Difficult, Very Difficult, Hard Very Difficult, Mild Severe, Severe, Hard Severe, Mild Very Severe, Very Severe, Hard Very Severe, Extremely Severe (with this category later subdivided and extended further into E1, E2, E3 ...).

Cromarty, Forth, Dogger ...

1967. Williams' Barn

The Ogwen Valley again, back after three years, and it was equally or more inhospitable than before. Snow flurries, dark, and no sign of Steve's tent.
So, nowhere to sleep.
I had hitched up from my parents' house in Weymouth to the Goldsmiths Club's Easter meet. The trip had taken almost twelve hours and my most memorable lift was from Chepstow with a civil engineer. As we talked, I described how I had given up my course in that subject at a polytechnic fifteen months earlier and was thinking of becoming a teacher after completing my degree in maths and physics.
'Nah, don't do that,' he advised. 'The wife's a teacher. Wants to change the world. Don't go into teaching. Go into civils. More money.'
When he dropped me in the wilds of mid-Wales and drove off (an expensive roar, a beautifully engineered road), it confirmed my feeling that I would not have found my tribe among his like.
Subsequent lifts materialised sporadically until, after dark and only three miles from my destination, they seemed to evaporate completely. As I set out to walk the road from Capel Curig, a couple stopped their car and took me to Williams' Farm where they were also staying. The tents in the field were pegged down against the night, there was no pulse of life discernible anywhere. I slithered about in the slush trying to remember the colour and style of Steve's tent. I even called his name outside a few of them, a muted sort of call, and then listened for any response, praying for a rapid unzipping and a welcome into a warm and comfortable fug.
But no sound came from any of them. Their occupants were all sealed in silently against the night – or out

somewhere enjoying themselves, if such a thing were possible. Gusts of wind picked up some of the surface snow, pulled it around and flecked some into my face.

All activity ceased. There was nowhere for me to go, nowhere to find respite. The cold, blank realisation of my predicament was just about to knock all hope to the ground when the couple who had given me the lift loomed back out from the dark and offered me their car for the night.

The back seats of small cars are never luxury sleeping spots. But this one was dry and out of the wind.

Moving my position through that long night, I tried to redistribute the discomfort through my body. This leg then that one, stetch, bend, tuck. I reflected on the supposed character-building nature of adventure. This shoulder squared, the other pulled back. I tried to remember more about the claims that physical adversity increased fortitude and endurance. I also contemplated the effort it would take to undertake another twelve-hour hitch-hiking trip back home at daylight.

But when at last, at long, long last, a thin, indifferent light began to creep across the field, my rescuers returned and extended their generosity with porridge and a mug of coffee. The visibility, the hot food and the kindness all lifted my spirits and Steve's tent suddenly became very easy to spot. He too had spent an uncomfortable night and was entertaining thoughts of returning home. But, having some company, seemed to buoy us both up enough to hitch into Capel to buy some supplies. The London University Mountaineering Club owned a hut, Casseg Fraith, where we were allowed to cook some food even though all the sleeping spots had been booked by others. Fortified again, we prepared to sit and sleep out some of the afternoon in Steve's tent when we heard our leader, Mark's voice outside.

Mark Vallance was a year ahead of me at Goldsmiths and I knew him vaguely because he and I lived in the same hall of residence. He had a reputation as an accomplished climber with serious Alpine ascents already under his belt and a period spent living in India. He was also a methodical organiser and had soon gathered other club members together from scattered locations and installed us in Williams' Barn, a venue, I was to learn, that was infamous in climbing mythology. That it was an ideal base for a week's climbing, and perfect for learning the discipline and rigour of mountaineering life, was attested to by the fact that we were sharing the barn with a troupe of army cadets and their officers.

The barn had a central gully down which liquids of some variety must have once drained. To either side were stalls with concrete partitions, originally for beasts during particularly inclement weather. A thick layer of straw was scattered in these stalls where we were to sleep, our club to one side of the gully, the boy soldiers on the other. The central aisle was to be used for cooking as best we could on primus stoves. Outside, an individual toilet, dark and cold, was shared by all alongside a cold water tap and a small stream for washing both our utensils and, should we choose to, ourselves. After the car back seat and the waterlogged camping field, it was luxury.

Mark put together a programme of climbing activities for the half dozen of us in the barn and we managed to coexist in a most unlikely juxtaposition for a few nights until the army moved out. The two contrasting cultures nevertheless provided occasional moments of great distraction.

'Would you like your beans fried, sir?'

'Eh, yes please, Simpson'.

One of our club members, Andy Handford, who I had met briefly at college, had been hired as a temporary instructor for a group and, when this employment ended mid-week he joined us in the barn, bringing three very welcome boxes of supplies that had been extra to requirements. The stalls in which we were sleeping were not quite wide enough for somebody of average height or above to stretch out completely and it was necessary to sleep with knees slightly bent. When Andy moved in to share my stall, he effectively blocked some of the draught that had been causing me to experience bitterly cold nights and I was able to sleep slightly more comfortably from then on.

We seemed to form a relaxed and agreeable climbing partnership and, as he was slightly more experienced than me, I felt confident joining him on routes that Mark recommended and tutored us on. In the stall as we tried to settle to sleep at nights, we began to exchange life histories and our various hopes and ambitions. These loosely formed and wandering philosophies of life seemed to chime with each other's and with the times.

We were both relatively able at mathematics, a deeply unfashionable subject among most of our fellow students at college, but we also craved a wider and more purposeful set of cultural experiences. I felt a strong sense of kinship when I learned that he had previously given up a course in mechanical engineering at a London college of advanced technology.

It was 1967 and the past seemed to be fracturing. The future, although ill-defined and unpredictable, was hurtling towards us all at an unstoppable rate. Only to the quick-witted and nimble would modernity bestow the fruits of progress.

'Simpson, have you got your waterproofs on under your denims?'

1967. Shadrack

Coffee bar rockers, heavy in their leathers, straight from the haunts of my youth. Becoming an anachronism by the mid-1960s but still very familiar. Coffee bar rockers, heavy in their leathers, speaking only in Welsh, however, was a completely new experience.

Andy and I were in the Tremadoc village café, a short walk from the mighty bulk of Craig Bwlch y Moch, with the climbing guidebook for the area open at one particular climb.

> ***Shadrach*** *180feet Very Severe*
> *Goes up the middle of Shadrach Buttress*
> *A splendid climb, probably the best at Tremadoc or indeed anywhere in the area.*

It was the last day of our week in Williams' Barn with the Goldsmiths Club and today we were on our own squaring up, 'psyching up' we called it, for our biggest ever climbing challenge, one that would be a watershed, lifting us at last out of the category of 'beginner' or 'novice'. This would be our breakthrough into the first of the serious grades – Very Severe – accomplished without technical help or morale boosts from others. And without a fallback strategy. If we failed, the consequences could be beyond Very Severe.

We had been climbing steadily all week. Every morning we woke up in the dismal barn and picked the straw from our hair. Taking care not to set fire to the mounds of it scattered around, we cooked breakfast on our primus stoves. Outside the barn we washed in the stream as best we could, toughening up in attitude every bit as much as in our muscles.

Mark was our guide to all the classic climbs of the region – and to their history and mythology. He was also an extremely astute judge of our abilities and at matching these to particular climbs.

Round in Llanberis we were introduced to the likes of Spiral Stairs and Flying Buttress, routes polished by generations of novices making their first careful steps into a lifetime climbing addiction or, sick with anxiety, swearing to any deity to never again treat the horizontal world, the everyday surface of human existence, with such contempt.

One day we walked up into high, lonely Cwm Silyn, a steady two-mile uphill plod from the car to the corrie. I was designated by Mark to climb with a chap called Chris and we set off to inch our way up a long V Diff route called The Outside Edge. As we climbed higher, we met the cloud. The wind swirled it, thick and wet, around us and when we at last reached the top of the cliff, all that was visible was the small patch of ground at our feet. Above us, the peak reached even higher and merged into the cloud. Below was a white emptiness.

And we were lost. We did not know the safe way down and feared stumbling over a crag. So, very tentatively, we followed a faint scree path, ensuring that we could always retrace our steps if needs be, until at last we heard Mark shouting from somewhere below, guiding us down.

If we emerged from our barn in the morning and found snow falling silently but with serious intent, we drove south for an hour to the more temperate climate of Tremadoc. Winding down through valleys, with cloud-shrouded, snowy peaks above and placid grey lakes below, Meg's mini was a red streak through a landscape of grey and green.

For our first climb there, Mark led four of us up a classic Severe called Poor Man's Peutery. The sense of fresh air beneath the feet, the lack of any solidity, can bring a terrifying experience of exposure. You try to close your ears to the malign voice hovering in the air and sneering

'You do not know what lies ahead. But you know that retreat is impossible. This you do know'.

At the top, the sense of triumph over the power of despondency, the discovery of grit deep within the character, generates euphoric releases of tension and a joyous sense of camaraderie. The view though counters this riot of adrenaline. Calm and orderly, the village of Tremadoc going about its business, the sand dunes, the dam across the lake, the sea, quiet and timeless.

Thanks to the luxury of having two cars available and because of the continuingly bad weather at Ogwen, we returned to Tremadoc twice more that week. As well as guiding us towards all the best climbs, Mark also provided an expertly graded set of tasks that brought Andy Handford to the point where he could consider attempting the independent, 'on sight' lead of his first VS. Nowhere near as bold, I was more than content – I was privileged! – to serve as his second on the rope.

Although we had finished our cups of tea, we were still dry mouthed with anticipation. The bikers in the cafe filled the room with an exotic weave of tongues but we were oblivious to it and locked into study of the guidebook. Even though every word had burned itself into our memories over many months.

Start: At a curving chimney at the foot of the face proper.
(1) 60feet. Climb up to the chimney and squirm up inside it to a block belay. Or climb outside the chimney. Strenuous.

Those words, '*squirm*' and '*strenuous*' spoke volumes. Awakened fears and apprehensions that could only be assuaged by physical contact with the rock. No matter how much reassurance Mark had given us that morning, we would not know or feel their true implications until we were rising slowly, irreversibly, higher and higher above the ground. Until we were committed.

(2) 50 feet. Move up left and over a mantleshelf, then follow steep slabs to a rotten oak and a huge, perched block.

The rockers were teasing the waitress. There were roars from the adjacent tables. As outsiders, we might be the focus of their curiosity, antagonism, or indifference. It made no difference. Every atom of attention, every readying against anxiety, was locked into those words - '*steep*', '*rotten*', '*huge*'. Dear God, the very sentences haunted us, even '*move*', '*mantleshelf*' and '*perched*' provided no solace, no prospect of a resting place.

(3) 70 feet. Step awkwardly up into a little corner above, finishing out on the right.

We leave the café. Reach the cliff. Uncoil the rope and tie on.

He nods at me. I nod back. He sets off.

I pay out the rope when I feel it pull. A foot or two, then nothing. Sometimes a rapid urgency.

'... *awkwardly ... awkwardly ... awkwardly ...*'

When my turn comes, I concentrate on removing his running belays, on the next immediate task, on calm consideration.

At the first stance, both tied on, I transfer his runners back to him.

There is little talk, the focus is the climb, the business at hand.

I nod. He nods back. Then he sets off again.

That magnificent panorama gradually reveals itself again, demanding our appreciation. And we ignore it.

The hours mean nothing, our timepieces are the sky and the afternoon's light.

And, eventually, we are at the top, exhausted and exhilarated.

'*... finishing ... finishing ... finishing ...*'

Changed forever.

Fifty years later, in 2017 and after a full life, Andy died at his home in Colorado Springs.

*

Fifty-two years later, in 2019, rock engineers abseiled down the line of Shadrach. Using only crow bars and a small car jack, they dislodged a thirty-ton block that was becoming perilously unstable. The block took with it another hundred-ton pinnacle as it crashed towards the ground in a cloud of dust.

A climb of such gargantuan significance was no more.

1967. A Firm Constitution

'If you do President, I'll do Vice-President'.
And so it was decided. The others agreed and somebody wrote the decision down on the slip of paper required by the Student Union. It was my first experience of committee decision-making, if the rabble around the pub table could be said to constitute a 'committee'. Andy would be the figurehead for Goldsmiths Mountaineering Club next year, and I would be his deputy.

I wondered about the responsibilities that the role would bring and whether I could fulfil them. I had been one of the few sixth formers my school did not make a prefect and had adjusted to the facts that I was not 'officer material' and had not been born with that prized streak of leadership potential running through my character. It was the 1960s after all and the absence of such qualities could easily be displayed as a badge of pride. But here I was, by accident or default, a Vice-President for goodness sake.

An Officer.

Of sorts.

One of the few duties required of me was to help organise our trips away. Another was to attend the Student Union sub-committee, the Athletic Union, that represented all the various sports clubs and societies in the college. Although London was swinging as a pendulum do, membership of this group seemed to be reserved for those square of jaw and with hair trimmed to within an inch of their lives. Health, fitness, and clean living emanated from them in a fashion that would disgust much of the wider student body.

I approached the first of these meetings with some trepidation, understanding from films and novels that such social arenas were conducted through sophisticated ploys and machinations within which the unwary would perish and the well-prepared and ruthless flourish. I was fortunate to be riding shotgun to Andy, who seemed to possess none of my fears and reservations.

'And now we come onto the main business of the meeting,' the chairman said. 'Allocation of funds for the coming year'.

Football wanted two new balls, a couple of theirs had become worn and would benefit from replacement. Badminton bid for a new set of shuttlecocks as the flights on their current ones were becoming tattered with frequent use. On round the table went the discussion with each representative making their group's bid. I was ready to disappear under the table but could sense Andy beside me stiffening in his posture, preparing to read from the piece of paper in his hands.

'We need five new ice axes,' he announced when his turn came.

'Five ice axes,' said the chairman slowly as he added these to the list he was compiling. 'And how much would they cost?'

Andy's tone was sombre and measured as he gave a figure that would obliterate the total budget for Football, Rugby and Cricket combined. The chairman paused from his scribbles, the other representatives around the table looked at each other in alarm.

I had never felt such power, such control of the moment, albeit only by association with the cause of this disquiet. This was the cool and calculation that had taken Andy up Shadrach and many subsequent routes in the past year. I merely nodded when the chairman looked at me, still paying out a rope to Andy in terms of steady support and responding to shifts of nuance and tension.

The chairman repeated the figure. A decade's worth of table tennis bats and balls cascaded to the floor.

Andy kept in balance and moved up steadily and smoothly.

'That's each,' he replied.

'Each!'

'Well, we are taking out beginners. Onto the hills in winter. And if something – '

'Is this for the cheapest versions?'

'Traditional ice axes are cheaper but we – '

'Ah! Alright, traditional ones. Surely these will – '

'The trouble with traditional ice axes is that they can snap – '

'Snap! They can break?'

'Yes, wooden ones can. That's why the club needs these new ones. They're made from hiduminium.

'Hiduminium?' Swimming spluttered. 'What the devil is hiduminium?'

Andy paused before answering. He seemed to be searching quietly within himself for the nerve to make the next move just as I had frequently seen him do on the cliff face.

'The thing is …' he said slowly, as if carefully pulling himself up through a delicate sequence of thin moves, '… the college can't afford to compromise on safety, especially when beginners – '

'Five, does it have to be five?'

'As I say – '

'Could you make do with less?'

'Well, we would have to limit who could come out at any one time, but I suppose we could. As I say, though, if – '

'Four. How about four? That would be a massive hole in our total budget anyway'.

Andy drew a breath and lowered his gaze, as if having to risk all on a tenuous and hidden foothold. To one side of us, Tennis, and to the other, Trampoline, were also holding their breath.

'Four?'

He had to move. We all had to. Remaining in that position was unsustainable, the inevitable could only be prevented for so long.

Slowly, silently, he rose. This was it – keep going now – don't faulter. And – phew! – we reached it. The ledge. The massive, commodious ledge.

Andy's offer of settling for three was rapidly accepted without dissent.

The club's new equipment would be available for use by members and, with Steve, we would be making our first journey to Glencoe in a couple of months as the snows of winter fell.

1967. Glencoe

Climbers in those days aspired to become mountaineers and mountaineers, in their turn, inevitably craved expeditions.

The Alps were an ambition, already visited by my companions and mentors. Andy had spent a few weeks in Zermatt the year before we met. Mark already had early ascents of formidable routes there to his name. Bob, unconventional even by climbers' standards, had eschewed the accepted progression and instead sought out British mountain environments that were rough, inhospitable and deeply unfashionable.

Although more tentative, I was ready for my next step. It was November and the snow and ice beckoned. Our friend, Steve, had a car and the college club now possessed its hiduminium ice axes. This was the time for the snow and ice, for Scotland and winter climbing.

We reckoned we could slip away unnoticed from our courses for three days on a Wednesday morning in late November. I was anxious about this transgression and urged Andy and Steve to arrange for our departure to be as low key as possible. I had to attend an early physics lecture, then I could sidle into the student canteen for our rendezvous and discrete departure.

Discrete?

Andy had commandeered several tables and piled them high with a tent, ice axes, ropes, rucksacks, primus stoves and food. He stood before it all, grinning triumphantly. Our cover was blown but his enthusiasm and a sense of our upcoming, outrageous adventure readily swamped my embarrassment.

Outside, drear November was pressing down on Lewisham and New Cross, squeezing remnants of artificial light out from the buildings and into the gloom, as we loaded this equipment into Steve's VW Beetle in a nearby side street. And then, late morning, we were at last away.

Creeping through the city's sluggish traffic, our hearts were already far ahead. On The Great North Road, dripping with hitchhiker mythology. At Scotch Corner, final outpost before the impossible North. Pushing on across Rannoch Moor, audacity and emptiness. Among the ghosts, still lost and wandering, still betrayed and desolate, down into dark Glencoe.

In second gear around Hyde Park Corner.

*

One of our ambitions for the trip had been a winter traverse of the Aonach Eagach, the five-mile ridge that bounds the Glencoe valley to its north. But when I looked out from the tent that first morning, only a few hours after our arrival, the mist was down almost to ground level and there was no question of attempting it. Instead, we decided on Bidean Nam Bean. Here though we were unable to fulfil our intention of a long session kicking steps on the snow. We found plenty of the white stuff near the head of a subsidiary valley but were forced to place each boot gingerly on the snow's crust only to fall through most times up to our thighs. That evening, having abandoned the peak, we escaped into the tent and fell asleep exhausted at some ridiculously early hour.

The next day dawned no fairer and the cold, the damp and the cramped sleeping conditions all did battle with my resolve. Back in London in the preceding weeks, I had sustained myself with dreams of peaks, snow-crowned and crowding around us in skies of brilliant blue. Of being strong, determined and bold. Instead, here, now, our second morning slid into being with no more energy, no more pristine enthusiasm, than our first. And I, its doleful scribe, lacked the will to hack once more up into the cloud.

Steve and Andy were still keen to work on their rudimentary snow and ice techniques and calculated that they would find more conducive conditions on the side of Buachaille Etive Mor. They set off determined to cut steps across snow slopes with their axes. In contrast, my mood was suppressed by the brooding, hidden heights pressing down from all sides. My priorities that day were to pursue the solitary, the melancholy and reflective, and I opted to walk the few miles along the road to Ballachulish and back. A plodding pace, the autumnal weariness of the valley bottom and the idea of majesty disinclined to reveal itself, all enveloped me that day as I wandered so very far from the pounding distractions of life in South East London.

The weather on our third day once again ruled against the Aonach Eagach but Andy had a contingency plan – Ben Nevis via Carn Mor Dearg. Over the map, we computed Naismith's rule, then added margins for drizzle, our physical state and our inexperience on snow. This calculation told us that we needed to pack the necessary for a probable high-level bivouac that night. The drive around Loch Leven added more time to our schedule but we were eventually walking through the Fort William distillery and up into the substantial corrie beyond.

We reached the place where we calculated we had to strike left for Carn Beag Dearg and were soon on steeper rock and heather. Our pace slowed and our individual zig zags wove ragged abstractions on the unfriendly hillside. Steve was dropping further behind and, after our waiting for him a couple of times, he announced that he would hold us up no longer but would pick his way back down slowly to the car and wait for us there.

With just the two us, we could struggle alongside each other and converse more easily. But something was happening to Andy. Usually so competent and organised, he was beginning to talk in sentences that meandered in their middle and lost direction. Given how much of our route – miles of serious, committing terrain – still lay ahead, I decided that we should think again when we reached the ridge above us.

Once there, we found a space between the boulders where we could huddle and, although wet, escape the wind that claimed the ridge. With exposed fingers, we searched our rucksacks for food with which to restore our fortitude when, suddenly, the cloud, the very fabric of the sky, seemed to part and open before us. There, instead of layers of sky or distant landscapes, there, seemingly within touching distance, a huge expanse of black and dripping cliff. Its apparent magnitude was overwhelming. Framed all around by mist, any sense of perspective was lost. Either this massive section of cliff was almost at our fingertips and horrific in its proximity. Or it was some distance away and of Himalayan grandeur, of an equally terrifying scale.

We scrabbled for food, eager for calories to settle our dispositions and hurry the return of rationality. We pulled open tins of sardines, then, having forgotten an opener, hacked into tins of rice pudding with our ice axes, stuffing handfuls of both into our mouths. Flecks from fish tails, globs of rice and blood from cuts to his fingers speckled his beard but Andy the mathematician, the careful logician, came back to us as we ate. And the decision to retreat then came easily.

The awkward rocks on our descent required concentration and our eyes were fixed on the ground before us. So, it was some time before we paused to glance back at the way we had come. But when we did, the mist had parted and we could see a gigantic snow face beyond our previous stopping point, its dimensions also distorted so that it assumed Alpine proportions. And high on that face was another climber, alone, with ice axe thrashing and moving fast.

It was Steve! He must have reconsidered and powered back up the mountain attempting to catch us.

Our shouts were taken on the wind, futile. Then we remembered the whistle in our emergency pack. But blasts on this also failed to attract him. We attempted to shout in unison, first without and then with a countdown. Nothing stopped the little orange figure – and the mist came in again. When it next parted, we blew blasts on the whistle, shouted again and flapped our arms and just before the visibility crashed again, he turned and signalled in recognition.

The afternoon light had faded as we three eventually reached the car. We had failed, very short of our aim but, although deeply weary, we were not disconsolate. At the least, Steve was not blindly chasing phantoms on into the night across the hostile summit of the Ben.

1967. Saturday Night and Sunday Morning

Reading lists!
Those stipulated by our courses of study, we picked at in a desultory fashion. Those whose reputations circulated by word of mouth within the climbing world, we gorged on. A key characteristic of many of the biographies was their culmination in grand attempts on the world's biggest mountains – the Himalayas.

Our early excursions felt expeditionary too, albeit on a smaller scale. For us, the biggest challenges often involved travelling to and from the mountains. Hitchhiking presented its own notorious and unpredictable schedules. The use of a college minibus, when available, simplified procedures dramatically and a private vehicle, although very rare among my contemporaries, granted the luxury of far greater choice of both destinations and companions.

On these long journeys, climbing tales, from our own limited experiences but also from these classic works, filled the hours and the enormous distances travelled. And never had we needed a night time's worth of stories, such a near inexhaustible supply, than on our return journey from Glencoe.

*

Another night in the tent, as had been our intention, was just impossible. We all three agreed. Although only Steve could drive, the journey back from Glencoe to London through the night was much more appealing than another night in wet sleeping bags. We were entering the final month of 1967, the most optimistic and liberating year that we had lived through, but there was none of that mood as we packed the tent in the rain and dark and left, not having seen the tops in three days.

We did not know how long the journey back through the night with only Steve driving would take. Nor could we guess how cold and uncomfortable a VW Beetle without a heater would be. But, wearing much of our damp outdoor gear, we luxuriated in being at least out of the weather and sitting down. Stories from the mountaineering books we had read sustained us through the early miles and we amazed ourselves with the amount of detail we had retained.

*

The return journey nearly ended in the early morning before we were hardly back in England. Andy had fallen asleep, crunched up among our equipment on the back seat, and Steve was growing more and more subdued. To keep him awake, I tried engaging him in conversations about climbing adventures from our joint reading. Longhi's fight for survival and Toni Kurtz hanging just beyond the reach of rescuers on the Eigerwand. Amputated, frostbitten toes being swept from the train truck travelling across India after Herzhog's failed attempt on Annapurna. Disturbing stories all of them. None of them soothing bedtime tales to fall asleep to – or so I hoped. We also sang every song we both knew – Beatles, Roy Orbison, Gilbert and Sullivan. Down alongside Loch Lomond, through the outskirts of Glasgow where the pubs were emptying out in a menacing fashion.

Steve was looking less and less involved, crouched over the steering wheel and staring intensely out into the night. He joined in with each song that I managed to dredge from memory, a few words behind and in a loud, insistent voice, somehow detached from the moment. Stuck for the second verse of a Buddy Holly song, I became silent for a while. Steve also fell silent and then he fell into my lap. I managed to grab the steering wheel and we somehow avoided the ditch at the side of the road. When he said sorrowfully that he needed to sleep, I knew that he meant it.

Not much further along, just outside Carlisle, we found an all-night truckers' cafe. Despite its stained net curtains and the water-filled ruts in the car park, it seemed like an oasis. Steve fumbled his way into the Beetle's little back seat while Andy and I went to seek warmth and refreshment.
Our shilling bought us two mugs of tea with plenty of sugar.
Our presence brought us suspicious stares.
There were empty plates on the tables, some containing uneaten bread, and Andy dared a quick foray to gather these spare slices. Some we ate but the rest we turned into a selection of sandwiches for Steve when he came round – HP sauce, tomato ketchup or sugar. We had time to kill if we were to allow him to sleep and we knew we had gradually become more accepted by the drivers when one big fellow came over and said 'Here you are, boys, I couldn't eat these last two slices'.

*

The car had stopped and Andy was waking me up. Steve needed to sleep again.
'Where?' 'Knutsford?' 'Where's Knutsford?'
Steve and I mumbled something as we passed each other in and out of consciousness, me coming round, him going under. The patterns of the lights on the sides of the big gleaming tankers in the car park were mesmerising and Andy busied himself in the food box.
'We'll make some porridge for Steve'.
It was the last of our supplies and, thinking of the porridge as we both began to shiver, brought back some colour to our existence.
'How many of these saccharin things do you think?'
The tube of saccharin tablets had been one of Andy's brainwaves and it enabled us to cut down on carrying bulky and potentially soggy bags of sugar.
'Should I put in a few more than that?' he asked.

And as he tapped the tube again, a blockage cleared, and an unexpected stream poured into the pan.

'Hell! Never mind. It will be a bit sweeter and that'll help warm us up'.

Nothing moved among the silent cylinders of the lorries and, as we waited, it slowly dawned on us that it was too cold for our porridge to ever reach boiling point. So, we ended up in the men's toilets with the primus stove and pan on a ledge above the wash basins and us loitering, wrapped in soggy sleeping bags. When we finally tasted it, the overpowering, biting staleness of the saccharin-soaked mess hit the backs of our throats and we had no hesitation in throwing our last food, pan and all, into the rubbish bin.

*

The light eventually came and with it names more familiar from our trips to Snowdonia – Brownhills, Coventry, the A5. These broke through into a dream world that was tormenting me with images of savage mountain environments, lost souls hanging from ropes, cars upside down in drainage gullies. Waking from each catnap, the taste of saccharin grew ever more intense.

Within this swirl of consciousness, we had somehow then arrived at Northamptonshire and Steve was saying that we needed to get off the motorway.

'We won't be able to get enough petrol at motorway prices to get us home'.

So, at each junction after that we had to drive around the roundabout looking for signs of a garage. We were fortunate to find one fairly quickly but a hundred yards or so from the pumps, the tank surrendered its final drop. We had to dig deep for the reserves of strength necessary to push the car for that final stretch and onto the forecourt. The accumulated jumble of coins from each of our pockets could buy just enough fuel, we calculated, to get us home.

We continued down the motorway heady with relief – and with a lack of food, sleep and any semblance of civilised discourse. Through London eventually, eighteen hours after leaving waterlogged Glencoe, and across the Thames with an exhaustion masquerading as grace. Home to a conspiracy of motorways and mountains rising up and fully claiming every final fibre of my consciousness.

And so, thick tongued and muddled, to sleep.

1968. West Penwith

Bodies among the dunes, scattered and sleeping wherever they had stumbled. The sun now stirring the blood and pulse, embracing the world, bringing us back into a shared paradise. We could never be so complete again nor such exotic strangers to each other.

Twelve hours or more the drive had taken. From London, dragging westwards and exiting the city, debating routes and trunk roads. Spirits high, crushed tight inside the minibus, securely sealed in wonder, doubt and expectation. Some still singing, chatting, chuckling, others drifting in and out of the short summer night. The dawn growing red and unimpeded over Dartmoor, where all this had started for me. Where these ambitions had first taken root, where I was free while others seemed locked down and set in concrete, career or fear.

We returned for the second time to West Penwith and the very end of England in 1968. Seasoned old hands now, we referred knowingly to cliffs, climbs, pubs and pasties. But really, I was a stranger still to this extreme tip of the country and play acting at familiarity. The West Country had always had an arbitrary boundary for me. Growing up by the sea in Dorset, I had felt sufficiently regional and firmly beyond London's sprawling hinterland. Surrounded by coast only a mile or so from my house in most directions, I had never been denied sand and sea, cliffs or rugged rocks. But as the urge to wander and travel grew in adolescence it was to the city, the capital, rather than further west that I had been drawn.

Sennen Cove, Chair Ladder, Bosigran. We had talked in the college bar and cafes of these proud cliffs, lusted for their dreamy ochres, reds and greys, the furry lichen on their boulders, the crystal quartz that sparkled in the sun and sliced into any finger ends that gripped or squeezed too tightly. We had plans for each, a list of climbs we might attempt if our boldness rose with the open skies, if our strength consolidated and grew after each day's exertions. The ozone, the rumble and boom of waves below us, and the excitement would urge us onwards. Upwards. We would dance on slabs above the sea, inching our way towards the next stance, united in a shared defiance of Nature's might and a readiness to meet her challenges.

On our previous visit we had been guided by the club's older hands. We were shown an Easy Way Down at Chair Ladder, respectful of the guidance that helped us pick our way down the walls of this Cathedral-By-The-Sea. We climbed in convoy up its highest section, slow and steady for hours on a straightforward classic. We were guided towards suitable undertakings for novices at Sennen, routes that we might climb on our own without supervisory oversight. We were led safely across the traverse at half height above the ruthless sea at Bosigran.

Now, in our second year, we were toned by experience in the mountains, hungry after the abstinence of a winter city. Far bolder and more independent, we had our list and a determination. Straight to it, we returned to the rock platform beneath the cliff at Sennen. Its golden architecture had stayed with me through the intervening year, but its grandeur seemed to have increased. The waves below the platform patrolled caged and restless, and after the shock of a spout of water blowing high into the air and drenching us, we were motivated to move quickly towards the vertical.

This area was first developed for climbing during the Second World War when specialist commandoes trained here for invasions by sea. The emphasis then was on scaling cliffs as swiftly and efficiently as possible, grappling irons and all. When we were first climbing, the emphasis had shifted to the elegance and technical difficulty of particular lines of ascent. Demo Route, a famous and serious enough challenge for a middle grade climber, embodies qualities from each era. The first pitch requires strength and finesse or a desperate thrutch inside a chimney lined with laceratingly rough rock. The top pitch requires a daring spirit and a steady, assured progression through a series of bold and unnatural-seeming moves.

In 1967, I had followed Andy up this climb as a tentative second. But this year, I had my sights set on leading it all, including the top pitch. From a small belay stance about forty feet above the starting ledge, the climber has to place hands at waist height under a huge, hanging flake of rock and lean out backwards with feet against the wall below. Assuming this position is relatively straightforward but, once there, any further movement, including a retreat, seems impossible. It feels as though relinquishing any hand or foot hold will result in your whole, backward-leaning body peeling away from the rock.

That day though, a fire developed during a winter of training, powered me on into the improbable and I was able to move confidently – no, much more than confidently – euphorically – on towards a more upright position and then up with increasingly large holds to the top of the cliff. To safety and security. To a sense of realising myself as a climber. And as a fully grown, autonomous adult.

The cultures of wartime commandoes and mid-1960s youth could not have felt more different. And yet, we were little more than a generation apart. We had been carrying much more of the ambition that had driven them than we could possibly realise.

*

These climbs have drawn me back over the years.
I last led Demo Route, still confident in a wildly different age and culture, on my fiftieth birthday.

1969. The Word on the Cliff

Communication in the climbing world. I loved its mediaeval character. An oral culture, almost pre-printing press and thriving by word-of-mouth.

You could be in a pub in South London, say, talking about a very specific piece of granite, a feint protuberance an inch or so long perhaps, one hundred feet up some obscure cliff in Snowdonia. And you would both know exactly the coarse contour of that handhold, its improbable location and its texture. You would have shared an identical feeling of 'thank-God relief' as your fingers located it at the end of some extended, blind reach. More than just shared knowledge, this was a common experience rooted deep in the body, beyond the cognitive, beneath language.

Two strangers in animated conversation and immeasurably connected. At some moment, this tiny patch of rock had held both of your lives. Actions that were primitive, prehensile and familiar. Irreducible to words. Essential for survival.

You learned from others, directly from mentors and those you respected. You also learned to weigh the credibility of these sources, the quiet authority of steady types, the wild words of the bullshitters. Again, essential for survival.

I was enthralled by the lattice-like inter-connectedness within the community of climbers, the characters I met at the bottom of cliffs uncoiling a rope, or sharing a cramped ledge halfway up a route, or mulling the day's achievements in a climbers' bar of an evening.

My diaries of the time reflect the delight I experienced in feeling part of a fraternity – and it was at that time exclusively male in membership - that met, dispersed and then reconvened in a haphazard fashion across all the major UK climbing areas. For example, a fellow worker selling deckchairs on Weymouth beach told me that he did a bit of climbing. While we subsequently tackled a route on the Portland cliffs one evening, he mentioned my friend, Mark, and asked whether I knew him, saying that he had watched him in action in North Wales earlier that year – and that he had hitched a lift in our college minibus!

It kept happening. Somebody on a ledge in Cornwall would reappear in the Peak District. Another in the Lake District would know one of my climbing mates in London. I found these two or three degrees of connection intensely fascinating. I had become a member of a guild, a brotherhood, closely bonded with people who were in every other respect, strangers.

Through such meetings, you could build a picture of climbs on your 'wish list'. There were guidebooks offering brief descriptions of these routes, of course, but I was always hungry for the reassurance – or a warning – that could be provided by a real live person familiar with each inch of the climb. And someone hopefully knowledgeable about my abilities and limitations as a climber.

'Is it as hard as, say, Crackstone Rib?'

'Can you abseil off if you have to? Is there a good tree or something?'

'The crux move at the top, is it really that hard?'

Not all communication was through these face-to-face encounters though. The leading magazine for climbers in my early days was called 'Climber and Rambler' but my friend Andy and I knew it as 'Stumbler and Bumbler'. It drew our disdain because, in both its content and graphics, it seemed to embody a stuffy and decidedly outdated approach to climbing and mountaineering. And it aged decades further overnight with the appearance at the beginning of 1969 of 'Mountain', a magazine with dazzlingly contemporary production values. It took a world-wide perspective so, despite its appealing features as an actual artefact to hold in one's hands, it contained fewer articles and photographs of climbs and places within my orbit.

A major rendezvous and the central source of information for crag-starved Londoners during my Goldsmiths years was the YHA shop just off Charing Cross Road. Tony Willmott, the young assistant in the climbing equipment section already had a national reputation as a pioneer of new, high-end climbs in the Avon Gorge.

Tony was known to regular visitors and way beyond as 'Mouth'. If you wanted an hour of his latest explorations, his forceful opinions, his recommendations, you stayed for an hour. If you wanted more, you arranged your visit to allow for more. If you could withstand a battering for even longer, you just surrendered to a verbal tour de force. If you actually wanted to buy something, and this never felt mandatory, you made an opening request as early as was possible in the stream of consciousness. At the next gap, you might be offered a '10% club discount'. More anecdotes at breakneck speed would follow, then a breath, then the bill rounded down. Another volley of enthusiastic storytelling, anecdotes, assertions and invective. A further purchase later added to the pile to make up for the new shortfall in the bill, maybe an additional discount or rounding down, then on again. More renegotiations than in any Kathmandu marketplace. The pile slowly growing, the stories never ending.

But our stories are taken on the wind. In 1971, aged only 23 and after pioneering some of the hardest climbs in the country from a very early age, Tony Willmott lost his footing on wet, easy ground at the top of the Avon Gorge. I like to think that he would have been telling companions about his latest exploits, voicing his impressions, giving his opinions in wild and fulsome fashion, as his foot slipped or he stepped backwards into the void.

1969. Carnedd Llewelyn

At the end of 1969 and perhaps seeking some icy astringency after cossetted Christmases, our club arrived in North Wales for a week of winter walking in the mountains. The original plan had been for us all to camp in the LLanberis Pass and this we did for a couple of nights. But the cold was extreme, even by the standards we had expected from that austere valley in its deepest, dark trough of winter. Some rapid consultations between us led to the discovery of a camping barn with spaces that belonged to Scottie Dwyer round in the Ogwen Valley. Although the main roads were passable, the track up to the barn was sealed inside thick ice and could only be reached by chipping away at it as a group some time with our ice axes.

Scottie Dwyer was a legendary figure in British mountaineering circles, especially for pioneering first ascents of demanding rock routes in the Welsh mountains just after the second world war. We found him to be a man of very few words and his barn to be accommodation of very few amenities. And it was debatable whether the temperature inside differed in any noticeable way from that outside. We slept on the creaky metal frames of bunk beds and, lying there, I could see next to my head, clear bright moonlight and a starry array through the large gap between the stones of the wall. The wind showed no respect and darted about our living area as freely as if in its natural domain. But we were together and could pace about the room, attempt to cook standing up and communicate with each other far more easily than between tents scattered about a windswept, frozen field.

New Year's Eve was approaching and expedition-style planning for a trip to some local pub was taking place. But Andy and I had our sights set much higher – to the top of Snowdonia's second highest peak, Carnedd Llewelyn. We had decided that we would bivouac for the night on this summit, partly to test out a piece of equipment that Andy had constructed with an industrial sewing machine, partly as 'good training for The Alps' and partly as an escape from the often-bleak surroundings of a Welsh pub on whatever the occasion. But mainly, if we could be honest about it, so that we had a tall tale to subsequently tell. An act of absurdity - Hunt's 1952 Everest Expedition somehow allied to *Les Evenements* of 1968.

We set off from the barn at around mid-day and settled into a steady ascent carrying large packs. The weather deteriorated on the higher reaches and as the dark descended before four o'clock, so too did the snow. We chose a spot just below the summit, a gently sloping bank of snow, and began to dig a trench that could house Andy's 'bivi-box'. His construction was essentially a box of red nylon, just big enough to shelter two people. In fact, although the comparison is unfortunate, it could best have been described as about the size of a double coffin. The intention was to place the bag in its trench and then secure it with four ice axes, one attached to each of the top corners.

With some difficulty, we positioned newly acquired insulation mats inside the tent, then our sleeping bags and finally, having removed only our waterproof outer layers, squeezed into the tight space where we prepared to spend a very long night. A New Year's Eve, far from festivity. Once inside, we attempted to excavate a small space for our gaz stove at the front of our tent using a billy can. Through the night we boiled snow in the pan and sustained ourselves with hot orange drinks.

We passed the time by making up silly songs (I still know them) and talking about *'The Purpose Of Life'* and, believe it or not, *'The Purposes of Education'*. We were both studying maths at the time and killed the bitter and desolate small hours trying to devise, without pencil and paper, the equations and models that described the range of solutions to the problem of whether one got more wet by running or walking during a rainstorm.

Because our tent fitted fairly neatly into the trench we had dug, we were protected from the main effects of the wind. But because it was made from nylon, the bag accumulated a massive amount of moisture from condensation so, although not bitterly cold, we were nonetheless pretty drenched all night. As well as having to keep raising the roof to avoid being buried by the continuingly falling snow, we also had to regularly excavate our stove. This involved taking off one woollen mitt, which we were wearing in our sleeping bags, and then scrabbling at handfuls of snow. The stinging pain from the cold made two of three movements the maximum bearable before withdrawing the hand into the relative warmth of one's armpit in an attempt to recover some sensation while the other person took over.

All those pints of hot orange drinks presented a problem later in the night as we were hemmed in and unable to get even colder and wetter by leaving our sleeping bags and the box. The creative but delicate, and slightly insanitary, solution is probably best not detailed here. But we did nonetheless continue to use the billy can for further drinks afterwards.

It carried on snowing through the night and we took shifts to push the new snow from the roof to avoid being completely buried. Maybe there was the odd catnap. It was a long night and we were in that claustrophobic box for about fourteen hours, until what little light the new day was going to grant us had been realised.

When we returned down to the valley later the next morning to the rest of our group and the luxury of Scotty Dwyer's disgusting barn, we were full of it. They had spent the night in the pub drinking in the New Year. I've spent many similar alcoholic evenings and they tend to blur into each other in memory.

But the night on Llewelyn stands out and has sustained me through life with its defiantly absurd assertion of the Life Force.

THE ETHELS – WINTER

Ethels Day 12 – 8th October

Blakelow Hill (Bonsall Moor)

A very murky morning and my cycling group decide to ride out to Bonsall Moor where, hoping that the heavy mist will remain our friend, we plunge into the murk to seek out the trig point on Blakelow Hill. We dump our bikes and use maps or instinct to guide us over and under barbed wire, through gaps where the limestone walls have collapsed, past witches' claws on dripping hawthorn branches.

I had been told of a friend being escorted off the land after being intercepted by an angry farmer on this hill. On *his* hill. It was to have been my friend's 'first Ethel' and it became his last.

Consequently, we move as silently as possible, figures shifting into and out of view, muffled shapes abroad among the heavy air. Our whispers are subdued, avoiding brittle syllables that can cut across air. We lose each other, disagree about the likely lines of walls, reconvene, then help each other through the wires.

We find the trig point and pose for photos. Then back into the gloom, the same haphazard route through the vaguest of mazes.

Back at the bikes, chuckling at the subterfuge, our modest achievement, our undetected accomplishment.

And then downhill, freewheeling into Bonsall, and indoors to the bustle and hiss of a coffee machine.

Ethels Day 13 – 10th October

Axe Edge Moor, Cheeks Hill & Oliver Hill

Having failed to reach Cheek's Hill last week, I am returning for a second attempt, this time after much closer study of the map. I park on the narrow lane to the north, intending to approach from the opposite direction. Turning, as it were, the other Cheek.

And what a joy to be straightaway on new ground. Only a few miles from where I lived for five years, yet a whole unexplored landscape. The feint path along the ridge to Axe Edge Moor provides an elevated, open aspect and there is just enough of a route-finding challenge to keep me alert – to keep looking, calculating and judging. Continually breathing it in.

I have it all to myself. Ridges to the far west melt in the afternoon light, giving the impression of a country deep at rest. It seems unlikely, impossible, that people inhabit any of this terrain, the folds and unseen dips, and that steady intercourse proceeds.

I am back to the lane at a shattered sign fixed to a post, its warning about abandoned mine shafts blasted by gunshots, its message made more sombre. From here an obvious track takes me to the summit of Cheeks Hill and its disintegrating sheep pens and walled path. These abandoned places always radiate an atmosphere of resignation, as if their stones fall, unobserved and one at a time, according to some unknown, irregular schedule. The effort to remain standing surrenders in the silent purity of autumnal light.

From there I drive down to Flash and follow a short path across farm fields up to Oliver Hill. From this scrappy top the views are magnificent. Wonderful, wonderful vistas, all relaxed and warming in the beautiful October sun!

Ethels Day 14 – 13th October

Kinder Scout

The toughest Ethel so far. And the highest of the lot.
Six of us take two cars to Hayfield, driving all the way through a mist that we hope will burn off through the morning. It doesn't.
Instead of William Clough, we decide to take the path up to Sandy Heys, which is a first for us all. The Downfall is in a wet and windy mood and offers no encouragement to linger. So, we press on westwards while the mist turns more definitely – and more defiantly – to rain. As if to reinforce this sense of haughty malevolence, the wind picks up too. There is no shelter for a lunch spot, so we sit in full waterproofs scattered across sloping slabs and laugh and chatter, bolstered by the delightful absurdity.
It is an effort to stand up again, cags and over-trousers creaking. Bodies too. I blow the rain drops from the end of my nose as we set off again. We become more subdued as the realisation takes hold that there is no quick and easy escape for us from these conditions. We plod on until we reach the trig point at Kinder Low and I experience once again that strange, child-like realisation that these isolated, stoical structures stand immobile through all conditions. While we eat, sleep, rest or play, they are there. In storm, in ice, in scorching sun, the same. Fixed, impervious, unaffected. A fanciful musing, fey almost, but also a sort of comfort.
We gather and discuss our options as the light signals its intention to retire early today. Three will continue directly to the descent route and three will press on into the interior of the moor to seek its actual highest point.
The map shows our destination to be little more than half a mile away and we try to navigate on compass bearings

across a watershed between streams. The lie of the land, though, is obstinately non-compliant and, as ever on Kinder, we are pushed from side to side to avoid the trickiest groughs. We know that we are not holding our precise course and attempt to take note of the ground beneath our feet to aid our return. And although the visibility is down to a few feet, we search ahead for any signs of a slight prominence.

The ground neither rises nor falls to any definite degree. The half mile seems impossible to gauge. Our remaining light is limited. Our resolve and determination are wavering. Our project is a folly.

We see a sloping rock shelf emerging from the mist ahead and it feels slightly higher than its surroundings. We also calculate that from the time we have spent we must be somewhere nearer our intended destination. So, we decide that this will do. And I suppress my niggling doubt that, really, it won't.

I adjust my compass bearing through 180 degrees. We turn to retrace out steps by means of the features I have been trying to commit to memory – the patch of gravel, the collapsed bank of peat, the trickle of stream, the stagnant pool and the pointed rock – and none of it is there! The little ground that the mist allows us to see looks totally unfamiliar.

We all feel it, the sense that we are in a very lonely spot, in rain and wind that bids us no good. I attempt a confident, reassuring tone and set off in the direction the little, red-tipped needle indicates. It takes a little internal conversation, one familiar from past mountain incidents, to insist that I follow the compass whatever and control the fickle instincts that would lead me one way and another.

The trig point re-emerges. Thank goodness. It has been a good lesson in trusting to the bearing and holding one's nerve.

As we descend to Edale Cross, the mist parts briefly and we are granted a view of the enormous flanks of interlocking hills at the head of the Edale Valley, magnified many times by the dramatic contrast to the hours of close, wet mist that has accompanied us all day. The dark now comes to find us and we finish with a long descent down the bridle path to Hayfield. There is little conversation. I am sealed completely inside a cocoon that has allowed some composure through the challenges of this wild and precious day.

Ethels Day 15 – 22nd November

Longstone Moor

The winter is anxious to be in full swing and the air is beginning to bite. But the sun, still keen to be ripening and enriching, casts late autumnal reds and golds across our fields and the moor above. Little Longstone barely notices our passing as we set out, so settled and deeply self-contained are its dwellings.

We leave the road and our route rises through orderly fields, the grasses trimmed and tidied by grazing sheep. The walls are in good repair, tumbling only occasionally to hint at a wildness that can be seen in the distance and in all directions as we climb. Farm gives way to forest, and in clumps of empty woodland, there is darkness, dustiness and little sign of life.

The transition continues and we are over our final stile and onto an uncultivated scuff. Up here, in a less orderly world, two figures in a vehicle are lumbering across the ground. Not a land rover but an ordinary family saloon making a tortuous traverse of the land. As they come closer, their age becomes more apparent. They are considerably older than us and seem purposeful in their efforts and acting in tandem. They are checking their sheep they tell us when we ask, able to manage this task now, brother and sister in their later years, only with the aid of a car. Stubbornly continuing in a role, clinging on to one, that has defined and shaped their lives.

There is little undulation across Longstone Moor and its highest point rises only slightly above the surrounding ground. But the perfect conical cairn that has been erected here forms a stately prominence, confident and at home in the flood of afternoon sunlight. We linger, nibble a late lunch, and take in the sweep of hills all around.

I have only crossed this moor once before. It sits inconspicuously in the map and has always evaded my exploratory urges. So, it is a surprise, a delight, to experience how large and remote an area it seems to cover. We walk on to the east across easy, level ground and in the distance familiar-looking edges come into view. Frogatt? Or maybe Curbar?

Lines of scree and rubble gouging the ground suggest something beyond natural weathering and displacement. Lead that folded into limestone over geological time was discovered here by the Romans and then scavenged or systematically extracted by later forebears. Now, these workings are abandoned and ignored, apart from the occasional, fenced off, collapsed hole.

Turning to the south we cross more rough ground and arrive at Longstone Edge with the land all laid out below, washed with sunlight as if for our inspection.

It is time to descend, back to the quiet confidence of the village, to its settled self-assurance.

Ethels Day 16 – 25th November

Ecton Hill & Wetton Hill

They stand about, these hills that border the Dove and Manifold, confident and quietly independent. Some have been chosen for the Ethels list, others snubbed. But they nonetheless endure as a community, custodians of the landscape.
It is the second glorious winter day this week.
From Wardlow, I cross a couple of fields with the scarp of Ecton Hill like a headwall blocking the view. Down a steep and awkward muddy bank to arrive in the bottom of the Manifold Valley. From here up the other side past a dwelling with the full range of gothic features – tower, turret, battlements and drawbridge – leaving hardly any space in which to live.
I check my map carefully as the path structure looks complicated and as I rise, I glance across at hills that now feel like old friends – Carder Low and Pilsbury Hill among them.
How wonderful to now be able to name them all. Before I had driven past and admired them for more than forty years, unable to distinguish one from another.
The shafts and tunnels of the copper mines that once bored and blasted their way into this hillside are evoked by restored buildings and explanatory plaques. The place is alive with the grunts of industry, the fear and the exhaustion. All around but also dead and gone.
From the top of Ecton Hill, I walk south along the rim of the Manifold Valley with nobody in view. Just me and the sheep. That's the way we like it, the sheep and me.
The route is not obvious as I drop onto tracks with occasional isolated houses and farm buildings appearing as if from nowhere, seemingly occupied by no one.

Wetton Hill now comes into view, another mighty flank barring the way, and I navigate tracks to the barrow at its highest point by means of a rising diagonal line. It is tiring work, and I lie down at the top in a scoop shielded from the sharpness of the breeze.

It will be an effort to leave this ancient place of rest and air and sunlight. A place above the worried rush of time.

Ethels Day 17 – 20th December

Wolfescote Hill

We park in deserted Biggin and take the track upwards from Dale End. At the narrow lane that leads to Biggin Grange we continue towards the hidden defile through which the River Dove flows. All is quiet, the ground exhausted, the day just ticking by.

The lane seems long and undistinguished despite the beautifully contoured hills, the silent sentinels, that line the far bank of the valley. The road surface deteriorates and becomes a pitted tarmac track. Ivy has clawed its way up the trunks of beech trees. Some lean on the point of collapse, echoing a sense of indifference that haunts all around the day. Occasional sounds from the Grange – a human voice, clear but toneless on the thin air, or a door slamming – have an unsettling effect.

How to access the open country and the hill's top is not obvious and I get in a muddle with the map. The ground we want seems locked in and locked away with trespass our only option. Then we locate the rusty gate and its stubborn catch. It is alien and unwelcoming but, once through and climbing rough ground and the limestone striations, our pace becomes purposeful, and our spirits rise.

From the summit we can see again the sleeping village and the dot where our tiny car must be. This hill that from below seemed so unprepossessing assumes full stature here, its watchful presence extending over distances, over a land whose breadth and undulation derive from eons long, long before our human strictures, our puny, feudal claim.

Ethels Day 18 – 22nd December

Wardlow Hay Cop

An early start, the land strange and eerie in the moonlight.

We are purposeful, the five us, sharing out breakfast supplies and equipment at the car. The chatter and the chuckles soon fade. The climb up becomes a silent affair. We are locked inside layers to combat the cold and there is a deep frost on the ground. We reach the trig point with a stiff wind across the top. The air is keen and indiscriminate, and our eyes water as we look east towards Longstone Moor. We are still ahead of the rising sun, the ceremony of the solstice, but a sense of imminent arrival is clawing its way across the grazed ground.

We unpack stoves, coffee and the ingredients for a fried breakfast, a spread to cater for all dispositions. The laughter resumes. We become busy, the bustle helping to counteract the penetrating chill.

I am stiff with bending and crouching when our leader says

'What we could do with is a trestle table'

and disappears behind a dip to drag one out! A table for us, brought here yesterday and hidden in anticipation.

The fun and absurdity fuels even greater cheer as the breakfast is dished out, coordinated as best we can. Hot food, hot drink. Its heat ingested hungrily, its finer culinary aspects subsidiary.

We are high above the surrounding land as the sun edges above the horizon without fanfare or fabrication. It swells as it rises in silent domination of the dawn. Our ancestors, our own blood and flesh, dwelt in deep connection to this spectacle. I am divorced from such

rituals, although aware of a strong but ill-defined sense of awe.
Meanwhile, below us on the main road to the north, the lights of cars cross the Peak District.
The trivial round.
The common task.
East to West.
West to East.

Ethels Day 19 – 28th December

Chelmorton Low & Sough Top

Day after day of thick mists and rain have made walking on the hills less appealing. But we are finally out from our midwinter burrows today.

The village is damp and deserted, seeing out the last, exhausted days of the year. We park opposite the Primitive Hall where the few short hours of daylight douse our surroundings in austerity. Along with fire thorns from a garden pyracantha, our jokes and chatter seem like the Life Force's last efforts at resistance.

The short, steep pull up to the twin barrows of Chelmorton Low then kills any idle conversation. These hummocks, as with all sites of burial, chastise my tread. It is an outrage to be here, and on such an afternoon. Would that I could step so lightly as to be above the ground and totally of the air. An air that clings to exposed skin like cheap liniment.

From twenty miles away or more, I have orientated myself by means of Chelmorton's scarp, its skyline asserting an ancient elegance in all directions. But today, as we descend, I also appreciate for the first time the striking geometry of the strip farming, walls as if gouged across the land, determined to endure.

To linger for a while longer outside this century, we should walk the few miles to Taddington. But we don't. We drive. We have hearths and homes, and night will fall with no allowance made, all of a piece with this dispassionate day.

Unlike Chelmorton Low, Sough Top does not assert its presence but is tucked away behind water board facilities and among high, cultivated fields. We climb up steeply from a little lane and make a map reading error which necessitates some back tracking in our search for the trig point.

Over decades the Peak District has grown familiar, so much so that there had seemed to be no surprises left for me, no new, first-time revelations. But this Ethels project has brought out the previously insignificant and unexplored. Massive tracts of land, magical corners, new names and a revitalised topography.

'Look! That must be Fin Cop, it can't be anything else. 'Look!'

Ethels Day 20 – 29th December

Lees Moor

Very late in the year, mid-winter, the sun is mimicking autumn. Feigning warmth. Our track is puddled with a golden light. Stones beneath our feet have a summer crunch but we know the afternoon will be of a limited duration. There will be a descent later through darkening woods. No lazy lingering before the finality of night!

Although this hill looked a relatively slight undertaking from the road, it is presenting more navigational challenges and awkward terrain than I had been expecting. Vehicle tracks impose their own order, and we use some of these to gain height. The degree of landscape fashioning smacks of a busyness, of rearranging for rearranging's sake. But no doubt, the management of timber, or maybe the recreational slaughter of birdlife, necessitate these thoroughfares.

Finding the exact highest point on this densely forested top demands much attention to the map and some reference to the altimeter. In among the trees themselves, the going is tough over fallen logs, abandoned to the custody of ferns and draped in moss.

I have a friend who sometimes talks of being lost in these woods decades ago when still a teenager. As the wind picked up and the light faded, and with the descent route far from obvious, he confesses to a creeping sense of fear.

But today, after so much mist and rain, unvarying and without respite, the setting sun exerts a powerful draw.

On our way down, we stare in silence for a long time like creatures of the veldt or plain, as if mesmerised.

As if facing some imminent, irreparable loss.

Ethels Day 21 – 31st December

High Wheeldon

From the north it is a pyramid, an unnatural construction, its lines too perfect, too symmetrical, to be born of ice or river or geological disruption. It has been placed here, some vestige of a alien intelligence, a superior civilisation. A gift, a reminder or, perhaps, a warning.

From the east, where we are parked, the dimensions become more reassuring. Still huge, and blocking out the winter sun, the ridges nonetheless have some weathered irregularity. The hill is recognisably of this area, formed and seasoned here.

It is a short push from the road, first a dip and then an unrelenting climb. Only a quarter of an hour or so but steep enough to require a stop for breath, echoing over decades from those slogs at altitude back when. Footsteps almost cut into the slope, impressions from the boots of those who have come before. A silent company still here and present in the chill air.

At the top, gathering around the trig point, we cannot but stare at the ridge of hills switch-backing away before us. Like the spine and tail of some gigantic monster from the deep, its scales and fins break the surface as it thrashes wildly in all directions – Hitter, Parkhouse, Chrome and Hollins Hill.

The spectacle is enormous, the air keen as sheet metal, bringing tears to our eyes. So, we retreat back down below the skyline. Others are on the hill, their voices half holiday high jinks, half wonderment. We have scones and coffee and invite the strangers to join us.

This outdoors brought others together, built strength and solidarity, gave sustenance in times of need.

And still it does, reaching out beyond the confusions and the shallowness of now.

Ethels Day 22 – 2nd January

Grin Low

The afternoon will not be long with us, the light is thin and filters between smooth trunks of leafless trees. Children's occasional shouts pierce the stillness, their games a secret somewhere further along the track. Occasionally, people appear and then disappear as they wind their way upwards on undulating, subsidiary paths. We climb in the companionship of woodland, sheltered from a conspiracy of wind and rain.

We reach the edge of forest where a gate admits us to open hillside, trails and hummocks taking us towards the summit tower. The wind is beginning to buffet and this sturdy, round construction appears to offer some shelter, drawing the various wandering figures towards it.

We touch its stone wall, everybody seems to. It is solid, indifferent to time, unmoved by storm.

But the intention of the weather is now unmistakeable. We pull our hats further down over ears, raise and tighten our hoods, as the first smack of hail hits our faces. The others scatter, denied companionship, all hurrying towards more substantial refuge.

Alone again, hunched inside layers, we make eye contact and chuckle, muffled though our laughter is, disquieting though our shaking from the cold.

Ethels Day 23 – 3rd January

Cown Edge & Lantern Pike

A fine Dark Peak walk on mainly unfamiliar ground. We park high on a minor road and make a steep ascent of Cown Edge. It is cold and windy up here, scratty grass and scrub and with views of the shiny, high towers of Manchester and aircraft from continents afar dropping from the sky down to the airport.

From here we can also take in the huge panorama of Bleaklow and Kinder Scout to the east, and various other Ethels to the south. The extent of these views! Hills and ridges outnumbering each other as if to crowd out the senses. It takes time, discussion and reappraisal to gradually put names to most of them.

Cown Edge, the remains of a high quarry, a dark, broken gritstone rampart, forms the eastern edge of a majestic, wide tract of land. If it were lower down and sheltered from the elements, it might be possible to imagine Jane Austen's ladies or others promenading. But the ground is too rough for the refined and the altitude too unrestrained. It suits us well though and we raise our gaze and fully take in these precious perspectives.

Lantern Pike looks miles away, far further than the map suggests. The track there takes us along the Pennine Bridleway, a section that the three of us had omitted through weariness on a cycle trip through the area a few years ago.

Lantern Pike welcomes us as we climb its eastern flank and from the summit we are again rewarded with a landscape that is growing ever more familiar, ever more enticing, as each Ethel is reached.

We return by a lower route. We have done our climbing for the day. Blackening skies move across our path and threaten. But neither snow nor storm materialise.

Instead, a rainbow!

Ethels Day 24 – 9th January

Harthill Moor

Sunday morning and they're all out – hikers, joggers, doggy people.

This track up past dour Cratcliffe Tor is well worn by memories. We make our way under its watchful scrutiny. A hermit lived here once in a cave, deep among his privations.

The stone giants of Robin Hood's Stride are frozen solid now, rooted to the spot, their epoch past. Old friends gone too, but still lurking here in various forms. Small children played on the rocks, a picnic was once spread out. Absurd challenges, daring, scrambling. Laughing.

On to arable land, long since subdued and settled, raked into pasture, churned into slurry, fenced and barbed. Fields slant down towards coppices, each neatly walled and circumscribed. Neatness and orderliness prevail, muting the roar of history.

We cross farmland, pick our way as best we can around the ruts from tractor tracks. A large agricultural machine straddles the skyline. A modest sign hints at some religious institution tucked discretely out of sight.

The trig point too seems tidied away into the walled corner of a field as if an embarrassment or afterthought. Electricity's shock tactics have also been employed to keep us from our destination and a little ingenuity is required to effect a breach.

The top of Harthill Moor makes no great claim to prominence but, far from all the other busy weekenders, we can pick out some from the growing set of Ethels that have already consumed our energies.

Ethels Day 25 – 14th January

Chinley Churn & Eccles Pike

Beautiful, strong winter sun is drawing out warm colours from the gritstone and casting deep shadows into the hollows. It is a day on which to feel alive and to be thankful for it.

I have been up around Chinley Churn only once before, about thirty years ago, and found it a much bigger piece of land than I had imagined from down on the Glossop Road.

The track leaves the hamlet with its scattered houses and rises gently though small, thorny trees, fierce guardians of the upper slopes. My map suggests that I can make a strenuous ascent up a steep, rocky gully and be at the trig point far more directly, rather than continuing on the long arc of the path.

But it is a tough climb and I have to stop more than once. Blackened gritstone walls have collapsed in places, gone their own way, and their barbed wire trimmings are rusty. Nearer my goal, however, the walls are taller, more substantial and the spikes along their top crueller and more ill-intentioned. An electric fence completes the barrier but the purity of the light and my light-heartedness put a spring into my jump when I decide to go. I clear it by a furlong. Thank goodness.

The trig point is substantial and well-maintained and, tucked down in a small depression nearby, I am completely sheltered. The sun's warmth has the intensity of late spring, of summer even. But the piercing clarity with which its light is delineating every feature, both massive and tiny, near and distant, this belongs to winter, to no other season.

My sandwich bursts with flavour, the coffee from my flask is a work of sophistication. I could stay here for a long time.

I begin the familiar routine of trying to name the many Ethels I can see. South Head and Mount Famine opposite, of course, and the huge sweep of Kinder's western edge. Bleaklow beyond, to the north? Down towards Buxton, hills that I now know by name individually rather than as just anonymous features in a broader panorama. But directly north, is that

Lantern Pike? It seems too close and not quite distinctive enough in outline.

I check my map and the Ethels app on my phone. I am not at the designated spot. That is still a walk away, a good half a mile.

What a glorious inconvenience, I am being forced to tread more of this landscape, to walk the edge of the abandoned Cracken Edge Quarries. The small outcrop of rocks ahead is my true destination, this extra distance a gift.

I eventually circle back along the western edge of the extensive plateau, the sun's heat beginning to lessen but its light still proudly scattered across the sky.

It is a short drive around to the lane below Eccles Pike, the few steps up to its summit an even quicker journey. The view back to Chinley Churn is spectacular, the sloping strata that support the plateau now visible, the magnificent size and structure now revealed.

Dog walkers join me, the access here is very easy for those overly reliant on cars, the detritus from their visits everywhere beneath my feet necessitating very careful steps.

Ethels Day 26 – 16th January

Gautries Hill, Slitherstone Hill & Eldon Hill

A misty day with some wind and a threat of rain that never really materialises.

We set off from just outside Peak Forest and climb steeply up to Gautries Hill. We have no views from the top. On the way back down we see an injured rook that seems to have been strangely incapacitated. It flaps a few wing beats into the air and then crumples to the ground again, its legs, body and wings all seeming to give way at the same time.

Eldon Hill is hidden in mist and thus seems very high and distant from the track below. The route is not obvious – across fields, steeply up through a small forest, then marshy ground around a large pond before a rough track climbing at a forgiving angle. Map and compass work ensure our success here. Gradually, the huge quarry that we are skirting becomes apparent as the mist lifts a little.

At this stage, we decide to add Slitherstone Hill to our itinerary as we are so close and to save having to return for it some other day. Barbed wire prevents us from reaching its very highest point but we are close. And what an experience!

From a very rounded, nondescript hill and in a claggy mist, we are afforded partial views of, for me, stunningly new perspectives on familiar hills. Never has Win Hill looked so impressively pyramidal nor Mam Tor such a brooding presence. All of it is new, striking and unexpected.

Then a return to navigate up Eldon Hill and down the other side to gaze for the first time into Eldon Hole - a savage slit straight down into the underworld.

And finally, a break in the mist, the light playing tricks and revealing layers and layers of hills masquerading as sky, as clouds are also transformed into land. Some very late sun to finish with, to hint at what might have been a very different day.

Ethels Day 27 – 20th January

Lord's Seat, Mam Tor & Lose Hill

A continuing run of completely clear, cold days so off to the Great Ridge from where I can look back and spot last Sunday's hills, this time without their *'entourage of mist'* (to borrow Kathleen Jamie's poetic phrase). It's a continuing delight to be able to name far more Peak District hills than I ever could. Why had I never sought to do this before?

First along to Lord's Seat, shut out from the camaraderie of the paragliders - all male, of a certain age and build. If these had been groups of climbers I would be enjoying brief exchanges. But I don't share their expertise, the terminology with which to bridge the distance between us and would only offer touristy banalities if I tried.

A turnaround from that high point, back down to Mam Nick and then slotting into the procession up to the Tor (past a sign pointing 'To The Summit'). It's forty years or so since I climbed the frozen front face of Mam Tor with friends one December evening using crampons and ice axes. There had been no crowds shouting to their dogs, on that moonlit, icy night. Not one other soul, in fact.

These are the most crowded Ethels so far. I know I should be more tolerant and I do make an effort to cheerfully acknowledge the many people I pass. And I do know that those brave and dogged pioneers did not work so hard to create a national park just for me and one or two of my closest mates. But I am who I am and do love the hills best when they feel deserted, lonely and remote.

The Great Ridge sweeps away down to Hollins Cross, then up to Back Tor and ending at Lose Hill. Once the slabs run out, the muddy runnels are well-worn and slippery and I go over twice - an old bloke crashing to

the ground, dirty knees, a taste of grit and solicitous enquiries from the various (younger) witnesses.
And the pretence that I am still very much nineteen is severely challenged.
But not extinguished.

Ethels Day 28 – 26th January

Parkhouse Hill & Chrome Hill

The Peak District's finest hills, surely? Although modest in height (even for Ethels) they are probably the most mountainous in character - and in the approach and attitude required.

It will be thirty-five years or so since I first traversed Chrome Hill with my old friend and back then it was private land, so we had the extra challenge of keeping a low profile on high, exposed ground. I have also crossed Parkhouse Hill, the more serious of the two, a couple of times but when younger, climbing fit and surer of foot. And in dry conditions.

This time we start with Parkhouse Hill from the village of Earl Sterndale, the opposite direction to my previous traverses. But first I suffer agonising pains in both my feet for a few steps before realising that I have put a pair of my wife's size 6 boots onto my size 8 feet. A quick change and we are off again.

The views are immediately stunning. When I was younger, I always sought out climbing crags or the highest moorland wastes. Today, this landscape seems far more overpowering – a benefit of ageing! We drink it in.

Descending the far side of Parkhouse is much more challenging. It is a hands and feet scramble, made serious by muddy boots, indifferent handholds and sloping, slippery limestone ledges for the feet.

And in places a drop that would have Consequences.

My friend has packed a short length of light weight rope and a couple of slings, just in case.

The exhilaration and adrenaline rush put us in a skittish mood for Chrome Hill and we are soon huddled in a small cave on its far side singing songs and eating lunch.

The return route takes us down lonely Dowel Dale, the middle stretch of the punishing Buxton half marathon route that I struggled with decades ago.

A great day out on the hills, to be filed in the compartment of my memory labelled 'Fully Alive'.

Ethels Day 30 – 30th January

Aleck Low

Turning from the High Peak Trail, the route to the top takes a bit of finding. At first blush, I miss the tight gap in the hedge with its old wooden fingerpost almost hidden and returning to nature. Once through and scraped by the thorns, it is then a rising traverse across a planted field that seems huge, stretching up all the way to the horizon, seemingly more prairie than Peak District. Another field and then I am at the secluded summit.

Again, I am at one of those places that I have driven by for years, never aware of its existence.

A copse of densely planted trees, tidy and circumspect, crowns the top, seeing out the seasons. Beside it, among tiny undulations of the land, a trig point stands on its own.

Solid, sturdy walls topped with copious barbed wire ensure that it will remain untouched. Such excessive fortification! From the closest point, I gaze over the wall like some visitor to a quarantined patient. Screened from closer contact, there is an air of formality about proceedings, as if some protocol should be observed.

I mumble something before turning to track back across the fields beneath a grey and darkening sky. I am pestered by a sense of dissatisfaction, an incompleteness, as the dwindling light curtails another day.

Ethels Day 30 – 6th February

Stanton Moor

It's a short drive from home, for a pleasant Sunday stroll with our visitors. The way should be familiar, the lanes, the parking spot, the access to the moor. But it still generates some doubt, some debate.

From the car park, we walk a short stretch of road and then we are away among the rocks and trees and up through heather onto the elevated plateau. The Derwent Valley drops down to the east. Its ribbon of factories and houses from Matlock up to Rowsley seems close. Yet, our moor feels removed from habitation, far above the daily round.

Sandy tracks skirt quarries that have filled with grassy overgrowth, softening the blunt geometry of these old, abandoned workings. We can but wonder at the vanished industry, at the idea of bustle and activity.

On towards the patch of trees, the track now broad and puddle strewn. The silver birches, as we enter, tingle, chatter almost, as they catch a whisp of breeze. The going is easy, all ways leading to the central space, the focus, the Nine Ladies ring.

The cloud is low, the trees respectfully still. A lack of life within the ring, its history dormant now, the heavy sense of community suspended.

Tribes, relations, strangers, all gathering here. Woodsmoke and ceremony, the comings and goings, the seasonal shifts and the cycle of the year. We can almost see them, hear their hearts and sense their pulse. Become pulled into their activity, feel with them their Bronze Age sensitivities.

But we can't.

Back the way we came or via a wider sweep? We choose the new paths as clouds darken and descend. As the wind picks up.

Then the rain hits us, perverse and far from vertical. It is sudden and insistent, and we raise our hoods, tug urgently at zips and Velcro. A second blast and I chuckle at such spirited adversity. But then, immediately, a third, and levity vanishes with the realisation that this piercing cold and painful, pounding rain is here to stay.

Our quickened pace will ultimately bring us respite. We are not completely lost to these savage elements. Unlike those dwellers we were so recently among, their being so set against annihilation, their fortitude so terrible.

Ethels Day 31 – 23rd February

Durham Edge & Shatton Moor

My first time out with Ethels for a while. After all the recent storms, the squalls are still with us and when I have parked up I can barely get out of the car, let alone get kitted up.

From the start, in this new landscape, there is emptiness and distance, the washed-out colours and weathered winter sky helping exaggerate the scale of everything. Aiming for a ladder stile on the horizon, it seems miles away across rough ground. From there a squeeze on hands and knees beneath barbed wire and through a chained gate, some uphill and then balance moves to surmount a gritstone wall to the trig point. All that crawling around exploring in my muddy childhood certainly paying off!

Some retraced steps and then a track towards Shatton Moor. Extensive vistas and what for years was just undifferentiated wild country to me is now a detailed panorama of heights and scarps and peaks that I can give names to, wave upon wave of them. A gate to surmount, then a steep pull up the top.

And then – Wow! Hail and rain blasting away at my fragile coating of civilisation. I crouch down in a grouse shooter's butt but achieve little respite.

Traversing rough heather along the top, blown this way and that, I chuckle to myself deep inside layers. These Ethels are not the big mountains of my youth. But I tire more easily now, lack the stamina I once had and experience nasty stabs of arthritis. So, the sense of challenge, the discipline of keeping calm and continuing to think in the face of Nature's rages, produces almost the same fears, rushes of adrenaline and satisfactions.

I just love it and am so fortunate. And so grateful.

Ethels Day 32 – 27th February

Revidge & Merryton Low

Spring is nibbling at the edges of winter this morning so the time is right to tick these off my list.

On my occasional trips across the high road from Warslow to the Roaches area during the past forty years, I have often told myself that I should one day stop and walk a bit on its extensive wastes. Today is finally that day.

Revidge is a short walk over land that seems less typical of the Peak District but still familiar?

And then it hits. My home county! The heathlands of Dorset. And in it all floods. Hardy's tangled bindstems scouring the sky, Sunday school trips, fish paste sandwiches, cherryaid, the lot.

From the trig point old friends to the north - High Wheeldon, Chrome Hill, Parkhouse. In the very far distance, others. Those to the west named. And to the east a muddle which needs the map – ripped by the wind – to finally sort.

The remains of my friend's dog are scattered here surrounded by these many hills.

On to Merryton Low which looks inconsequential from the map, lanes on all sides and the top less than five minutes from the car. But from the first step up, a skylark is asserting a frantic monologue. Spring is extending into the high ground.

The views are, as ever with these Ethels, magnificent. The brooding spikes and shadows of Ramshaw never fail to hit me, as do their bigger sullen siblings, Hen Cloud and The Roaches.

Ethel Day 33 – 4th March

Shining Tor, Cats Tor & Foxlow Edge

Out and about in the mist. At The Cat and Fiddle it looks so uninviting I have to force myself out of the car. However, once going I warm to the task and enjoy the eerie atmosphere.

There is no wind and the mist lays fixed and heavy, an occupying presence. Traffic is mumbling and roaring back and forth on the tight bends beyond and below the hill. Sensations slip away and soon the world becomes more neutral, more resigned. It feels both unsettling and comforting at the same time. In all directions, the land stretches off into obscurity.

After an age, there are figures up ahead, their outlines fuzzy, their movements seeming theatrical and lumbering. Suddenly an utterance, carrying clear and clipped, disturbingly distinct in such a muffled world.

A few huddled figures at Shining Tor. Banter and waterproofs, a camaraderie of sorts. On, into an atmospheric wilderness. A painter, confident in her palette, might draw out, might finesse, the fine distinctions that lie around me, but I have to battle against my world being reduced to monochrome.

I know these hills from long ago, from when my children were young, from hikes and cross country runs. Today, I carry those memories in stretched muscles, the past sedimented in my being.

I have always approached Errwood by the track that passes the Spanish-styled St Joseph's shrine, a lonely and incongruous flourish of design. Miles from anywhere, cut flowers have been mysteriously placed here for ages, small bursts of colour alien to the bleakness all around. Today, though, I take the track less travelled, at least by me, up along Foxlow Edge and into a freshening, light rain. Down through ravines, down through dripping vegetation, where rhododendron have run wild and ravaged the collapsed estate of Errwood Hall.

I sit and eat a sandwich in the drizzle among the fallen buildings, musing that the blocks resemble memories, some solid in structure, others askew or misaligned and others still just worn completely into nothingness.

'*The foggy ruins of time*'.

Then it is time to regain all the height I have so casually frittered away earlier. With legs stiffening, with time mounting since I have last seen a human being, with resolve outsourced to fate, I try to focus down my efforts into a steady, mindless plod. And so, for a final solitary hour I rise, through unfamiliar terrain that is also all too familiar in its uniformity.

Level ground eventually, spirits lifting and a lengthening stride.

A sense of approaching completeness, a sense of rooted satisfaction.

THE 1970s

1971. Alps – The First and the Thirst

Our friend, Andy, arrived at the station in Zermatt with a gigantic rucksack on his back and an equally large one, obscuring his vision, on his front. His ice axe was strapped to the front one, poking up like a periscope. Three of us had arrived the day before and set up tents on the campsite. When we sat down on wooden crates to eat our first evening meal, he found that he had forgotten to pack cutlery, so he ripped off two tapering pieces of wood from his crate and used these as a stabber and lifter for the full three weeks.

Our first peak was to be the Breithorn, a straightforward plod up to 12,700 feet. It was without technical climbing difficulty and even the most careless of mountaineers would be unable find an appropriate location from which to plummet to their doom. Those scenarios would come a little later in our trip.

The first day, in late afternoon when the sun had lost some of its fierceness, we trudged up paths, then scree and finally patches of snow, to the snowline proper. We cleared a space among the rocks and pitched our tent at around nine in the evening before dining on bread and jam, tinned hamburgers and a big billy can of coffee followed by another of hot orange juice.

Although our small alarm clock had been set for 3am we overslept and were not awake until an hour and a half later. Hurrying to be off before daybreak and to make as much progress as possible before the sun's strength took its toll, we made a mistake that was to ensure that the unfolding day one that I would remember for the rest of my life.

We had forgotten our water bottles!

When the sun rose and quickly established itself in the heavens, its heat, the increasingly rarefied air and the exertion required to keep up steady progress up the snow slope, all meant that we needed desperately to replace our bodies' fluids. I have never before nor since known thirst of the magnitude I experienced that day. By mid-morning, we were feeling disorientated and crazy. We tried eating snow that we scooped up with the adzes of our ice axes, but this dried out our mouths even more. We tried leaving it in the sun on our spread-out anoraks but the bloody stuff refused to melt.

We eventually made the summit, the highest by a long, long way that I had ever been. The mountain panorama was spectacular, peaks in every direction extending far into the distance. The Matterhorn, its menacing proximity, its sharpened ridges slicing into a sky of faultless blue.

This could not be anything other than a significant moment in my mountain experiences, such as they were. More than that, it felt like a milestone in my life, an achievement that, even as a daydreaming and adventurous child, I could never have foreseen. And yet the splendour was as nothing to the dehydration, to the heavy draw of desperation.

We took a quick photo, then hurried to retrace our route. Immune to any sense of melodrama, I did in all seriousness consider hurling myself from the mountain top and finishing it all there and then rather than enduring hours more of this. My head was swimming and I fantasised about water constantly, willing to trade everything I had for just one deep draught.

At last, after about ten hours we reached the first flowing stream, back by our tent. I knew then that I would remember plunging my head into that icy water for the rest of my life. And I have. Spluttering and half-choking, unable to swallow enough and quickly enough to blot out the madness of the day, we somehow took our fill.

We made it back to the valley that night and spent the next day resting (and drinking) and then falling upside down on ropes in trees to practice the drill for crevasse rescue.

1971. Skye

It came at the speed of an express train. No, of a supersonic jet. Straight at me. Too fast to take in, too fast to compute, to make any sense of at all.

There was no noise, no technical wizardry. There was no artifice.

This was Nature, furious and cataclysmic, immense and overpowering. I was frozen to the spot, in awe and facing oblivion. If I had been able to, I would have fallen to my knees on this lofty, rocky ridge. I would have offered allegiance, supplication, whatever was demanded.

But the force, the immediacy, was overwhelming and I was turned to stone-like immobility. Frozen in body and in thought.

There in the cloud that swirled into Loch Coruisk far below, there in the air directly before us, were two shadowy figures surrounded by a circular rainbow, two beings with saintly haloes. Floating in the air. But then, without the slightest hint, rushing at us, becoming huge, their horrific speed threatening an overwhelming impact that would dispatch us into the sky, to tumble and turn and to plummet into the depths.

Up on the Cuillin Ridge, we were witnessing a Mountain Glory, something I had seen only the once before and then of nowhere near such magnitude. When I was able to steady my nerves, to blink and swallow and look again, some rationality crept back.

These strange phenomena are caused when atmospheric conditions allow the sun to cast one's shadow onto clouds or mist. Refraction of the sunlight also creates a circular rainbow - a Brocken Spectre - that gives the shadow its saintly, other-worldly nature. Then, as on this occasion, if the wind moves the cloud about, the shadow can appear to hurtle towards and away from the viewer at impossible, superhuman speeds.

Thank goodness for rationality. Without it, people would flee in terror, mass migrations might commence, civilisations change their course. Thank goodness for science, fact and measurement. But thank goodness too for Nature's wild excursions, for its power to humble and to terrify.

*

It was the Autumn half term and my wife and I were staying on the Isle of Skye, in the Glen Brittle Memorial Hut. Our companions were two friends we had met fairly recently through work and, although not really mountain people, they had become excited about this trip. Crucially, they had a car and, unlike on my only other Scottish trip four years earlier, their vehicle was comfortable and fully functioning.

At the hut, which slept about twenty people, we were the only occupants. How wonderful to be in such a beautiful, isolated place but with space and the relative comforts of hot showers and bunk beds. After the long drive from southern England and the ferry crossing at Kyle of Lochalsh, night was well settled over the land when we arrived. We wrestled unsuccessfully with the water supply but, after I had slept soundly that first night, a local farmer took a walk with me up to the burn where the pipe that supplied the hut had become dislodged by recent floods.

Our party was such that we were not able to avail ourselves of many of the mountain marvels that the Cuillins offer - eleven Munros along its classic seven-and-a-half-mile ridge to name, well, eleven – but we did spend four days alive in a sort of autumnal paradise. Although Atlantic storms can pound this coast and sea mists and cold air envelope the land, we experienced nothing but light of pinpoint clarity, sunshine of intensely nourishing warmth. The peaks were visible, their flanks reddened, the sea played in light-hearted fashion along the little beach where our track petered out at Loch Brittle. Fieldfares, redwings, oyster catchers, curlews, and greater black backed gulls, all occupied this territory. And everywhere, hooded crows, those highland hoodlums and my favourites.

We did attain the Ridge on a couple of the days, climbing up the long spurs from Glen Brittle, breathing a rarer air, fully appreciating the true limitations of human endeavour. We could not but know our place within the desolation of these mountains, within their planetary scale. And we were granted a Glory and a Brocken Spectre.

*

I have never returned to Skye and I have resolved never to do so despite being close by on the mainland many times since.

Some places belong only to my imagining. They are formed from snippets of conversation perhaps, a snatch of song, the odd photograph or a glancing account – an impression built up in a kind of absence. They contain a hint of longing but also something pure and not corrupted by experience.

Skye had been one such place. Then we visited and it became real and solid, a memory vulnerable to the potential effects of disillusion and decay.

Fifty years and more, and the rough, red rock, the switchback, airy Ridge, the wading birds, the shingle and most of all, perhaps, the melodrama of those mighty sunsets overriding a whole seascape – all have seeped back into their former, purer state.

And that is where they should and will now remain.

1971. The Cairngorm Tragedy

Trevor was to drive up to me in Buckinghamshire after work on the Friday and we would then travel on to Snowdonia and arrive in the early hours. One or two o'clock at best, we reckoned. It was an ambitious plan, probably a ridiculous one, but we both wanted to escape from our newly entered worlds of work and snatch a brief November weekend on the crags. As in our old lives.

Three hundred and fifty miles to the north in Edinburgh, a school party was setting off for the Cairngorms.

During the day, the forecasts warned of dire conditions across the Welsh mountains, so much so that Trevor had, very untypically, decided that it would be best to abandon the trip. This was an extreme move as we would usually have gone even if bad weather meant we had to forgo the actual rock climbing and be content with a wintry hill walk or, in extremis, a low-level tramp along the valleys.

My old friend and climbing partner, Andy, was by this time working for the local authority in Edinburgh as an outdoor pursuits teacher, taking school parties into the hills on various adventures. It sounded like a tough call at times. Especially the occasion when, setting off in a minibus he noticed a commotion in the seats behind him and on investigation found that one lad had smuggled on board a hatchet! 'I'd heard there was goin' to be kids from Glasgow up there', had been his justification.

My cancelled weekend turned into a routine domestic one. But on the Sunday word began to filter into the news that there was a party missing in the Cairngorms. I tuned in to each bulletin as further details emerged.

'*Youngsters ... school students ...*'

Details of an unfolding and major tragedy were coming out slowly.

'...Edinburgh ...'

I was unable to reach Andy by phone and began to fear the worst.

'Blizzards ... overnight ... mountain rescue ... '

He shared a flat with his boss, Ben, and surely one or both of them from a very small team must have been involved.

'Bodies ... failure to reach the bothy ... survivor ...'

Eventually, a more coherent account was available but only after a couple of days. Ben had indeed been leading this party of fifth and sixth formers. But not Andy. Ben's girlfriend Cathy, who was also familiar with the Scottish mountains in winter, had been enrolled to lead the less experienced students, by a less exacting route across the Cairngorm plateau to Ben Macdui with the aim of connecting with the others and spending the night together in the relative safety of the Corrour Bothy in the Lairig Ghru mountain pass.

The weather had been atrocious and too much for Cathy's group. They began to rapidly weaken in the ever-increasing onslaught of gale force winds, snow and cold, and it became obvious that they did not have the strength to continue to their planned rendezvous. She had desperately searched for any depression in the ground where a crude snow wall might be built to shield them in some small measure but in the end they were forced to bivouac close together on exposed ground in an attempt to garner some small degree of succour and mutual support.

The storm did not abate and the group were forced to spend all of the next day and a second night at their bivouac site. On the morning of the third day, Cathy was spotted by a helicopter crew crawling for help and, although dangerously ill, she was able to give the rescue team details of her group's location.

When the rescue managed to locate her party, five of the students and Cathy's young assistant instructor, had died. Only one was still alive.

I later learned that I had been unable to reach Andy because he was barricaded inside his flat with Ben while reporters besieged their front door and bombarded their telephone line.

This was Britain's worst ever mountain disaster and its ramifications cast a long shadow over the whole world of outdoor adventure as well as the lives of those most directly caught up in the awful tragedy.

1974. Reassembled in Iran

'Hi. Guess who this is?"
'Andy? What – ?
He should be in Iran or possibly Afghanistan by now. On his way to an unclimbed mountain in the Hindu Kush.
'Where are you?'
He had told us not to expect to hear from him for at least three months – and that had been only four weeks or so ago.
Four weeks, when he and his two friends from Edinburgh had rolled up their sleeping bags from our floor and repacked their clothes into their rucksacks. Four weeks ago, when I had watched them squeeze these items back into their methodically packed Land Rover.
I envied them their journey, the excitement and the adventure. But I also admired the determination that had taken Andy onto a week-long course at British Leyland where he had learned to dismantle the vehicle right down to its tiny constituent parts before reassembling them into a sturdy, efficient machine that would carry them across continents. Such practical skills and knowledge! Not for the first time in my life, I questioned the value of my flimsy academic accomplishments.
My wife and I had waved them goodbye in brilliant, early morning light, silently acknowledged the sense of loss, and then returned to hanging freshly laundered nappies on our washing line. Good drying weather, despite the smell that carried on the sulphur air from the local pit.
'I'm in Middlesex,' he said. 'I'm in Rehab.'
'Rehab? What do you mean Rehab? And Middlesex? What –?'
'We had an accident. Hit a lorry. I need to get better. They've brought me here, Mount Vernon.'
'An accident? What kind of –?'

'They're teaching me to walk', he chuckled.

He chuckled!

Gradually, I extracted the story from him and when his time ran out, I waited for him to insert more coins.

Somewhere in Iran they had swerved to avoid a boy on a bicycle and crashed into a lorry. The friend on the passenger side had been thrown out through the open door and, in shock, had run off deep into the scrub. The person in the centre had been restrained by her seat belt and, although bruised and shaken up, not seriously injured. Andy had been thrown from the driver's seat out of the vehicle and straight under the back wheels of a huge lorry.

Fortunately, the driver had braked and continued to do so, scraping Andy along the ground rather crushing him with the vehicle's full weight. Good luck though it may be, he was still left with an appalling set of injuries and, after we had hurriedly travelled down to visit him, he gave us the full account. Still chuckling – as if at some cosmic comedy featuring irony, fate and luck. And, no doubt, from the relief of being alive.

By an amazing coincidence, the accident was witnessed by a German doctor on a family holiday in the area. This kind, devoted man, like some biblical character, had arranged for Andy to be transported to a local village hospital where he had then performed a series of essential and urgent surgical operations.

One of his feet had been unrecognisable as a foot, Andy said. As was an arm. His right hip was dislocated. The angelic medic had realigned, readjusted and stitched these major wounds and reassembled him as best he could with the tools and facilities at his disposal, all this taking place without Andy getting word to his parents for fear of causing them alarm or worry.

Although these life-saving operations had been successful and the doctor had continued on his holiday,

Andy's precarious situation was far from over. The sanitary conditions in the hospital where he had been left to recuperate were so basic that he immediately caught a fever and ran a temperature of 39.5 degrees for two days. There were no nursing facilities nor any staff at all on duty at night, so he had to supervise his own medical care. In one instance, this involved fighting off being given morphine as a treatment for constipation. One of his arms was in a plaster cast while the other was on a drip. Bowls of food were brough to him but, unless a visitor to another patient came over to feed him in response to his gesticulations, it would be taken away again after a while. Another complex operation was required if he wished to use the toilet bucket beside his bed during the night. He taught himself to remove the catheter from his arm before using the bucket, to manoeuvre himself onto it, and then to reattach himself afterwards.

Despite such fortitude and self-reliance, it became clear to Andy that he would have to tell his family of his continuing predicament and seek their assistance. After managing to arrange access to a telephone and an international call, his brother responded rapidly by flying out. Air journeys were prohibitively expensive but fortunately Vincent worked for British Airways and was able to obtain a staff discount. Andy was strapped to a door and placed in the back of a van for a long, bumpy ride to Teheran Airport where the airline removed a set of seats so that he could be accommodated, door and all, on the next available flight home.

His recovery had accelerated once he began to receive a sustained package of expert care. Toughened by a lifetime of outdoor activities, his body continued to knit together. A spirit that relished adventure and experience powered him on through his recovery.

That and Lynn, a visiting American physiotherapist.

1977. Friends Like These

Although my climbing activities were curtailed in the mid-1970s by responsibilities resulting from being a wage-earner, a father and the owner of a dilapidated house in the country that required extensive work on my part, I did keep in touch with old friends from previous times. Mark Vallance had married Jan in Port Stanley at the end of his posting in Antarctica and they had returned to England and to the Peak District in late 1972. A few years later, through the kindness of a babysitter, my wife and I were able to drive across to their cottage one evening in 1977 to have dinner with them.

Our conversation flowed over a range of topics that preoccupy most young, married couples and before too long we were drawn into the world of work. I was settled into the early stages of a rewarding career but Mark was restless and ready to move on from his bureaucratic role in the Peak Planning Board.

He had a plan, he told us. But could comment no further. 'Would it involve you moving?' I asked. Employment was sparse in the area and, selfishly, I did not want my friends scattered any further away than was necessary.

No, he reassured me. They could stay where they were. He was intending to open his own business.

'A business! You want to be a businessman?'

I knew no businessmen; I never had done and indeed had assumed until then that I never would. We, after all, had come of age in the 1960s.

'Not just any business. I'm going to manufacture something that will revolutionise climbing'.

'What is it?'

'I can't tell you. I'm sworn to secrecy'.

'Is it clothing? That waterproof material that can breathe? I've heard that's under development. That could revolutionise climbing'.

'No, it's not clothing. It's bigger than that. But I can't say any more'.

And so saying, we tried to move the conversation to another topic. And failed completely.

As the evening wore on Mark's reticence eased by degrees and he eventually revealed that he was going to re-mortgage his house. Then, that he had been gleaning information from businesspeople who lived in the village and would give up his job to sink everything he had – time and money – into his manufacturing endeavours.

He would not be drawn into saying more but, at the end of the evening, and swearing us to absolute secrecy, he went out to his shed and returned with an object covered by an oily rag. He unwrapped it to reveal the 'Friend', a sophisticated piece of machinery consisting of camshafts, cables and moving parts.

He told us about its inventor, Ray Jardine, an American climber who had given up his job as a NASA engineer to spend more time on the rock and who was willing to grant Mark a manufacturing licence.

I tried to disguise my horror at the site of this huge, ungainly object and my concern that Mark was risking everything on such a foolhardy venture. It almost seemed to require two hands to hold and operate it and I could not imagine anything so heavy and cumbersome – and potentially expensive – hanging from a climber's harness.

On the drive home afterwards, I feared that Mark was making a terrible, disastrous misjudgement.

*

In January 1978, he took a massive fifty-foot fall while climbing on Millstone Edge.

Deliberately.

His fall was broken just above the ground, and he was saved from certain death.

By a Friend.

Mark had persuaded the popular BBC TV science and technology programme, 'Tomorrow's World', to film a feature on his new piece of climbing equipment after promising them footage that would provide compulsive viewing.

And after the showing the orders began building quickly from a trickle into a flood.

His firm, Wild Country, grew and grew and, in due course, became famous throughout the world.

I subsequently bought some Friends when I could afford them and, as a result, in my later second wave of climbing activity, my standard, my sense of safety and the depth of my enjoyment, increased astonishingly.

1978. Yarncliffe Quarry

'They're a good laugh. Got some big bikes. Race 'em down t' Peak District sometimes', he said.

It was not what I wanted. Not at all what I wanted. But it seemed to be this chap, Steve, and his mates or nobody.

I had a little more free time now, the odd half day at weekends, and could think about getting out climbing occasionally and hopefully recapturing the levels of confidence and skill that I had once attained. Andy was living in the USA and Trevor, like me, had a family and a job - and was living in London. The person in the Doncaster outdoors shop had recommended Steve as someone to contact about a local club but they did not sound like my sort of crowd. I needed friends who held my welfare in very high regard, took their time and took great care. Not big bikes and devilment!

Steve, however, was willing to give climbing together a try and for me to drive the pair of us over to the Peak District on the next Sunday afternoon. He chose Yarncliffe Quarry, which was new for me, and we set about gauging each other's competencies and trustworthiness, indirectly through stories about our past exploits, about successes and achievements but also things that had gone wrong. Lessons, if any, that had been learned.

As always with new crags like this one, I was eager to see the consequences of industry's once mighty battle with stone-faced, bare geology. To be among unfamiliar arenas with their lost echoes of drilling and blasting.

We were the only people there, drizzle was intensifying into rain and there was an unseasonal mugginess in the late April air. I deferred to Steve, who judged the conditions still suitable for climbing. The footholds were ample in size but sloping the wrong way. The dampness in the air formed an unsettling combination with the sand on the ledges, taking away the joy of movement on the rock. With old mates it would have been no problem to suggest wrapping it in. But with a relative stranger who was perhaps my only hope nowadays of a local climbing partner, there was no shared etiquette, no mind reading formed from outings in adversity, to help judge when to give the cliff and the weather best.

The drizzle was no longer drizzle, but rain. What had been merely unpleasant was beginning to feel dangerous.

'What d'you think?'

'I dunno. What do you think?'

We had done it, opened the conversation. After that, we rapidly agreed that the pub was far preferable.

So, settled with my half to his pint, and lowering the tone with our scruffy climbing clothes, we searched around for some common topic of conversation other than climbing. He was Yorkshire, I was from the distant South. He was at the local pit, a surface worker, and I had some fancy job that didn't sound like real work. I was university-educated, he had graduated from the local comprehensive.

There was the link!

I knew his school, I visited it regularly as part of my professional duties. And one of its most distinctive features, at least as far I was concerned, was its connection to Dartington College, a famous co-educational boarding school in Devon. These two organisations could not have been more different – one catering almost totally for a poor but proud mining community, the other for the off-spring of wealthy, ultra-liberal parents who were willing and able to pay for a radically different education, a primarily arts-focused regime, for their sons and daughters.

One feature of this social experiment was a student exchange, in which a group from Dartington would spend a term attending the Yorkshire comprehensive and living in a specially designated hostel. In addition to the usual curriculum, these students would also carry out some form of social research aimed at furthering their knowledge of life as it was lived in a mining community. In return, the local students spent a term in the splendour of the southern Devon countryside being creative, exploring their common humanity and deliberating on a world of differences. On first hearing of this scheme, I had applauded its barrier-breaking intentions, its heady idealism. But my knowledge was based on the words of its professional proponents. Theoretical. Rhetorical almost. What I had always lacked, and what Steve would at last be able to give me, was an honest, off the record, insight into this experience from someone who had lived it.

The week before I had stood with a bunch of husbands, the other halves of members of the local National Housewives Register. The conversation was cars and football and I had contributed nothing. With this climber though, as so often before, the subject was Life.

Nonetheless, I struggled to find the words and the moment.

Had the experience changed Steve? He had stayed in his village and was working, like his father, at the pit. But how did he view the world now and his place in it? Had his life's trajectory steered wildly off onto a new and enriching course?

'Best three months of my life ...'

We bought more beer, stared more deeply into our glasses.

'There was this girl ...'

1979. Renaissance in the Lakes

Towards the end of the 1970s, I had come to realise that climbing was a thing of my past. A hugely important aspect of my growing up, a key influence on who I was, on my values and how I judged what was important. And what was not.

It had been formative, but I was now in a different phase of life.

I had occasionally tried to interest new colleagues and friends, to take them out onto the Derbyshire crags once a year or so, but my confidence was gone, my body strength had sapped away, my ambition directed elsewhere. Various infrequent, shambolic attempts to rekindle the old spirit always seems to end in embarrassment and failure – stuck halfway up a gritstone edge, desperate for a top rope or trying to pick my way back down again.

What had once been fluent and joyful was now awkward and potentially dangerous.

It was time to grow up. And to grow old.

Except that, in 1978, Ken Wilson had published 'Classic Rock', a large format book of photographs and accompanying essays about classic British climbs. Like most developments in the climbing world at that time, it had passed me by but the next year, during a phone conversation with my old climbing friend, Trevor, he brought it to my attention and I sought out a copy.

It was wonderful to be able for the first time to savour close-up, action shots of particular moves and locations that I knew. Wilson, by virtue of his skills as a photographer and an editor, was the first to create a 'coffee table' book portraying what I had always loved but until then had been unable to share with others who were not climbers. More than just high production values, the word 'classic' here referred to what were also known as 'middle grade climbs'. Before then, the books and magazines usually focused on the most extreme end of the climbing spectrum. Wilson's book no doubt made good commercial sense, as it would appeal to a wider book-buying public, as well as allowing people like me, for the first time, to luxuriate in memories of past adventures. In those glorious bygone days.

In 1979 I received another phone call from Trevor. His friend Irwin was putting together a small group to have a look at some of the routes in the Lake District that were featured in the book. Did I want to join them?

I had not been in the bigger hills and mountains for seven years. But, my family was getting older, various house building projects had been completed, and the attraction of such an expedition was impossible to resist.

Did I have it in me? Could I risk being a drag on the party, a liability even? And with people I did not even know?

*

When viewed from below, Black Crag in Borrowdale swept upwards at an intimidating angle, going on forever until it touched the sky. All around, growth burst from every inch. The rocks themselves, the very ground, all seem engaged in this profusion, this reaching for the sky. The sun beat down on the lake and on the five of us, deeply enriching and providing sustenance right down to the cellular level.

We chose Troutdale Pinnacle. As well as having classic quality in its varied climbing and exposed positions, at nearly five hundred feet, it was one of the longest climbs in the area. Irwin and Trevor would take the lead and I had reassured myself that my companions were mindful of my limitations and uncertainty.

'We'll tuck you into the middle of the rope, youth,' said Irwin. You'll be alright there'.

And indeed I was. With five us climbing, our progress up the cliff was slow, all the better to soak in the unfolding panorama. Sections of the cliff offered exposed positions which set the blood coursing. Big holds for our hands and feet countered with assurances about our safety.

That combination of a terror in my being, the powerful engine for survival, challenged head on by a cool, calm rationality, has been an essential delight throughout all the best moments of my climbing. I am almost a bystander, a spectator, to this primitive battle taking place within me. It is so hard to describe to others, impossible to replicate in other areas of life, so sublime and completely life enhancing.

That is the type of answer I want to give when occasionally asked about the purpose, the pay off, the pleasure of climbing. And it is that moment. The pinnacle of the rock climbing experience. But I manage only inarticulate offerings.

On the stances between pitches, we were able to congregate together, all fixed to the cliff's solid bulk, while the leader for that pitch prepared to probe further upwards. There was banter, camaraderie, good cheer, while Borrowdale clenched us all tightly in its spell.

Thrilled with this ascent, and despite it being late afternoon by the time we had all 'topped out', we decided to take in the other easy classic of the area, Little Chamonix on Shepherd's Crag. Another steep ascent, pulling the muscles into action, the heart into joy. Open afternoon air to either side, disappearing ground below growing further and further away.

Late to the chip shop then later still to the pub. Reluctant to re-enter the everyday.

'We'll bivvy in the woods above Thirlmere', said Irwin. 'Not worth getting getting tents out now for just one night'.

THE ETHELS – SPRING

Ethels Day 34 – 8th March

Bole Hill (Burton Moor)

What a difference from last week's outing.
Dark Peak/White Peak
Solid blocks of gloom/Sunshine
Mists serious and silent/Birdsong
Empty swathes of moor/Dwellings
I park in Over Haddon with Winter making a pretence of being Spring.
Only one person passes on the other side of the road.
'Isn't it wonderful?'
'It is'.
'Derbyshire in March'.
'It's wonderful'.
'And in April. And May, June, July. All of it'.
'It is. It's wonderful'.
And then up across fields, all of it to myself. Paths in straight lines, close into walls or striking out diagonally across fallow fields, all green, manured and ready for growth. I love these faint tracks etched across lively green. Hardly discernible now but come mid-summer they will be deep, narrow grooves all among the barley, all among the maize.
For the second or third time on these Ethels, I fall from a stone stile. My head is perhaps too full of maps, photos, hope and metaphor. My knee loses concentration too, forgets its function. There is a hop, a step and a splat! No harm done, just muddy knees and palms – and a realisation that narrow paths above deep drops may for me be exhilarations of the past.
Crib Goch no more.
Bosigran no more.
Stanage no more?

Pressing on, gently uphill, musing that I am returning to my childhood, back to mud and crawling, in landscapes that I have travelled for many years in a tie, with briefcase and with professional demeanour. Back to where I began after such a long, long interlude.

Not much chance of reaching the actual Ethel top today what with a patrolling tractor, high walls, barbed wire and an electric fence. Another flashback, some lad from my childhood telling a tale –

'Johnny Symes' brother, he peed on an electric fence and – '

An erratic, cold wind has taken hold of the White Peak plateau by the time I reach Magpie Mine and I manage only a quick bite after adding layers. It is too cold to linger despite the spectacle of walls still standing and towers still erect.

Then it is the return journey, more or less automatic now and no need for a map. Concentration has evaporated and, striding back downhill to my starting point, whimsy is totally in control.

Over Haddon, Under Haddon, Wombling Free.

Ethels Day 35 – 17th March

Fin Cop

It's a mile or so along the high Eastern rim of Monsal Dale, tougher going, muddy and narrow after the tourist-trodden track veers away. A home to the Ancients, Fin Cop, with livelihood and lives to protect. Now it attempts to hold memories constant, defends them against time and erosion.

Down below it is 1980, early February, and a young man with his pregnant wife and two small boys step out for the first time into the sparkle and the snow. They arrived the day before and all their belongings are still in boxes. The children should be at school but are yet to enrol. This is the first day of a sort of paradise, an unwritten future that, in all its brilliance, demands full observance. Up above, the man is now much older. He turns the last corner of the wall. Those small boys are now a decade or more older than the young man below. There have been many futures. The man turns towards a small summit cairn and into a wind that rages across a mighty landscape.

Ethels Day 36 – 28th March

High Edge & Hollins Hill

After the flow, the ease, of the White Peak and the high abandon of the Dark, today it is the sheer brutalism of High Edge.

The overflowing refuse bins set the scene, sneering at those seeking the manicured and pastoral. Or the raised, exalted moorlands. Here it is the thuggish exploitation of geography, the concrete bunkers and the scoured ground. A different kind of awe, meeting force with force, geology with scorn. A hardened beauty accessible only to the stoical of spirit.

With relief comes the turn towards the familiar and expected, back to hills of comfortable proportion.

Ahead is Hollins Hill, modest, rounded, reassuring. Lightly trodden trails, horses standing in vacant idleness, gorse preparing, readying to spike the Spring with colour.

But instead, from behind each dip and turn, there is Chrome Hill screaming for attention.

'Look! See my ridges, see them sweep and cut across the sky!'

'Over here! Look! See my flanks, see them soar then plunge into my valleys!'

Ethels Day 37 – 24th April

Bradwell Moor

On this very day in 1932, on the hills behind us, the Kinder Mass Trespass. Ramblers from Manchester and Sheffield, quiet revolutionaries, took to these hills and were beaten for their trouble, imprisoned, robbed of their livelihoods.

Today, having been flattened by illness for weeks, I am picked up, elevated, by the weather, the view, the freedom and the right to roam.

On this very day, meanwhile, my Ethels pal, Alastair's, Dad was patiently pushing policy and precedent through committees, opening up the land by degrees, by negotiation – by inevitability.

The Right To Roam was not built in a day.

Whatever the relative strengths of these two pincer movements, between them they succeeded, and we have the Peak District National Park and all the others.

Thank you to all those pioneers, including Ethel Haythornthwaite of course, thank you for not giving up, thank you for your dedication and commitment. By taking the disappointments, setbacks and the blows, you made my life and that of everybody, so rich, so wonderful!

Ethels Day 38 – 5th May

Black Hill (Whaley Moor) & Sponds Hill

Still a bit groggy and disorganised after my strange illness, I am determined to prove to myself that I can do this. Can still get myself out, climb a hill, be companiable with myself.

My first blunder? Forgetting my phone with the map on it! I had been intending to walk from the road just west of Kettleshulme but have no idea where to begin. I try to guess how the hills, valleys, paths and tracks might form below the bottom of the Dark Peak OS map that I have brought. A challenging but fruitless task and I give up and drive around until I can locate myself on my map.

I am full of advice to myself, too preoccupied really, as I begin the short ascent of Black Hill. 'Don't push it'. 'Just one foot in front of the other'. 'Take rests'. 'Listen to your body'. 'There's no shame in turning back'. Thankfully, a pair of frolicking skylarks, a lapwing, and a couple of unidentifiable corvids high in the sky, prove more interesting and distracting than all this self-talk and twaddle and I am at the top, once more relishing scruffy, undisciplined moorland.

Lovely hill spotting from the top, new landscapes to the west, a panorama of Ethels to identify.

Then, back down and up the other side, on a metalled track. A steady and reassuring haul. Along the Gritstone Way towards the strange sight of what I assume is the top of Sponds Hill. From a distance it looked like a cluster of boulders and scree that could easily be adorning a summit in the Cairngorms. The scale seemed disproportionate and when I arrive, I find a bulldozer and an enormous mound of blue-grey fibrous matter which I later guess must be some form of supplementary sheep feed. And enough for all the flocks in the Peak District.

A dreamy descent then back to the car. So pleased to be out, moving, confident, catching the early summer and the strains of silence on the hills above the Cheshire plains and the Greater Manchester sprawl.

Ethels Day 39 – 12th May

Burbage Edge (Goyt's Moss)

These Ethels come in various guises: classic mountain peak (Thorpe Cloud, Shutlingsloe); smooth-contoured, rounded grandeur (Shining Tor, Mam Tor); guarded and remote (Kinder Low, Alport Moor); and almost too easily accessible (Sir William Hill, Eccles Pike).

But there is another category, the shrinking violets, the wallflowers, those never invited to the dance. The hills that I have overlooked for decades, assuming them to have no distinguishing features worthy of investigation. Sough Top was the first of these, back in January. And today it is Burbage Edge, up above Buxton.

A short pull up from town and we are on open moorland, a scratchy carpet of heather, a startled black grouse, a pheasant and patches of dark, boggy peat ready to encase and claim a misplaced boot. All about is uniform, the wastes seemingly extending for miles. But then, at the trig point the panorama opens startlingly. Miles of hills in every direction, thousands of acres, Ethels all about. We name a dozen already visited, guess at a whole load more.

Not insignificant at all. Solid, understated and modest, but quietly binding together their widely scattered family of hills, bluffs and ridges.

Ethels Day 40 – 16th May

Tissington Hill & Thorpe Cloud

From the map, the trig point on top of Tissington Hill looks inaccessible, some 300 yards from the nearest footpath and protected by a maze of walls. I assume I will have to be content with 'proximity' and save the prospect of views and a sense of minor triumph for majestic Thorpe Cloud.

I set off in mist, a thick claggy mist that reduces visibility and mutes Nature's many displays. The occasional birdsong sounds artificial, the solitary pied wagtail on the path in front a clockwork toy. All parts of some grand scheme to deceive.

But the reduced visibility becomes my friend and after crossing a number of fields deep with dew and rain, I remember and am emboldened by Theresa May in her fields of wheat. I deviate from the path, climb a gate with barbed wire and then a wall and enter trespass territory, heading into the unknown. My eventual reward? The trig point, there materialising right in front of me in the gloom!

Back the way I have come and the sun begins to break through. Fields, the rifle range and the broad pastures of Thorpe and then I am climbing slippery limestone up the eastern flank of Thorpe Cloud. Alone on the craggy summit of this mini mountain, there is enough clarity to be able to see down into the opening stretches of the Dovedale Dash.

How, when we ran, we had streamed down Lin Dale like otters, sleek and eager, and then screamed like warriors as we crashed across the river!

Ethels Day 41 – 17th May

Brown Knoll

When I was nine, I read yet another book about my favourite young adventurers. This time they were on holiday in a strange place called The North, camping near some high, exposed moorland under which a mysterious railway tunnelled. Down in the bowels of the ground nefarious characters, somewhat foreign looking or with rough and uneducated diction, raided trains they had misdirected onto some secret branch line.

Today, I am on that very moor.

I hurry up Rushup Edge – I rush up – onto the high ground and then stride along slabs leading further and further into lonely open hillside.

Away to my left, a ventilation shaft for the Gowburn Tunnel appears and I am rewarded with puffs of smoke from a train passing far below.

On then into ever more distant territory and finally the trig point atop Brown Knoll. Although I can see for miles I have had no sight of any other human being.

Until the trig point. And then there in the rough ground and with his back to me, is a portly man preposterously perched on a tiny, three-legged stool. I shout 'Hi' but he does not turn.

As I grow closer, I can hear him talking, presumably into some hand-held device.

I shout a greeting again, more loudly this time.

Still no response.

So, I ignore him and settle to my sandwich just a few yards behind him. Just me, him, the vastness of The Kinder Plateau and the Edale skyline.

He continues with his conspiratorial babbling. 'Smokey Bandit. G4S. Wilco.'

The Famous Five Go Off to Camp.

Only one comes back.
'Woof!' said Timmy.

Ethels Day 41 – 13th October

Kinder Scout (revisited)

Brown Knoll, up and back from the road below Rushup Edge, had been today's destination, a reasonable trek on slabs across empty heather.

I have bounced so joyfully along this track that the edge of the Kinder plateau, just a little higher and further, now begins to exert its inevitable pull. I have never completely sorted out to my satisfaction the topography of this area, easily confusing my Edale Rocks with my Edale Head, my Noe Stool with my Pym Chair, Wool Packs and Crowden Tower. I am tempted to press on. Added to which, our failure to be sure that we had in fact reached Kinder's very highest point last October has been niggling me through the winter.

So, with clear visibility and a punchy attitude, here is an opportunity. One not to be declined.

A little further along, I encounter several people who have emerged from the top of Jacob's Ladder, including three women who are asking a chap which valley they should descend in order to end up in Hayfield. Oh, how scornful we had been in our youth about people wandering into high hills ill-prepared. How smugly superior. And how, perhaps sadly, I still can be.

Kinder Low trig point is busier again with parties pausing for photos. Very different from that rain-sodden, wind-blown visit last October. I set off enthusiastically with map and compass - and altimeter! - in and out of dips and boggy ground, further from points of reference. Further from the known and secured. But emboldened, heart and soul, by the stunning blue of the open sky above.

I do love this high ground, the strange perspectives, the sense of gambling that everything will work out right.

The slight panic that comes from feeling unmoored and lost, of being forced to find and rely on one's own inner resources. The apocryphal tale of the eventual discovery a young shepherd's frozen body with his faithful dog still alive and curled at his side.

Today still presents challenges, manageable but enough for a certain piquancy, a reminder of bigger thrills and headier times. The tiny cairn, when I find it, is handsomely undistinguished. But it is a summit, bold and true, today.

Then it is all the way back, more miles than originally intended, more alive than ever expected.

Ethels Day 42 – 18th May

Crook Hill

Another day, another Ethel.

Just a little excursion today, up above the dams, under the threat of rain.

The climb is through sheep pastures, around a farm where dogs in wire cages throw themselves about in their metallic constriction, all their anger and foaming frustration aimed temporarily at us.

Beyond the yard and back in the calm, another beautiful gritstone summit. Just a few boulders tossed about the hilltop, another pleasing and unique natural sculpture.

Up pops a young Scouser with all the playfulness of a puppy, a puppy that has not suffered farmyard abuse. He has a canoe, it's inflatable, he'll attempt to make the next dam later. He's a climber, just quarries with bolts, indoor walls.

Not trad climbing though.

I point to regal Stanage on the skyline and begin a sermon. An old man unaware of how much time has passed.

Ethels Day 43 – 25th May

Win Hill

A 70 per cent chance of rain, easing to 40 per cent later. A mild hankering to ascend another Ethel, easing to a quiet compulsion soon.
You win some.
I approach from Thornhill through the Nature Reserve, a wide zig zag to draw the sting from the near 1,000-foot climb. First an open track, then back along a narrow winding path disappearing into a chaotic mix of woodland. Alone and muttering to myself about childhood explorations amid a froth of hawthorns.
The winner takes it all.
Turning again and onto the high moorland, perspectives opening out in all directions. A different clutch of Ethels on view today – both ends of Stanage, Higgar Tor, Shatton Moor, Durham Edge plus all the old familiars.
The plug of polished rock at the summit after the final steep push. Not the Lakeland tops or the Scottish peaks but an effort enough for me today. Not the thin air of my first Alpine ascents, nor the delirium of the Thorung La at 17,700 feet.
But a task tailored to my current capabilities, a satisfying sense of embracing my limitations, of dissolving into the miracle of still being here.
Win Win.

Ethels Day 44 – 30th May

Lost Lad & Back Tor

We are dwarfed beneath the great wall of the dam, awed by the gritstone gothic. Holding back our knowledge of the menace and the volumes it contains. The broad track beside the reservoir picks up our feet, lifts the spirit as the high ground exerts it lure.

On the first bluff, we stop to scan the emerging perspectives, the great threatening banks of cloud along the rim of Bleaklow, the skyline smudged and darkened as if with soot, ink and chalk. Then, improbably – impossibly – beneath our feet and barely cresting the water, a massive, lumbering Lancaster bomber, stumbling out of history into the here and now. It is too slow, too inflexible, too alone and too unnoticed. It staggers without sound around the next hillside and disappears from view.

Our world, our sense of time and place, must recalibrate The track deteriorates then reasserts itself in sizeable slabs, cast like dominoes across the hillside. And here, making its way like a furry concertina, a tiger hawk moth caterpillar. Boneless tissue and countless tiny legs, some incarnation of this creature survived up here last winter under packed snow and frozen ground. Hidden in the heather, masked by flecks of cotton grass, we hear the chortling alarm calls and the cries of curlews, then see them piercing circles through the sky with their curving beaks.

We are on Lost Lad, eating lunch, still drawn to the Edale Skyline's deep incision, the disdain of distant Kinder and the troubled countenance of mighty Bleaklow. So much to draw the heart, to give perspective, to stabilise the balance in the flow.

Not Lost but Found.

THE 1980s

1980. Buxton

We had moved to live in the heart of the Peak District. If I was to forge new climbing partnerships, it was now or never. But had I left it too late, was I far too old for this sort of thing?

I had a young family and a demanding job but surely one evening a week was a possibility? Where some men played five-a-side football or took part in Rotary Club events, could I not snatch a similar amount of time to grapple companionably with the grit and limestone?

The girl in the climbing shop told me that there was a local club, a nice little group, she said, with a range of experience. But would there really be anybody of my age, people willing to tolerate my rusty technique, my almost crippling levels of carefulness and caution?

She gave me the date and location of the next evening meet and I summoned the confidence to make my way to Ramshaw Rocks on a late spring evening. Could I possibly recapture some small part of the activity that so forged my identity in my youth? Was it possible to reclaim these aspects of character, these passions, or did growing older demand a reconsidered approach?

*

It was a clear April evening. The sun had reigned confidently through the day but night was now beginning to assert its claim. In an hour or so the temperature would drop, the light would go, but that was still enough time for a few short climbs on these otherworldly, jagged rocks.

I picked my way along the base and could hear climbers before I could see them. Loud cheers and guffaws. Boisterous blokey banter. Then, there they were, half a dozen young men, one of them hanging out beneath a prominent overhang, both hands jammed into a vicious crack beneath the roof, feet flailing, looking for any place of purchase. His body was shaking from the tension through his frame and his mates had moved in beneath him, ready to try to break his fall. The playful insults and rowdy encouragement continued nonetheless, even as they moved into position.

Not for me. Definitely not for me.

But one of them had seen me and nodded before I could slink away.

'You the Buxton club?' I managed to say.

'Nah mate, there's some others up there though', he said, pointing further along the track.

I could leave now and flee home.

Or I could risk humiliation through one final reckoning with the realities of my age, standing and responsibilities.

*

And I am so glad that I took that risk.

A cheerful, welcoming group were enjoying the rocks further along. Their standard of climbing appeared far more within my capabilities. Nobody was goading anybody to take more risks than they wanted. They were encouraging each other, however modest or cautious their efforts.

I mentioned my earlier encounter to them and my asking whether those people were the Buxton Club. Wide-eyed laughter was their response. Among those others, apparently, were figures with national reputations within the climbing fraternity. Fearsome reputations.

The local group, by contrast, seemed amiable and easy-going.

And it was among these people that I re-entered a culture and style of companionship that had so enriched my earlier years. Colour and vitality began to flow back into my life. These new companions were cautious but enthusiastic, ambitious but measured. Some were almost as old as me and one other couple had children and were therefore familiar with the juggling of time and priorities that participation would require.

The club held regular Tuesday night meets with a list of dates showing the crag for each evening and its corresponding pub for afterwards. I was able to develop more confidence and skill, get to know and trust other climbers, regale them with tales from my younger years – I was almost their oldest member! - and luxuriate in all their stories. They had little truck with committees, constitutions and codes of conduct and were thus a perfect contrast to my professional life.

Derek, in particular, worked hard at keeping the wheels of the organisation turning whilst avoiding any hint of self-regarding bureaucracy. A strong, competent and reliable climber, he made a special effort to welcome new members and help them settle into the group and it is certainly thanks to him that I was able push up my climbing grade safely and with a great sense of accomplishment.

Finishing routes in the dark became a significant feature. Derek and I often found ourselves forgoing the camaraderie of the pub in Matlock Bath to begin uncoiling the rope yet again beneath Wildcat Cliffs in another thickening dusk. The record, and again far too late for the pub, was being at the top of Medusa in Ravensdale at 11.20pm, having pulled up on every shadow on the top pitch.

Perhaps the most unexpected of these local adventures occurred one Friday in deep midwinter. I was walking home from work, briefcase in hand, head down and watching my footing on the ice and hard packed snow. Coming down the pavement towards me were my friends, Les and Del, who recognised me beneath my layers of winter wear.

'Tonight? Mam Tor?' they enthused. 'It's got to be. Perfect conditions. Crampons and axes. 7.30 in the layby at the bottom!'

Half an hour or so from home and we were to be climbing the frozen face of the Shivering Mountain, easily imagining ourselves in the Alps high above not Castleton, but some mountain village with its last lights twinkling miles below. Normally this shattered face of shale and soil would be highly unstable with any foolish venture onto it highly likely to have deadly serious consequences. But, after a rare run of extraordinarily low temperatures, the face could well be frozen solid and hence climbable.

And so it proved to be. We ascended carefully, to a small ledge that we fashioned from the snow halfway up, where we reflected on this perfect absurdity. Here, at the end of a working week and after the children's bedtime, with the night sky savagely clear and cold, we were transported to landscapes and times long since rendered inaccessible.

And we were reliving them to the full.

We accompanied the Buxton group as a family on occasional weekends away and over the years other babies were born. We even returned to places that I had felt were long ago abandoned to my youth – Snowdonia, the Lakes, Cornwall.

*

I retain powerful, sustaining memories from this period of running down sandy tracks at 'mothy curfew tide' and of coiling ropes in a wind straight off the ocean with gulls and fulmars screeching in the turmoil. A curtain of rain in a steady progression across a valley with the mountains opposite dissolving into mist. A chill wind picking up grit on a quarry top. The need to get moving, euphoria coursing through the body. Raucous laughter, muscles stretched and swollen.

If, along with my eight gramophone records, I could take one memory, it would be of those hours around the fall of night in mid-summer. Arms and legs would feel lithe and loose. The last figures, still in T-shirts and shorts, would be leaving the crag. The track would be unclear and the pace intense. Gear would clink like reindeer bells in the night. Sitting on the wall outside the chip shop in the warm air, the quiet of the village would make the skin tingle. Stepping through the pub door a wave of human warmth would break. There would be all the old stories again, all the anticipation and interjection, the shared bedtime tales that never grow stale, the laughter that bursts without a moment of calculation, the eyes alive, the bodies close together and all that blood and adrenalin coursing to a common pulse.

1982. Abbey Brook

'One of the most remote valleys in the Peak District'.
'Very easy to imagine yourself in the Lake District'.
The magazine gave a mouth-watering description of Abbey Brook. The walk it described began less than an hour's drive from our new home. I made a mental note but the opportunity to take a day's leave from work while the children were at school did not come about until the following February.

It was to be a long day and the light and weather might be a problem. But the thought of twenty miles or more of unexplored, wild country almost on my doorstep fuelled my anticipation. By about ten that morning, I was parked on the Ashopton Viaduct, the bridge where the Snake Pass Road crosses Ladybower Reservoir.

The Snake Pass! That name always excited me. On winter mornings in Buxton, I would wake up to the radio and the day's weather forecast. My work took me around the Peak District and this road often featured as one of the first in England to be closed by snow. I appreciated that such a prospect was seen as a major inconvenience, or worse, by many but I loved the excitement of it all. I travelled with a sleeping bag in the car, extra warm clothes, spare food and a stick that could be used to poke up through a drift should oxygen become in short supply as a result of a sudden snowfall. My work was of itself, and in the main, interesting and rewarding but the backdrop of possible meteorological melodrama made it pretty much perfect.

Today, conditions seemed fairly settled. There was a crust of snow underfoot but no forecast for more. The sky was overcast but in an indifferent rather than threatening fashion. As soon as I was off the road and over a stile, pulling upwards towards my first landmark, Crook Hill, my sense of being slipped effortlessly into a different register. Body as machine, mind as a feather in wind, huge horizons, past, present and future fusing into one, good cheer and optimism coursing through the veins.

A lonely hour or two and easy going over crisp snow brought me to Alport Castles, a magnificent landslip reeking of a lost history and significance. It was too cold to linger for a lengthy, late coffee break and I was soon descending towards Howden Reservoir and into a dark, silent wood. Nothing moved, not even a breath of wind, among the shadows and across the springy carpet of dead pine needles. I was particularly aware that I had seen no other person all morning and that any chance meeting here and now would prove unsettling.

Any encounter with a living person.

It was sometime later that I read the dreadful account of a man who had hung himself in woods somewhere around here. This doomed unfortunate had lingered, dangling undetected from a black branch, all the while as winter transformed slowly into spring. It was, and remains, a ghastly scene to imagine, one that ever lingers in the mind. How I would have handled discovering it that day in such a desolate setting, I still find impossible to contemplate.

Down at the reservoir, it was a long plod around inlets on a metalled road until I eventually reached the place where the River Derwent deposits its accumulated moorland waters into the reservoirs. On this road, I was passed by two cars. They contained the first people I had seen on the whole walk. And they were to be the last.

I walked on down the track on the far side of Howden Reservoir and although tiring noticeably, I was also anticipating my first sight of Abbey Brook. The way became a single-track, metalled lane and I mused on different forms of emptiness. Whereas deserted hillsides and moors have always enthused and excited me, man-made features such as lanes or reservoirs, when completely devoid of people, seem more sinister in character.

I was consequently relieved when I was able to turn away into the steep-sided little valley and begin my climb up Abbey Brook. The snow had accumulated in greater proportion here and I was more than ready to settle to a late lunch.

I calculated that I was probably two thirds of the way around my circuit. My body was acknowledging the distance that I had walked since setting out – and I was aware of the miles still to go. Although the layer of cloud had leeched away to reveal a greasy smear of sunlight, the daylight remaining was limited and at a premium.

Nonetheless, I needed rest.

When Andy Handford and I were climbing regularly, especially in winter and in the bigger mountains, we took exposure and hypothermia very seriously and were alert to their indicators. And these all came flooding back as I contemplated lying down and closing my eyes for just a few minutes.

I wasn't exhausted. Just a bit sleepy.

This was the Peak District not the Cairngorms.

I would be lying on snow but on top of my rucksack. I would have some degree of insulation.

It was February, granted, but that sun was giving off some degree of warmth.

It would only be a light sleep. A doze. I would definitely wake again after a few minutes rather than slide further and further from this world.

And I did wake again.

Busy in conversation with myself, I noted a little relief, perhaps even surprise, that I was still here. Then I told myself that time spent in idle musing was a distraction from the work still to be done, an indulgence I could ill afford.

Heavier now in my steps, I climbed out of the steep-sided valley to view a brilliant expanse of snow-covered plateau, broken only by gently contoured rises and dips stretching eventually to a featureless horizon. I could not see beyond to any defining features, to any promontory or edge on which to fix my sights – and a compass bearing. It was silent. Nothing moved. My interior monologue was all that shattered my absorption into this silent anonymity.

Until – woosh! From beneath my very feet a ball of snow shoots away, my heart racing with its suddenness, the impossibility of its speed. A mountain hare in winter pelage, its breath-taking acceleration turning to a flaunting spring and bounce once sure of safety. The hare's effortless adaptation to all around served to remind me that I was far from hearth and home, my natural environment.

Lost Lad, the map informed me, was my next objective but I could see only snowy miles. What a name for a landmark, its romantic ring and its dire implication. I was no lad and I had to work a little to convince myself that I was not lost. Now all that winter navigation – Dartmoor, Snowdonia, Scotland – must come into play. By all means, think and imagine when doing so serves you well. But surrender to the compass when you must. Accept its higher authority.

I tried to remain single-minded over the snows, to ignore aching thighs, and concentrate on the bearing. Puffing and plodding onwards, I covered ground and eventually the promontory of Lost Lad with its cairn came into view. From here it was a short final climb up to Back Tor where I could allow myself to acknowledge that the final miles were on relatively level terrain with, hopefully, some indication of a path.

Under a cooling sky that was hurrying towards night, the light was fading. The temperature was dropping. Ahead along this edge, miles away again it seemed, stood isolated towers squatting awkwardly on otherwise featureless land. The scale of things somehow became planetary. Movement was necessary however much my muscles demanded rest. The half-light must be exploited before it too dwindled and extinguished.

Along the Edge now, the going easy, the dream time begins. Thoughts as well as legs in motion. While the imagination swerved wherever, and despite some missteps and stumbles, the machine that was me progressed with an unquestioned sense of direction. This was the last hour of intoxication, of self-reliance. It was to be savoured even as I was hurrying its end.

Back at the car, the night was fully in command. Refreshed in weariness, purposeful despite an empty mind. Sitting down to rest and become warm, even with the winter still on my skin. To turn at last for home.

Should I ever wish for more?

1985. Hanging in the Balance

Summer evenings on the rock.
And right on my doorstep.
No need for arduous journeys, hundreds of miles to the mountains. No camping, bivis or barns. Easy to fit in following a full day at work and my own bed to sleep in afterwards.
Could it get any better?
Climbing regularly, I was building up my physical strength, exercising my judgement and consolidating confidence. I felt safe, efficient and accomplished, all qualities that would be needed and tested to the limit when the crisis came crashing through, unannounced and terrible.

*

A young lad came out with our club occasionally and, although he was tough and bold, the reckless streak to his character worried us older climbers and we tried to caution him with every means at our disposal, from quiet asides to threats of dire consequences.
On the evening in question our club was climbing on Wildcat Cliffs in Matlock Bath and he had launched himself onto Great Cleft.
Solo!
Solo on a route that is treated with great respect by the most accomplished of climbers.
I was climbing nearby with Derek and preparing to bring him up the line I had just ascended. As I looked down I saw that, instead of beginning to climb, Derek was busy untying from the rope. There was an even tone to his voice, an untypical and chilling seriousness.
'Just leave me here for now. Get a rope down over there.'
He is trying not to panic the evening.
'Get it down pretty quickly, Andy!'

The young lad is one hundred feet above the ground without a rope on Great Cleft and has been in the same place for too long. He is unable to move up and, we are all suddenly realising, is equally incapable of climbing back down. His arms are tensed and swollen, taking his weight. We all know the time limit for sustaining a position like this. It is seconds rather than minutes.

I untie, unclip, gather rope and run through the grass to the big tree. I have no opportunity to decline the challenge. Time, place and circumstance have all collided. No time for preparation; no time for consultation; no time for thought. Thank God that for once there is no root or rock to snag the trailing coils.

As I try to adjust my belay knot so that I can position myself at the edge and see what was happening, voices break out from below.

'Hurry!' 'Hurry it up!' 'Quickly!'

Forget the position. No time to fit my rope braking device, the Sticht plate.

He has no harness, nothing to clip into. Tie a wrist loop. I look at the loop I have made. Is it too small? What if he fell, his last effort having been wasted trying to force his hand through a loop that was just too tight?

'Come on, hurry!'

I gamble a few seconds more making the loop a better size, make one guess at the length and direction and throw it.

'Left!' 'Quickly!' 'To the left!'

God, whose left, theirs or mine? I flick it to my left.

'Hurry it up!' 'Left!' 'To – the – left!'

How far is he from it? is the rope lost beyond a couple of buttresses or just tantalisingly out of reach? I make to move it further – my left or theirs? – when suddenly a dead weight stretches the rope within my hands. My body tenses and I am pulled down into the grasses.

How has this rope come to be around my body and wrists? If I had just been holding it in my hands he would have been plucked free and gone by now.

'Let him down!' 'Quickly!' 'Come on, hurry it up!'

I pay out the rope, gripping it, fearing sweat on my palms. Each foot, check, grip, slide, grip, check. Will it start to slip?

This will take hours. How long can he possibly hang by one hand?

'Come on, hurry!' 'Lower – him – down – quickly!'

I try to close my ears to the voices. What if I allow the rope to run just a little bit? Perhaps get him down quicker. Can I brake it? Would I be able stop it if it starts to burn?

I am cursing my bare forearms and thin T-shirt as the rope moves methodically across my body. Moments before I had been delighting in the summer's warmth, my free, unencumbered movement on the rock. Now I am paying for my small share of ecstasy.

Is the weight still increasing? Any instant now the strain in the rope may cease and the rope twang slack with me recoiling backwards. I can already hear the crescendo in the voices as it happens.

I could go much faster with a Sticht plate. Mine is there on the grass. I can touch it with the side of my hand but I cannot let go of the rope. Staring at it, trying to make it appear on the rope. If only someone was here to fix it on. A thought I do not want intrudes. It would not be a case of the rope eventually pulling itself free from my grip. Rather, there would be a point when the weight and the burning were perceived as too much. However instantaneous, a form of decision would be made. A half-conscious argument with my strength would be won by a sense of the inevitable.

I stare at the scene as if it is already real and in front of me. The sweating increases. Great cold drops thud into my lap. The palms of my hands are getting even wetter. Please stop.

'Lower him as quickly as you can!'

I can see people tied to trees, each one with a second making a move somewhere below them. We could shout to each other but not one of them is able to fix my belay plate. How will I live with it? I know they will all say, 'Don't blame yourself'. But I could have gone slower or gone faster,

held tighter or let it run, not wasted time with knots, not worried so much about my own skin by rigging a belay. Suddenly. Did I belay? Am I tied to the tree or not fixed to anything on this cliff top? The jumble of knots at my waist looks foreign and unfamiliar. I don't remember tying any of them.

Before I can resolve this new worry, the rope becomes lighter. It moves from its position to reveal a sticky groove across my forearm. Can I let go? Is he on a ledge, or clinging by finger ends to a flake of rock, or can he possibly have fallen? Can I risk fitting the plate? If I dare to relax will the rope jolt taut again more furiously than before?

The evening has gone quiet. The flowers in the grass, small stabs of colour, stare back at me, intense and indifferent. I lie gripping a slack rope and begin to shiver. Please tell me what is happening.

Eventually the word filters up, the urgency thankfully gone. At the pub later the watchers fill in the missing details for me. They describe the onset of his shaking and estimate that there had been at the most a one or two second margin. They disagree about how he would have fallen, whether he would have bounced against the cliff where the angle changes. They tell of how he grabbed the knot as it passed and swung out by one hand as he pushed the other through the loop. And they describe

how he was lowered until they could inch out along a ledge and pull him into safety.
As normality creeps back, the tale is told many times.

1986. Eldorado Canyon

There was a decision I was dreading making. There was dislocation and disorientation heading my way. Over the previous two years, I had exhausted every option I could think of, and none had proved successful.

Now, at forty years old, I had taken only the second flight of my life, to Colorado Springs and my old friend Andy, hoping that the way forward might become more apparent here, five thousand miles from home. And, as on those mountain routes of old, I could maybe find the resolve and commitment to push on through my fear to clear, clean air, brilliant sunlight and the power of vast perspectives.

*

Because Andy and Lynn were busy setting into a new job, they arranged marvellous itineraries for me for when they were not free, and I met with various of their colleagues and local personalities. And their climber friends.

With Bruce, I visited the nearby Garden of the Gods, where spectacular towers of orange sandstone rose from the shrubs and scrubby trees of the park's flat floor. He usually climbed at a higher standard but graciously spent an afternoon introducing me to routes that he thought I would find 'interesting' – and possible! Sandstone is never the easiest of rock and I was briefly reminded of desperate struggles at Harrison's Rocks near Sevenoaks back in my student days.

I felt confident enough, once I had adjusted to the unfamiliar nature of the rock itself, to lead the easier climbs. One route, the three-pitch West Point Crack, included a long chimney with big pockets and stalactites for handholds. Pigeons were nesting in some of the depressions while others were full of guano a good six inches deep. The climb also involved stepping off a large pinnacle at the top of the second pitch and onto a steep wall, clipping a peg and then lie-backing boldly up the crack above.

Many of the routes here had names with drug references and after Silver Spoon, he led me up The Fixer, the most technically difficult climb I had, up until that time, ever encountered.

The Garden of the Gods made a strong impression on me

*

A few days later I set off to the north of the state in Andy and Lynn's camper bus where, if I wanted to climb in some of the classic areas there, I would have to face my strongly held reservation about not undertaking routes with people I did not know well, people who might prove reckless or unsafe *in extremis,* people who did not hold my safety and wellbeing among their highest priorities.

At Estes Park, I found the local climbing shop and talked to the staff there about the best routes in the area, how to find others who might wish to climb with me and where I could park my bus and sleep for the night. They recommended a parking lot on the edge of town that climbers often used and where there was a good chance of not being moved on by the police. They also directed me to their notice board where scribbled notes on cards said things like – 'Looking for climbing partner, Estes, Boulder area, lead up to 5.8, second 5.10' Then a name and a phone number. With some apprehension, I jotted down a few of these details.

I slept without disturbance, warm and comfortable in the Dormobile, in bed by ten and awake before light next morning. Outside there was a thin layer of snow so I turned over feeling supremely content and cat-napped for a while longer.

This trip was to be a turning point in my life however it panned out and, in addition to the confidence that came from daily growing more physically fit, I also benefitted enormously from meeting the positive and sociable characters I ended up climbing with after I had summoned up the confidence to start making those phone calls.

With Kent, a teacher from Denver, I talked climbing, education and Ronald Reagan as we tackled some testing routes in Eldorado Canyon. Then the next day in Estes Park, with Andy, an Ecology student from Fort Collins, we talked conservation, soil erosion and politics (again) as we hiked along Lumpy Ridge and ascended the breath-taking, 460-foot Pear Buttress, one of the best climbs I had ever done. And on my last day in the area, I met up with Todd, a lawyer with the Public Defenders Department and we squared up to the most impressive climb in the area – Bastille Crack in Eldorado Canyon. We talked about Life

*

'How long have you been married?'
'Seventeen years.'
'Happily?'
That's a precocious question from a stranger half my age. And this small ledge is hardly the place.

The Bastille Crack is reckoned to be not only the best rock climb in the area but some judge it the most impressive route in the USA. Its 350 feet follow a striking crack system divided into five pitches. It involves a glorious combination of face climbing, hand jamming and chimneying and, because he had climbed the route a number of times before, he generously allowed me the lead for the whole thing.

We roped up on the actual dirt road that wound its way up the dusty red canyon beneath massive walls and dizzy edges that seemed to bend into the sky. There was a power here in the scale of things. It seemed bizarre that, to belay me on the first pitch, Todd had to stand on the actual road itself while cars crawled past within a few feet of him.

The guidebook said that hundreds of climbers had fallen from the first section of this route, but I resisted the inner voice that advised me to retreat and hand it over to the younger, local man. No, treat this next bit like a Derbyshire gritstone problem, think of Lawrencefield and the pool and the silver birches. Put in a jam, lay away and put in another higher up. Lean out, stay in control and move up. Use some technique and you are there.

We chatted as we dealt with our belays on each stance, and he told me that his girlfriend had just left him and that he did not understand it. We stopped on one tiny ledge for longer than usual and shared our confusions across a generation before I continued, delighting more and more in the stretch against the undercut hold, the long reach and the wide bridge. Through my legs, on the track directly below, cars inched along, like tiny black toys on a child's bedroom floor.

Emerging at last from the shade onto the summit and into the full heat of the Eldorado Canyon sun, I was making decisions. Feeling much stronger and supremely alive, despite being parched and tired, I belayed myself to the timelessness of that mighty mass of rock and began to take in the rope.

1986. Longs Peak

I had been warned about Daphne and still I went.
And the wild night we subsequently spent together in restless embrace is one that I will never forget.

*

I was finished, '*burned out from exhaustion*', and grubbing around in a large, square plant tub.
Here, in Boulder, Colorado, the door of the apartment next to Ray's opened a crack and in the dim light from its porch I could see his neighbour silhouetted. A stocky man of medium height and in his left hand, possibly a gun.
'Can I help you, bud?'
'Ah, I'm a friend of Ray's. He said it's alright for me to stay. The key's somewhere in this soil, in this corner. If this is what you call a planter'.
That was how Ray had explained it to me.
'The key is buried in the northeast corner of the planter outside the door,' he had said.
'What's a planter?' I had asked.
But he had already moved on to cautioning me about Daphne.
And now his neighbour was viewing me with increasing suspicion, and in my abject weariness I was contemplating sinking to my knees and begging him not to shoot me.

*

Early that morning, I had victualled up with a gigantic stack of blueberry pancakes. Longs Peak was a big undertaking and I would certainly need to draw on a mound of calories to get me up above 14,000 feet and back down again safely in a day. My portion was not the largest available at the diner, but the huge pile topped with blueberries and cream nevertheless defeated my determined attempt to take on board a full day's worth of fuel.

I parked on the high road, at about 9,000 feet, where posts supplying oxygen were stationed at regular intervals and one large, middle-aged man had a mask pressed to his reddening face. He did not seem to need my assistance, so I set off on a well-used track up through forest and out onto open hillside.

The weather pattern had been stable in previous days with an absence of the late afternoon thunderstorms common to the area, so I had judged my plan to be feasible. Flogging upwards, I fell into a reverie about the similarity of mountain paths everywhere. The geology differed, and the soil and vegetation, but there was something about the scars worn by many thousands of boots, the relentless uphill, the arrangement of rocks, large and small, and the vibrancy of the local earth, that all felt so well known, even on this unfamiliar continent. The mountain track has been a constant in my life, an environment in which something essential and unchanging resurfaces in me every time.

For my first rest, I sat among the coarse grass, consumed some water and a cereal bar and relished the warm air on my face. An animal – a marmot! – was lumbering over the rocks towards me, seemingly unafraid. I had seen plenty of these creatures in the Alps but they were always elusive. One shrill warning from their scout and then the group would scatter in all directions and disappear swiftly into their various burrows.

'Don't be frightened,' I called. 'I won't hurt you'.

And frightened it wasn't. There was determination in its movement and as it came closer, I realised how big it was. It had the face of a beaver, or how I remembered such creatures from nature films, and when it revealed its nicotine-stained incisors, I began to fear the consequences of a bite.

'Go away! Shoo! I've got nothing for you'.
It stopped, some dozen feet or so away, as if considering its options. Was it after the food in my rucksack or just being clumsily sociable?
'Go on, go away!'
Could I possibly consider throwing a stone at this confident, independent-minded hill dweller? I was, after all, on its territory, not it on mine.
It stared at me for a while longer and then contemptuously turned and shuffled away, resolving my ethical dilemma but leaving me feeling a lesser person for what I had contemplated.
More uphill, now with body and mind operating independently of each other. The former was engaged in a slow, steady Alpine plod, that I learned first from Andy in Zermatt. The latter was lost in the 'meditation of the trail' from Kerouac on Desolation Peak.
The climb eventually levelled off and I entered the Boulder Field. At an nearly 13,000 feet above sea level, this is a vast expanse of rocks bounded by cliffs and, at its further end, the Keyhole, a window into a whole new landscape to the west. The Boulder Field had originally been my objective for the day and there was now a decision to be made. I had seen neither person nor creature since the Marmot-from-Hell and this majestic mountain arena, so distinctive and so challenging to sensibility, was encouraging a boldness and ambition within me. Perhaps I could pick my way carefully across the Boulder Field – territory in which a twisted ankle could easily occur and with possibly calamitous consequences – and at least look out through the Keyhole to the continent beyond? I judged that I was moving well and that the altitude, although it was beginning to tax my breathing, was manageable. I could take it in stages and make considered, careful

calculations about when to proceed further and when to give the mountain best and retreat.

The crossing of the boulders demanded strict concentration and the journey took me a good hour. The pancakes and especially the cream were beginning to have an effect and the dreaminess being induced by the altitude was combining with a growing nausea. Below the Keyhole I just had to climb up to look through into a completely new panorama and, in doing so, found again the motivation to push on for at least one more section.

The Ledges comprise a near horizontal traverse of the far side of the mountain, relatively level going but in places exposed enough for a slip to terminate the Project – the Project being One's Life! Battling against my unsettled breakfast and forcing myself to breathe more slowly and deeply, I decided to make a tentative beginning to The Ledges. I could see hills and peaks for miles and being alone up so high among them was giving me a strength and determination that I barely recognised as a part of me.

I reckoned that I could complete this crossing and even perhaps commit to making the summit before evening began to descend. And at the far end I met my first and only people, a couple who complimented me on my achievement so far and assured me that the next section, a snow gully, was solid and at an easy enough angle not to present too great a problem. Then I would be only a stone's throw – or a boulder's collapse – away from the summit itself.

Fighting my way up the slope, using the ice axe I had carried all the way, was arduous but relatively safe. I was talking freely to myself now, voluble in my encouragement and cautions. No need to feel self-conscious. I was completely alone up here in the thin air. Just me and my multiple personalities.

As I neared the top of the gully, I picked up a colder wind and when I was eventually able to peer over its very top, I could look straight down the sheer, vertical Diamond Face of the mountain, one thousand feet or so to the scree and boulders far below. If the pancakes, cream, and altitude were not making a serious enough assault on my composure, then the exposure and the lonely enormity of my surroundings stood a good chance of completing the job.

Lying flat on my stomach and forcing myself to continue looking down the face, I instructed myself to drink in the sensations, to recognise my own strength of will and my ability to look fear in the eye. To laugh at threat and adversity.

A final couple of hundred feet of rock scrambling would lead to the summit. But I was tired and the afternoon was well advanced. The wind had picked up and turned cold and was blowing flecks of ice into my face and eyes. This was not a place to linger and I abandoned the final section, known as the Homestretch, and instead began a speedy but careful descent.

The route back took several hours and, although I was careful with my footing, I was also lost in reverie for great stretches, as if my mind had had its fill of spectacle and the here and now for one day. On the open hillside below the Boulder Field, I allowed myself to stretch out and sleep for half an hour or so, and thus fortified carry on down and enter the woods as they became thick and mysterious, extinguishing the daylight.

Adjusting to the dark, I was disconcerted by the sounds of gunfire somewhere ahead, by whoops and shouts, bottles and tin cans shattering. Just good ol' boys letting off a little steam, I told myself! Just the final obstacle before I could secure myself inside Andy and Lynn's camper bus, freewheel down the twisting canyon track, hit Boulder and locate Ray's apartment from his scribbled directions.

So, despite my desire for respite, this fifteen-mile climb with its 5,000 feet of ascent and descent was maintaining its challenge until the very end.

*

Ray's neighbour was thankfully convinced by my story about the planter.

'Yeah, that's where he keeps the key,' he added as I continued to grub around in the compost of the plant tub.

'Ah, this is it,' I said, my fingers finding the metal. 'Thank you for your help'.

'You're welcome, bud,' he replied. "You're gonna have to watch the dog!'

And Daphne, a Great Pyrenees, made her presence known the second my key entered the lock. A volley of barks erupted, a body slammed into the other side of the door and, like a tide drawing back over pebbles, she began to growl in an ever more menacing fashion.

'Just keep talking to her,' Ray had advised. 'She will make a lot of noise but she won't actually bite you. And she will eventually calm down.'

'It's alright, Daphne,' I said limply as I inched the door open a fraction.

A snout and bared teeth appeared in the crack. Daphne clearly intended to rip my limbs from me, to shred my skin to the bone, in a manner used by her kin to deter sheep-stealing wolves back on their native turf.

'I won't hurt you,' I offered, even more pathetically, and then edged the door open another inch or so.

The neighbour had obviously seen enough and made to go back into his home, shaking his head and possibly chuckling.

Step by step I eased the door open further whilst remaining ready to pull it back closed immediately should Daphne indicate that she was about to initiate a more direct, paws on – fangs on – strategy.

But as I moved forward, she retreated by just one small step and then another, hackles still raised, barking, snarling and growling all the while. Each tiny move on my part was matched by one from her and I began to feel that her sound and fury would not indeed translate into her teeth deep in my flesh.

'You're a good girl, Daphne. A good girl. I won't hurt you'.

And inch by inch I moved in through the front door as tiny step by tiny step we maintained those same few feet of distance between us. The heart-in-the-mouth moment was when I began to close the door behind me, cutting off any means of retreat should any slight misreading trigger a change in her intentions.

'Let's go into the kitchen, shall we Daphne? You good girl. Let's go and find something for us both to eat'.

The longer we were together without her actually attacking me, the more my confidence returned. But as I eased open the fridge door, she returned to a more agitated and vocal stance. This was clearly a new level of trespass.

'You are a good girl, Daphne. You really are'.

I was ready to sleep, despite the new rushes of adrenaline that the dog was stimulating. The day had been just too long.

Ray had told me that I could put down my sleeping bag on his single bed but as Daphne and I made our way into that room, continuing our dance with her still facing me and moving backwards with each step forward of mine, it became apparent that this was the final patch of territory that she would defend. As she jumped up onto the bed, her barking became intense.

'It's alright. You sleep there, Daphne. I'm just going to lie down beside you on the floor here.'

It was with great relief that I stretched out on the floor. Even with Daphne towering above me!

Her hostility seemed to be decreasing in volume. I was not intending to move anymore, and she seemed to sense it. And then, without warning, she slumped from the bed and her massive bulk pinned me to the floor.

I tried to stroke her back with my free hand, while she lay on top of me, shivering and whimpering. She nuzzled her face against mine and I could feel all the anxiety and aggression dissipating from her body even though her shaking continued. It took all of my effort to ease her gently from me and, with both of us relieved of our fear but still muttering and snorting occasionally, we drifted off together into a companionable sleep.

1987. Christmas on the Rocks

For the first Christmas I was to spend on my own, I entertained the idea of doing something dramatic, to make a feature of my being alone. The idea that kept returning was a bivouac, perhaps on a summit in the Lakes, to watch the sun come up. In the end, though, I settled for a little more in the way of creature comforts, - hot baths and a four-ring cooker, - and planned a walk up on the deserted Kinder Scout plateau.

But now, because I had not been able to bring myself to set the alarm, I was too late for even that and I was awoken by three telephone calls that came ringing in on Christmas Day in the morning. As I fumbled with my dressing gown, I thought I must have left the bathroom light on. But it was bright sun, the first in well over a week, and the very present I had wanted.

'How're you going on, youth?' It was Irwin, my climbing partner of two days before, taking himself away from the tree and presents. We talked about my intended long walk in the Peak, about subsidiary valleys with strange rock formations and isolated groves of trees. The next callers were my sons, making unselfconscious contact. My youngest recited his whole list, item by item, right down to the last orange in his sock. And then, all within half an hour, it was my mother, sharing her pleasure at the freshness of the morning.

I dithered with sandwiches and a flask. The Derwent valley and then back along the Edges would be quiet, I decided, it would suffice and I could have most of it to myself.

At the car park, I realised how wrong this was. Along the paths, groups of often two or three generations, were everywhere. Through Padley Woods, where I expected to hear the river below me and imagine myself in distant mountains, I was stuck behind two young couples with Dalmatians and loud conversation about an art exhibition. Even as I nodded and smiled, I was wishing them away from this place to their meal tables and firesides.

At around two in the afternoon the crowds finally thinned out. I had walked so fast in my bad humour that my back was damp, and I soon became chilled when I stopped for lunch on the hillside above the River Derwent.

Along Curbar and Frogatt Edges, the people seemed to re-emerge, and I was angry with myself for not having made more effort to get to Langdale or at least up onto the peat moors of Kinder. At the top of Frogatt, I changed into my climbing boots and left my red socks and rucksack arranged where they could not fail to attract the attention of a passer-by. Without a sac on my back, I felt buoyant and scrambled down to the bottom of the cliff. I selected my climb aware that crowds could all walk along above while an injured person lay unnoticed below in the shadows among the trees as night fell.

I had a headful of voices and ideas that would not stop, and because of them I was attempting to move up before checking that my holds were secure. A misplaced foot scraped down the rock and stopped me. Only a couple of weeks before, a leading climber, a standard setter, with a powerful physique and temperament to match, had slipped and fallen to his death from a nearby climb graded no harder than this one.

That did it. The whirl of words and images clunked to a stop like fruit machine cylinders, fixed into place and able to be put to one side. Now it was possible to attend to the balance between fingers and toes, to be aware of the unhurried transfer of tension through my body and to move in a controlled manner. The sand on the ledges required extra attention, making my hands slightly uncertain on the familiar gritstone.

Safely back on the top my impulse is to run as fast as I can, with breath bursting, over the tussocks towards White Edge, inevitably to catch my foot and splash face first into the boggy ground. I catch myself laughing out loud, - the sound is almost frightening, - and I quickly check that I am still alone. On to the track again, aware of the speed at which the light is changing. The hand that scratched the cirrus across the sky also hurries me over the boulders towards the evening.

It is a thin light, like watered down milk, but it has given me sustenance this afternoon.

Just before the gate I overtake an elderly couple and am drawn to a scrap of their conversation. It is as though I am meant to interrupt them, as if it would be rudeness not to.

'I'm sorry, did you say you've been on Kinder on Christmas day? Was anyone else there?'

'Oh yes, hundreds. We didn't go across the top, the mist came down. We're in our eighties now.'

Something bent or stretched or missing arched his arms and legs and bounced him along like a puppet.

'We're not television people.'

There was a tear of cold on her cheek.

'There must be a lot of food wasted at Christmas, the police were directing people in and out of Sainsbury's where we live.''

I tried to say something about ugliness, about Crisis at Christmas, and about still being on the hills at eighty, but my attempts felt clumsy and ingratiating. They talked and I beamed at the end of the afternoon on their faces.

'We'll have our dinner tonight at our daughter's. We don't have turkey, we like a piece of beef.'

We stood at their car, with me wishing I could embrace them both. He blew his nose with the full gusto of old age and then we parted, wishing each other well.

On through Longshaw, at last peacefully alone, - in peace and fully alone. The light is playing funny tricks. Although the sun has dropped into low clouds and the hills to the west are turning black, the track and dead bracken are tinged with purple. After the abrupt sunset, this creeping colour on the land is unexpected. I am walking loosely now, tired in my thighs and beginning to roll, my thoughts moving in waltz time.

The people are gone, the solitary sheep are turning pink, the air is becoming colder.

There are stars in the east and throughout the heavens.

1988. The Annapurna Circuit

The irony of it. Despite all my precautions – I had avoided for months any friend with the slightest snuffle – I managed to end up on the big day flying towards Kathmandu with an intense attack of diarrhoea, taking it with me rather than bringing it back.

At first, I found it embarrassing to be grilled by Holly about the delicate state of my insides. However, this was part of her role as group leader and she was making sure that none of us weakened too early. The trek around the Annapurna range required all eight of us to be fit enough for one hundred and sixty miles of walking and the thin air at an altitude of seventeen thousand seven hundred feet.

The paraphernalia for our trek – tents, kitchen utensils, food and in the higher treeless zone, firewood – was carried in huge bundles on the backs of porters. We were heavy with guilt for the first few days as they trudged so slowly in the great heat. However, on the higher, precipitous paths, at their natural altitude, they were to race easily ahead of us as we cautiously picked our way and be laughing around their fire as we entered camp each night.

By the end of the first day's trekking, strong emotions had consumed many of us. A mile or so from our camping spot we were joined by the children, big smiles and varying degrees of proficiency in the English language.

'Hello! What is your country?'

They walked between us, holding our hands, grinning up at us and leading us to their village.

'Hello! What is your name?'

Having given my own children all the usual warnings, half of me wished these youngsters were far more suspicious.

'Hello! You give me pen!'

Acutely self-conscious, we were paraded before their equally trusting and welcoming parents. The girl from California retired early to her tent that night to weep at the intensity of the day.

I remained outside later than everybody else. It may have been sensible to settle at dusk, to get into a good trekking routine, but I needed to feel the thickness of the air on my face and to touch the baked ground of an unfamiliar continent. I was drawn towards the village's single room dwellings. Through the open doorway I saw two bundles on a trestle table, the tops of tiny human heads and the tightly swaddled blankets around their infant bodies. There was no other furniture except the saucepans on the wall and I assumed that their parents were sitting out of view on the floor near the candle.

There was something reassuring in the austerity of the clay, wood and metal and it gave me the confidence to wander alone for a mile or so along the track alive with clicking, trills and whistles from unseen mouths.

As we approached each village on subsequent days, we were greeted by clasped hands and bowed heads, - from women at their pots, toddlers in filthy vests and wellingtons, or whoever.

'Namaste!' they said, meaning 'I salute the God within you!'

We were careful in our responses and easily drawn into the sincerity of the ceremony.

I had known that all my cultural assumptions would be easily shaken but there were others in our party who were far more hard-headed. Pam was a New York lawyer paid to defend her company's instant dessert. If anybody trifled with its textures or flirted with its flavours, she had the courtroom skills to extract a sum the size of Nepal's gross national product from the perpetrators. She was determined not to idealise the poverty or submit to sentimentality and yet, on the fourth day, she confessed herself overwhelmed by the relaxed and purposeful sense of existence she was witnessing in each village.

Because of the continual changes in altitude, our journey was one through climatic zones. It was like starting from subtropical Africa and, within the space of three weeks wandering to northern Norway and back. So, on the first day, there were banana trees and rice paddies. After six days there was the deep cut of an Alpine valley, the straight trunks of the conifers and the beginnings of the Buddhist influence on the architecture. And at ten days from the road and eleven thousand feet above sea level, we came to the high mountain desert of the upper Manang valley, where yellow dust replaced the soil and forces from the sky had shaped enormous sand spires.

We stayed here for a day, washing ourselves and our clothes in the cold glacier melt and wandering among the closely clustered, flat roofed dwellings of Manang. Everywhere prayer flags clattered in the wind, the characters fading and the material itself disintegrating as the holy words were taken into the atmosphere.

Beyond Manang habitation quickly disappeared. Juniper and gorse scratched a prickly existence in a landscape ringed by Big Peaks. The sun's light took on heaviness and great gulps were needed to assuage the body's thirst for oxygen. 'Don't worry if your tent mate's breathing sounds unusual in the night' Holly had warned us. I learned not to bother about him but felt no easier when my own lungs went on their occasional flutter.

We came to camp in a bleak canyon below the Thorung La as a cold air sliced the last light of afternoon. Conversations were desultory, the mood sombre and the ground hard as we tried to gain rest before the exertion of the next day.

We were up at four the following morning by the light of constellations I had never seen in the West's polluted skies. All the apprehensions had been voiced in the previous twelve days, now it was each person in their own time, a plod over scree and snow, upwards for three, four, five hours to the narrow gateway between two landscapes. All the while, the drama of a day unfolding was played upon the gigantic backdrop of the Annapurna range, the pink upon the ice fields, the night slowly abandoning its strands of indigo to the bottom of the deepest valleys. Muzzy headed and thirsty, my day's water gone by ten in the morning, we greeted each other as we arrived through the summit snows.

After descending from the pass, at a tiny village, a fourteen-year-old boy, who looked no more than ten, attached himself to us for the one-day journey between his parents. He insisted on carrying Holly's rucksack.

'Me por-dar' he beamed with a new status that would, if he was lucky, all too soon be his only means of livelihood.

Our sticks tapped out the miles on the stones of the Kali Gandaki, a valley that to the north becomes the forbidden corridor into Tibet. We wrapped our faces against the dust storm and bent into the wind as thunder colours rumbled above us. This old salt and silk route took us, at twice the depth of the Grand Canyon, through wild lands between the interlocking feet of the massive Annapurna and Dhaulagiri mountains.

In the days that followed, we dropped first to the cool greenery around the firs and pines and then later to the humidity among the banyan trees, the hot sulphur springs by the river and the shadows in the rhododendron forests. We climbed Poon Hill before dawn and applauded the sun as it rose above a skyline full of rock and snow pyramids.

We usually walked in various permutations of two and three, sometimes peeling off the outer layers of our lives, but always returning to a steady level of small talk whenever we came together for communal meals.

Dumper trucks with slithering loads of ballast chugged around us on the twentieth day as we walked into Pokhara, the composure of the mountain trail still in our footsteps.

Is this when our journey ended?

With the sight of an old woman sat by the roadside, breaking a boulder into smaller pieces with a hammer? Or us bemused among the crumbling two-storey buildings on the city's outskirts, or giggling to be moving so fast again as our taxi dodged cows and bicycles?

Or, in Pokhara market, me glimpsing my reflection in a small mirror, the first time I had seen my own face in almost a month? Seeing a younger man, tanned and healthy, unencumbered. A stranger who was at once also deeply familiar. Someone with whom I had lost touch. As if reunited after a lifetime.

Was it that evening at our camp beside the lake when the porters, with a petrol canister full of rakshi, sang and danced for us? The most worldly of the men becoming, with the chanting and the rhythm on the drum, the most sensitive in their portrayals of dragons, princesses and rescuers as they turned their fingers and limbs against the firelight. Or, with senses high, Holly and I pulling the excited Nepalese inwards with each chorus of our crass offering, the Hokey Cokey? Singing songs as the evening dwindled, and Temba, the head man, holding us with the hint of a familiar theme within the alien lilt of his offering. And just as he was finishing, us managing to detect the melody of 'Oh my darling, Clementine'.

'In 1973 ...' he explained '... on Makalu expedition ... the Japanese ... they teach me'.

Did the journey end with me crawling into my tent after Auld Lang Syne, still chuckling at the incongruity of it all? Strengthened by the dignity and self-respect I had witnessed daily and knowing a little more about life lived between the poles of self-reliance and inevitability? Moving my sleeping bag so that the rock beneath my hip could tuck into the small of my back before sliding happily into sleep?

Perhaps it finished back in Kathmandu with Susie pleading to two young and eager traders with their tourist souvenirs. 'Please don't try to become like us. You have something very precious here, something we have lost and desperately need'. And them replying, 'You have a car, lady? Your husband, he has a car too?'

Or maybe it was in the small hours with half a dozen of us locked in a cavernous warehouse at Delhi airport while a problem with the tickets for our flight back home failed to move towards resolution.

Was it definitely over by Amsterdam's airport, perhaps? With its massive displays of luxury goods in the brilliant morning light – a groaning excess of cameras, watches, phones, jewel-encrusted vulgarities thrust into our faces everywhere. Breath-taking in their superficiality, fatally blocking us from a grounding so necessary for sanity.

When did our journey end?

Answer, it hasn't!

'Hello! You give me pen!'

'Namaste!'

1988. Whistling Down to Jomsom

We come into Kagbeni, crowded, closed, Tibetan streets, a river through the road, a complex, a jumble of lanes, dark alleys that narrow beyond vision, openings out onto the wide flood plain of the Kahli Gadanka, figures on the stones moving against vast stretches, the mesa-hillsides, the flanks of interwoven mountains crumpled into a landscape that becomes Tibet, a magical place, lunch in the cool upstairs of a rest house, chapattis, peas fried in onion, tinned chicken slices, and tinned fruit, decorations formed from an old Colgate tooth powder tin prominent among the iconography, our boots cracking the new mud floor, a puppy crapping among us, Susie bringing in a ten week old baby, his mother's jumper folded under him as a nappy
... and out into the valley, all in scarves and bandannas, against the winds coming up from the south, and into the Kahli Gadanka, the wide flat valley, the beach between the feet of mountains, the muddy wanderings of the split river, the laughter at the slippery stones, the sight of an old woman piggy-backed by her husband along the narrow side track, smashing rocks in the search for ammonites, and the beginning of trees on the hillsides, and yellow flowered gorse and a purple clover in the stones and the dust rising up like a cyclone in the distance gathering momentum before dipping and then setting off towards us
... and the five Nepalese girls travelling back home to Jomsom, arms swinging, shawls over their faces, and the huge curving rock faults, and the thunder colours further up, and the Eiger-wall face on the north east of Nilgiri appearing in the clouds that take on dust haze layers of shade above the ever-darkening hill ridges, while a wild, drunken Nepali attaches himself to us, reeling through the canyon waving his stick until we shake him off, and

we join the Nepalese girls who giggle at my attempts to sing through my bandanna, then they sing to us, leaning forward in earnestness and against the wind, and on across the pebbles and packed earth, white everywhere with surface salt, and into the bumpy mud mainstream of the town, an ugly mixture of Western influences, but not before we have seen riders in the valley corralling horses and the relations walking out into the wild land to meet the girls

... and we arrive to porters and loads in the main street, some confusion and words from Temba and we step inside a hotel, with a round of apple brandy and it is the worst image of the remote lands, where a dissolute German and a local leer and press rakshi onto Krishna who shares some with me and out, head spinning a little, into the street, around the back of a rest house, to find a crowded camping space like a bombed out refugee camp, children watching, dogs that creep, and huddled people breaking wood for fuel

... and in the mess tent our young travelling companion whom Holly will mother and keep beside her in the night to deliver to his father in the morning, and he wide-eyed as he eats with us and takes three helpings of soup, and then outside at 8.30, as the lamp burns, only Susie and I are left with our diaries, a dog is yelping and laughter, coughing and conversation comes from the porters' campfire and all the changes that we have seen today from the town below the Pass to the entry into Tibet through Kagbeni with the cherry blossom and the moonscape, other planet, other consciousness and the tapping of the stick on the miles of stones to the one-horse, bombed-out resting place, have left a patchwork day, a richly woven, threadbare cloth of a day, a rags and riches of experience.

1989. Tour de Mont Blanc

I had known that my lack of planning would catch up with me sooner or later. And here, so early in the proceedings, that reckoning was taking place as we passengers spilled out from the overnight train into a dismal dawn at St Gervais.

Two British lads watched with a sneery superiority, as I emptied my rucksack onto the station platform, searching for French currency with which to buy a morning wake-up coffee. With everything scattered before me – and under their patronising gaze – I began to pack in an orderly fashion what I would need for the ten-day, one-hundred-and-ten-mile, hike through the mountains of France, Italy, Switzerland and then back into France again.

My strategy had been to get to the Mont Blanc area with the jumble of things that I might require and then sort myself out before starting the walk proper. To jettison anything that seemed superfluous once there and to repack in a more coherent fashion. I had indulged this ramshackle approach up until the night before as I boarded the train at Gare de Lyon at around midnight.

In the couchette compartment I became pathetically aware of my ignorance about the necessary conventions. Do you just strip off? Is night wear de rigueur? Do the men let the women have the carriage to themselves first for such purposes? How does one find out, jammed cheek to jowl – and the other cheek to another jowl – with five strangers? Hoping for guidance from the glamorous Parisienne lady almost pressed against me taught me the first, principal lessons:

You do not speak!

You do not establish eye contact!

You do not acknowledge the existence of the other!

Somehow, we managed the task, the experienced leading with practiced efficiency, the hopelessly wrong-footed copying as silently and as best we could.

The comical was left behind though through that long night as I slithered around on my mattress, sweaty and pursued through brief snatches of sleep by dreams and demons. A couple of feet beneath me, as we careered through the night and through France, metal wheels were racketing on metal tracks, fifty years almost to the hour from the commencement of World War Two.

*

Le premier jour

My two contemptuous countrymen gave me a tip – to ignore Andrew Harper's guidebook that we were all following and gain height early by taking a tram up to Col de Voza. I had last been in the Alps seventeen years earlier and was eager to see again their peaks piercing blue skies and their glaciers cutting a course through the limbs of mountains. Instead, a thick mist hung like grey jelly between each tree branch and out across the meadows. After disembarking, the walk took me through pleasant, dripping forests up to the edge of Glacier de Bionassay where, once again, I was disappointed with the dirty, unwashed appearance of this icy architecture. The otherwise thick and murky silence was punctuated by the sound of eerie trickles and the occasional crack as stones and boulders fell from the melting ice.

La deuxième jour

My haphazard approach had continued through the first day, mist and rain adding to the atmosphere and then my temporarily losing the route completing the picture. But my dortoir in Les Contamines was clean, comfortable and nowhere near full and more than compensated for my rather lacklustre first day. The evening then improved further as I enjoyed the company of various fellow TMB hikers in the nearby bar, especially relishing the stories told by an older Scottish climber, Donald and his friend Elaine, of wild adventures on the formidable Etive Slabs in his home country.

In the morning, I spent some time cashing traveller's cheques and attempting to organise small packs of the three different currencies that would be needed over the next week and a half. As I stashed bread, cheese, garlic sausage and fruit into my rucksack, I began at last to feel more in control of events and ready for the challenge that lay ahead.

The day's walk of about ten miles ascended steeply up the side of a forest-clad ravine, accompanied by the continual roar of racing waters. The path then opened out into a valley bounded by a huge rock wall, snow speckled against the skyline. From then on, pleasant climbing, never too long or too steep, brought me up to the Col du Bonhomme. In good time, I had risen approximately the height of Ben Nevis and, as I seemed to be going so well, had to decide whether to push for another couple of hours.

As I came to the Refuge Col de la Croix du Bonhomme, its ramshackle three-story wooden construction and its remote location high in the mountains, made the decision for me. The clinching factor was the toilet, a tall, thin timber building anchored by hawsers at the side of an enormous drop, a location that obviated the need for sophisticated plumbing and afforded any seated visitor who cared to look straight down a terrifying perspective!

Inside the refuge, the concierge, a full-figured Italian woman, explained the various sleeping and eating arrangements. There were various British guests staying that night, all doing the TMB. Frank and Rachel were keen cross-country skiers from Cheshire, David and

Elaine "serious" walkers, they told me, from Grimsby, and Derek and Alan my fellow, disapproving travellers from the Paris train whose conversation consisted of little beyond their obsession with calories expended and taken in.

Later we grouped together in the candlelit main room at one end of a large, old wooden table as others, staff maybe or possibly long-term residents, crept from hidden rooms with hanging blankets for doors. These half dozen strangers sat themselves at the opposite end of the table and chatted quietly in French and only amongst each other for the whole evening.

I had sometimes wondered what became of the Woodstock generation, whether they had all drifted into conventional lifestyles – semi-detached and suburban. but here they were, surviving on a mountain, seeing out the years behind blankets, in dark and dusty rooms, by candlelight. Stardust and golden and back in the Garden. In that mellow atmosphere, with substantial plates of mountain food and, in my case, a whole litre of red wine, we Brits found many topics of common interest. Our whispered conversation generated a warming bond of camaraderie as the night outside tightened its grip on our flimsy structure and the bare mountain side.

Or maybe it was just the wine.

Le troisième jour

At last, a clear, pink sunrise and it was a pleasure to get up and out from the de-oxygenated bunk room. Outside, frost was locking the ground, causing me to reconsider my plan to spend some nights bivouacking at altitude.

Washing was to be in freezing water from the glacier melt outside. The toilet was to be for those with a sense of adventure – and an absence of vertigo.

I was the last to leave the hut but made good progress up scree and boulders. Feeling alive, alone and strong, I left my sac and took a detour up to the Tete Nord where I obtained my first big mountain view. With confidence soaring, I put away my map and guidebook and planned to follow the contours of the hillside to save unnecessary ascents and descents. And in doing so, I ended up in a perilous position trying to cross a steep bank of loose shale above a drop into a river. Pouring with sweat and with the rucksack feeling very heavy on my back, I had to retrace my steps. The footholds held but I continually dislodged handfuls of small stones as I scrabbled for holds. It was a lesson in not losing concentration and thinking I could do without the map.

When I had managed to get back to the solid hillside bank, talking to myself all the while – 'Take it steady, you're still alive. Think. Keep thinking!' – I lay back in the grass, celebrating survival, drinking water and putting away a large lunch of bread and garlic sausage. And all the while, grasshoppers were springing through the grass or into the void, happy as ninepins.

I had lost between two and three hours.

Il sesto giorno

On the days following my misadventure, I drank in the experience of still being alive with heightened senses – the Peuterey Ridge in spikey silhouette and the summit of Mont Blanc in mist; squashed beneath the eaves of the Elisabetta Refuge; a clear, crisp morning with the Miage glacier tumbling down to the little Lac du Miage, where miniature icebergs floated in the aquamarine water; in the absence of a cheaper alternative down in Courmayer, paying for a room with a bed and bath; eating tagliatelle bolognaise followed by escalope of ham and cheese in the town with Dave and Elaine.

On the sixth day, because the meal in Courmayer had been delicious but expensive, I needed to institute a more austere regime for a while. So, soup and bread the previous night was followed by coffee and bread for breakfast. At lunchtime, huddled down behind a ruined building at the site of the old Elena Refuge destroyed by avalanche in 1961, I brewed up my chicken and sweet corn soup as crowds began to arrive and watch me eat.

This financial discipline proved to be no hardship. I was, after all, seeing for the first time areas that had dwelled in my imagination for decades. From a green, round whaleback ridge with a great sense of empty space all around, I could look back at Mt Blanc and even, in the haze of distance, the Col de Seigne that I had crossed a couple of days earlier. From beautiful, lower pastures, with marmots running everywhere, the Grand Jorasses grew in magnitude, looking to me every bit as big as the Himalayas.

I found it thrilling to be crossing the high mountain passes that constituted unmarked borders between countries and as I climbed up further to the one between Italy and Switzerland at the lonely Grand Col Ferret, the air grew decidedly colder and a mist descended. It was too chilly for stopping so I dropped down quickly to softer and more sheltered Swiss hillsides and met up again with Frank and Rachel.

We walked along companionably until a massive boom filled the air followed by rumblings as if the ground itself was disturbed and about to break open. We speculated that it might be blasting or perhaps thunder but neither fully accorded with our previous experiences of suchlike in the mountains. That it was neither soon became apparent when the noise continued with the hills in every direction seemingly shaking with the blasts. I eventually concluded, after some rapid bursts that must be gunfire, that the hills were alive with the sound of war games. And we learned from the local paper the next day that military exercises had indeed been taking place in the area and that the Swiss Minister of War had visited and been much impressed by the 'exercise de infiltration and exfiltration'. Welcome to Switzerland.

La Fouly was neat and ordered with every shutter newly painted and noticeably different from Italy just over the border. After a late and boozy evening with Frank and Rachel, I turned in about 11 and was just getting to sleep in my dortoir dormitory when the soldiers in the next room started to have a party. Their machine guns were lining the walls of our corridor so grinning and bearing it rather than complaining seemed the sensible option.

Der achte Tag

People had been talking of a bad weather forecast and my guidebook was building up today's walk as a 'rugged mountaineering route'. In the event, the weather held and I found the 3,000-foot ascent little different from that of a peak in the English Lake District. In fact, and despite our liberal approach to demi-litres of wine in the refuge the night before, I arrived at Trient, my destination, the earliest of any of the days on the tour.

After particularly extensive views from the Fenetre d'Arpette followed by close views of the spectacular Trient Glacier, the walk through the quiet village with its widely spaced chalets proved a tranquil conclusion to my day.

Until I passed the boy soldiers.

Around a small, monumental tower, two young men and three girls were chatting and guffawing in the lingua franca of flirtation. The boys, with their tunics undone, were smoking cigarettes and laughing, their rifles resting by their sides. They watched me as I shuffled past, avoiding their glance by focusing on my footsteps and maintaining a steady plod.

Then, in a universal language again unmistakable, there was a sharp command from one of the young men. I decided to ignore him, to play the tired,

uncomprehending foreigner and maintain my pace. Quite quickly, the order was barked again but his time accompanied by the ratcheting sound of a gun brake being released. 'He wouldn't do it, there is no way he would shoot me,' I told myself. 'In the back, for God's sake!' But I did nevertheless wonder whether I would feel anything if he did. The briefest burst of intense pain before all feeling ceased?
Forever.

Der neunte Tag
There had been no bullet, but bad water brought catastrophic consequences in the night. Various of the walkers, my occasional companions, had recently experienced violent bouts of diahorrea and vomiting and, in a tightly packed dormitory where access necessitated stepping over others and negotiating two sets of rickety ladders, I joined this carnival of misery. The toilets were two floors below my little sleeping platform, bright modern facilities, cavernous and tiled to magnify the slightest sounds as echoing blasts to the sleepers above.

After a long night of such manoeuvres and waking the whole dormitory, I could barely make it to the breakfast table. Somebody kindly made me a pint of tea and I could do little but stare at it and the peach placed beside it. While Alan and Derek maintained their continuing obsession with consuming calories, I forced myself to tackle the drink and piece of fruit.

I could easily have been persuaded to stay in the gite at the edge of the village to sleep and recuperate although the mortifyingly quiet nature of the place made it seem like somewhere in which to go mad. Duncan and Elaine had both been ill too and the three of us decided to make our way slowly over the pass back into France where the Gite d'Etape at Trelechamp had a widely shared reputation for being particularly welcoming and nurturing.

Packing my sac required a massive effort and the others helped lift it onto my back. The Swiss army were all over the hillside with their mortars and shells and we were allowed along the path at intervals. And so, we walked over the col, out from Switzerland to the accompaniment of explosions rocking around the mountains.

I have never needed to exert discipline of the level required to keep my focus solely on the next step, and then the next, all morning. Somehow, this trudging upwards one movement at a time delivered me to the highest point at the Col de Balme and then all the way down to the welcome ministrations of Mme Sylvia Mugnier at the gite. Among this warmth and succour, I took immediately to my sleeping bag for a couple of hours and then, with some effort, managed the best meal of my trip, a lovingly prepared dish of fish in a gratin sauce topped with shallot, white wine, butter and chives. After such a long, slow and taxing day where I had learned for the first time in my life that I possessed so much more strength and resilience than I had ever envisaged, after all that and it being over, I could luxuriate in these depths of warmth and nurture.

I contemplated staying for a second night. Or, for the rest of my life.

Le douzième jour

A number of the people I had bumped into along the walk had become ill and decided on the morning of the tenth day to remain in the cheerful and homely atmosphere of the gite for another day but, as I was feeling much improved, I set off for the final two days to Chamonix. Our goodbyes felt surprisingly emotional, we had forged an odd camaraderie parting and meeting over the hundred miles and massive total ascent.

Walking on, spectacular views of the area – again all new to me – opened up. The Aiguille Argentiere with its detached tower like some organic growth and then the Mer de Glace, its level, winding course giving it the appearance of a mighty river stopped in its tracks.

On the eleventh day, I managed to change my ticket for an overnight train from Les Houches that evening and thus save myself from having to hang around for more than 24 hours.

*

Somehow, I slept, battle-hardened and weary, through the couchette experience and was at Gare de Lyon by 7am, around the Mero to Gare de Nord by 8. But the bad water from days before, or some new malevolence, had business with me still and I spent the period waiting for my train home kneeling at the edge of an empty platform. Kneeling and retching, weak and wretched, while pretty girls in the height of Parisienne chic, clickety-clacked past me on high heels on their ways to work.

I hoped they could step over me, pay me no mind.

I wished I could wither away and disappear.

1989. A Taste of Life

Boxing Day morning, the telephone, and Les did it probably the only way you can, every word a hammer blow in one short sentence.
'Bob ... Andy ... dead ... avalanche ... Christmas Eve'
He went over the details while the words thumped into a sense of disbelief.
I didn't know what I wanted to say or where I wanted to be. My trip to the Lakes with a lot of people I hardly knew lost its appeal. The fancy dress party on New Year's Eve was the last thing I needed. Scratching around at home in that deep dip between Christmas and New Year, however, seemed equally daunting.
I drove to Buxton to be with old friends. In different houses we started the same conversations and were unable to finish them. Children, recently gorged on excitement and novelty, now took their place in the solemnity of the feast gone sour. In one house, friends busied themselves blasting heat against pans of beans and spaghetti hoops. In another we sat in the half light, the computer monitor ignored as it flashed out new attractions. It was where I wanted to be and there was nothing to be said.
I never really climbed that much with Bob Brevitt or Andy Poole although I knew them well as part of the Buxton Club. They did seem to be there stitched into my life, weaving in and out of the incidental and touching moments of significance and intensity.
I went to the Lakes insisting to myself that I would turn around and come back home the moment – the moment what? I didn't know. They were climbers and would understand. They asked about the details and I knew very few of the answers. I wanted instead to talk about the sandwich boards and the posters Bob used to stick all around the town, high on hoardings and railway arches,

in the middle of the night. I wanted to talk about Andy setting off on the first pitch of Gash Crag only a few weeks earlier and how, when he looked back down to us with water running all down the mountain and with rain in his face, he was grinning.

But the week progressed and I relaxed into it. We froze up on Pike's Crag at nearly three thousand feet because Irwin assured us it would get the afternoon sun. We huddled, six of us, on the stance halfway up Nape's Needle, thick ice in the depressions that should have functioned as holds, with only a packet of extra strong mints between us. We took a day in the valley on Wallowbarrow Crag but found no respite there. And on the final day, we squared up to Overhanging Bastion.

I hardly knew the chap I was accompanying and I hardly knew whether I wanted to climb anything challenging ever again. I did know that I was probably biting off more than I wanted to chew in my present state and at this time of the year.

Beneath the wall Nature was in retreat, damp with winter. Waterlogged tree trunks and branches gave way beneath us and our boots smeared fresh moss across the boulders. The north face of Castle Rock soared and leaned above us with all the confidence that I was lacking. Andy, Bob and I had shared this knowledge of our place in the scale of things.

I was unsteady on the climb but getting up it. Thankfully the ramp was his pitch and I sat perched on the spike and belayed him, leaning back over two hundred feet of air and vertical rock. We had also shared this welling sense of delight in our own audacity, tiptoeing up walls while giants slept.

The crux did not turn out to be the problem I had feared and I relaxed onto the ramp.

'It's easier than I was expecting,' I shouted.

'You're not there yet,' his voice came back. 'There's a sting in the tail'.

I crouched, bunched up at the top of the ramp, my head against the bulge that blocked the way. The only alternative was to step down from the ramp and stretch my foot a long way sideways, three hundred feet above nothing, and place it in a small nest of stones and gravel. I practised loading my weight against an uninspiring sideways pull, limbs at odds with each other being pulled through uncomfortable angles like a spindly music stand. Daring myself to move the centre through and beyond the boundary of retreat. Every bit of thought and memory, every hope and aspiration now disappearing into that extended step across, locked in and lost, focussed to the exclusion of all else. The seconds seemed to take over and set their own pace as tension and slack played against each other through my arms and legs, back and neck. Extreme care now to avoid the giant.

At last, my left foot landing in the nest and all the release, endorphins in the brain stem spilling over into the whole body, cymbals crashing and the giant roaring and being so alive, pulling into the rock with arms stretched, and leaning out, and we had known and shared this saturation of delight when we could have roared like giants after all the delicacy of step and the holding of breath, but it's not over and this is nowhere to rest, arms draining and hands having to pull on 'rickety tusks', and all the sensations of flight and euphoria to be slammed back under control.

Great, stern, sharp, father words of rebuke inside the head put the body back into a tight discipline. I uttered a quiet obscenity and it caught on the cold air. And all the poise rushed back again for the next big move.

And as I stood with him on the top I realised that I had shared with Bob and Andy many times this switchback of experience, the sheer assertive sense of being, loose and raucous and able to fill a whole mountain landscape with its energy, and then in one flick of the senses change to a racing metabolism, speed frozen into the frame of some threatened, tiny creature, stretching the instantaneous into the accurate and precise.

Our arms and our grins hung with the weight of the climb as we shook hands on the top, two people who barely knew each other. The air was keen as sheet metal, and we hurried to coil the ropes and get moving.

The cold grey understatement of a late December afternoon was absorbing the shoulders of Helvellyn.

Bob and Andy were all around me on the hillside as the light went down on that last day of the decade.

And they'll be coming home a little later than the rest of us.

THE ETHELS – SUMMER

Ethels Day 45 – 7th June

Alphin Pike, Featherbed Moss & Black Chew Head

Here we are in the far Northwest of the Peak District, all new landscape for me. Not some insignificant, distant corner but huge tracts of land, startling spikes of rock against the skyline, high remote moors, reservoirs that are both playgrounds lower down - ice creams, sailing clubs, cycle ways - and higher up, sullen tracts of water, deserted dam walls.

A steep pull, barbed wire to surmount and a tax on breathing for the first hour or more. But then we are at the top of Alphin Pike. From here, almost level ground for a few miles, skirting the magnificent moorland above the southern rim of the Chew Valley. Peak District edges get no more compelling, but today's feels very special because I am seeing and treading it for the very first time – and so late in my love affair with the area. A long and delightful traverse, the hillside below vivid and extravagant with new bilberry growth, and we are at Chew Reservoir. There it dwells, high, isolated, haughty and municipal.

Then map and compass, experiencing the frisson that comes with pushing one's body on across difficult terrain without way or marker. Always I have some silent debate about trusting the bearing and suppressing the erratic and spontaneous. After half an hour or so of rough ground, a hare lolloping ahead of us through last year's heather at one point, the trig point for Featherbed Moss comes into view. Just where it should be. Just where I had never doubted it would be. Just when I might have cast aside my calm and the rational.

Lunch and a sit down on springy, hollow-sounding peat and then on again, another bearing but this time with a clear view for miles of flat, unending emptiness. The map shows that we are walking the lines of boundaries, one foot in North West England, the other in the East Midlands. Or in Greater Manchester and High Peak. We eventually come to an absurd barbed wire fence running straight across the wastes, where one might half expect to see a sign saying 'Derbyshire. Keep Out!' or some such.

From here we accompany the fence across indefinite ground to find the 'summit' of Black Chew Head. A grand and ominous sounding name for an insignificant pile of stones, the slightest of cairns barely rising above the scruffy vastness all around.

Then it is retreat along a boggy path, the elevated reservoir again and, with the miles accumulating in our muscles, a welcome metalled lane falling all the way back down to our morning's starting point.

Ethels Day 46 – 17th June

Ashway Moss

Today was to be the day 'Those Northern Ethels' were faced, three tops in the very north, just outside Holmfirth. They have niggled me for the past nine months, knowing that in their northern reach, a long day awaited and would sooner or later have to be faced.

We are away early, breakfasting in Glossop before driving on to the Holme Moss tower. Sacs packed and adjusted, sunblock on, extra water for temperatures predicted to reach the 30s. And then we meet the notice saying that the landowner has closed the moors and access is denied!

'The sin of property we do disdain
No man has any right to buy and sell the earth for private gain'

After a quick burst of righteous fulmination, with 'World Turned Upside Down' playing in my head, we reconsider and head off to Dovestones Reservoir and Ashway Moss.

This hill involves a steep pull with little respite. We meet many people, including a teenager with her boyfriend who, on reaching a stile, asks 'What do I do here?' There is a holiday atmosphere all about, the sun and the spectacle bringing the people out from the conurbations. The joyous air affects even me. I accept the crowds, almost embrace them (figuratively).

We have the summit cairn to ourselves and enjoy a lunch with views over Saddleworth Moor, munching, chatting, resting.

On returning to the car and because the sun is still fierce, I make for woodland shade to read and think again about that ragged band they called the Diggers and who claimed the land 'a common treasury'.

Ethels Day 47 – 18th June

Snailsden Pike End, Dead Edge End & Britland Edge End

A day of strange names and empty wastes - Little Twizle Clough, Riddle Clough, Reaps Moss, Great Grains Clough and many more.

On the map, this area, 'Those Northern Ethels', looks vast and relatively featureless and so, in the main, they prove to be. Hence the grandeur of Ramsden Clough is an unexpected delight. A deep ravine, splattered with bilberry, ravenous for the eye's attention.

Route finding is at a premium. Map and compass, reading the weather, anticipating detours around impassable land, estimating time and distance, all keep the mind busy while the body acknowledges any early warnings of fatigue and struggles to find a rhythm.

From the long, rounded summit of Snailsden Pike End we look across an extent of land that may be barely navigable. A mile or so on the map here looks like a day's journey under the darkening sky. After calculations, best guess estimations and the setting of a compass bearing, we enter the fray and strike out across rough and ominous terrain.

We proceed, we make headway hacking through the heather and checking our course. The sky grows darker and rain or storm feels like a possibility. Time ticks on and then, in the most anonymous and remote of landscapes, my foot falls through a hole and thuds down a couple feet. The pain shoots through my ankle, and I hope that no serious damage has been done. A rescue would be near impossible.

No serious damage has been done.

We make for and attain the skyline and the trig point of Dead Edge End (my 80th Ethel) – a bit Edgey, not at the

End and certainly not Dead. From here a trodden path, so welcome, and we can lengthen our stride, raise our gaze and feel a new spring in the ground.

It is still a long trek to our third hilltop and then the car but we are accompanied by the calls of curlews and the companionable presence of golden plovers with their mournful calls piping across the barren land.

Ethels Day 48 – 30th June

Margery Hill & High Stones (Howden Edge)

Two remote Ethels today from the very top of Howden Reservoir, up onto deserted moors, the hillsides folding with ease into each other as we follow Cranberry Clough. The water that tumbles down over stones worn smooth in the bed of the stream is stained a rich brown with peat, sand and soil. The lovely valleys that slice down from the high ground of the Dark Peak, on the northern edges of Kinder and Bleaklow and here, remind me of discovering Dartmoor in my teenage years. The exhilaration and sense of emancipation that these landscapes, these colours, this section of Nature's palette, always bring.

Solitary outcrops like Bull Clough Head are scattered about these high, open places, impassively seeing out the centuries. The occasional cairn is piled beside the track. We have no need of them today but they remind any wanderers that, far from summer, these places can conspire with wind and snow and visibility to unleash a lethal, unforgiving rage.

The vegetation at the top of Margery Hill has cleared into a fairy circle around the trig point. There is nobody here, nobody discernible, and Margery has long since surrendered a name to the vagaries of time and season.

Once again, the views are overpowering. Away to the east are the vague outlines of industry, towers and turbines, and densely concentrated conurbations. At the other three compass points though, only wild, outrageous openness, no people, no dwellings, no sense of boundaries. There, to the very south, hovering in and out of the haze and distance, that tiny protuberance, could it possibly be Minninglow? We attempt to reckon the miles. There to the north, no question about it, that's the mast of Holme Moss. We are located along some huge dimension of the Peak District.

On now along Wilfrey Edge, the high ridge, with purposeful strides. Past weathered sculptures bequeathed to no gallery, to High Stones.

From here, the county top of South Yorkshire, we survey the patchwork hillsides below us, attempting to pick out a feasible descent. First, steep steps down, tough on the knees and balance, and then a search for the path. It gradually manifests itself from the heather, with the knowledge that others, nameless and gone, have worn this slight track over the ages.

Signs that the civilising reach of Howden Clough is extending upwards come with the first silver birch saplings, then tall and improbable foxgloves and thistles searching around for stray companions. Onwards down to woodland, the canopy of tall, dying pines creating deep shadows but, where light does penetrate, busy concentrations of new deciduous growth.

Eventually, the wide track beside the water and a few people.

It is still a long walk back around the top of the reservoir to the car.

Ethels Day 49 – 4th July

Alport Moor

Up from Fairholmes onto the high ground of the reservoirs' western flank, the maps, printed and online, are in good-natured disagreement with the actual ground beneath our feet. We make our way, this way and that, through forest, along path and track, rising all the while. At the crest, we step onto open ground and are straightaway aware of the extended plateau, the majestic Rowlee Pasture, across which we will now walk for hours. It is relatively easy terrain and it is possible to converse two or three and sometimes even four abreast. And how the conversation can flow whilst walking!
I usually tend to value solitary contemplation. And yet, on moors, mountains and coastal cliffs – heck, even sometimes on bikes – it has been the chat and conviviality that has enriched me just as much.
So today we make our way with cheerful exchange along to Alport Castles. Down to our left the Alport Valley blazes with vivid greens, rich and luxuriant. With oxbow lakes even. Away to our right, the far horizon above the reservoirs, hills and tors that we have so very recently reached only through toil, now reduced to tiny pimples on the skyline.
I have been across this huge whaleback at other times, slightly earlier in the year, and been surrounded by an immense cacophony of skylarks and pipits, alarmed by the footfall across their nesting grounds. The sky has been a-twitter, full of common concern, of watchful agitation.
A stop above the Castles, where the shattered land mass lists like a stricken battleship, falling away into the depths, going under at geological pace.

The onward journey now takes us across a featureless expanse of land, the distant, ridge of Bleaklow providing only a minimal, vertical rise.

Except.

Except for a tiny white dot, almost too small to see unaided. A trig point standing lost amongst the moor's muted hues. We reign in our sociability, lengthen our stride and fix concentration on this, the only landmark. From here, we again scan horizons, attempt to superimpose the map, the directions, onto all this emptiness. We make a judgement about our final destination, the rounded and undistinguished point of highest elevation.

More application in the pace and we are eventually there. Although it is mid-summer, the wind, the lowering clouds and the heavy hemisphere of sky above – magnificent but not without menace – all caution against lingering or relaxing for too long. Sheltered down in a peaty dip, we eat our lunch and muster remaining energies, replenish our commitment, for the long walk back the way we have come, the eleven-mile round trip. As we return, we spot a lone figure materialising from the groughs and have a brief, shouted conversation. He is trying to reach 'Grains In The Water', a wonderful but remote and lonely spot. I remember the last time I tried to do so and failed, and the long, exhausting day that resulted.

I shout 'Good luck!'

Alport Moor is one of the strangest Ethels. It has hardly any 'prominence'. Bleaklow Stones, to the north, and the huge, thuggish tumble of Grinnah Stones are higher, far more distinctive and ostensibly more deserving of inclusion on the tally.

But our objective today has taken us somewhere far more subtle, where our efforts, our human frames, have

brought us through seemingly unending tracts of unvisited, unspoilt country.
Slowing at the end of a long day but happy.
Weary but fulfilled.

Ethels Day 50 – 14th July

South Head & Mount Famine

South Head is a dignified presence. It rises imposingly above Chinley, almost Alpine in attitude. The meadows on its lower reaches seem laid out as if on offer to all while its higher reaches grow increasingly steep. Forbiddingly steep almost. Like some Matterhorn with its solemn authority, towering above the village and the land below, watching the years go by.

But well might it display its stern demeanour. It has had no effect on the extent of litter in the layby where I park. Nor on the violent potential of the crazy, speeding vehicles as I pick my way back along the main road to find the first footpath.

Once through a gate though and a small patch of gorse, up beside a broken wall and over the first rise, and all that is left behind. Out of mind, that modern excess and despair is soon sealed in its own bespoke defile and the sky, the hills, the vistas open out and claim all my attention. No map can tell you how suddenly and how beautifully the Peak District can exert its timelessness and ancient pulse. It is a lasting wonder but surprises me every time.

Although the way ahead, straight up to the top, is clear and apparent, I am having difficulty with my navigational instincts this morning. North is to my left I know and yet the GPS on my phone seems to turn the world through ninety degrees. This could be a worrying disparity, indeed a fatal one in mist or snow or around precipitous drops, but today it is just a niggle. A worry that the material and the mental are somehow out of kilter.

It is steep to the top and I pause a few times before the crest is finally reached and a summit cairn can be seen buried in a mass of scrub. In such circumstances, it is hard not to talk a little to oneself, to chatter good-heartedly about the immense good fortune that has brought me here, now.

The grass around this summit mound and all the surrounding land has been expertly manicured by the sheep creating an air of leisure, conducive to rest and relaxation. And I lie down and stretch out after my sandwich, quite sure I can wish to be nowhere else. Just below, the Pennine Bridleway weaves its way between here and Mount Famine, a yellow ribbon rippling out of view. I cycled this way with friends some years ago and we still joke that it is the only trail where we have had to push downhill as well as up.

A brief walk along this track brings me to the path up over Mount Famine, so named apparently because of the meagre living that this ground could provide to those once dependent upon it. Now a peaceful calm surrounds the place, a sense of unhurried existence. The fields below look productive and cultivated and this area ticks along at its own pace, undisturbed by the armies that traverse Kinder beyond.

The ridge drops away to the north and I am quickly back on the bridleway and then the road. But the traffic cannot unsettle or undermine me now. The mown verge beginning to bleach in the heatwave can be tolerated. On a wonderful, two-hour trip into the high hills and back I have gained a shield of quiet confidence against these depredations.

Ethels Day 51 – 18th July

Bleaklow Head & Higher Shelf Stones

Forty degrees on the most remote, high moors is a sobering prospect.

When it is wise to protect against the most severe of winter weather, we know the routines, we have the gear. But today.

Today is a 6.30am start, muesli at the top of the Snake Pass 7.30, walking into the interior before 8. Watching the pace, drinking water, worrying that the very ground is vulnerable in extreme heat. Worrying about the future and wishing for leaders who could begin to measure up to its challenge.

An hour on the Pennine Way or a near approximation and we are at the high, open clearing around Bleaklow Head. A few steps to the very highest point and then the Wain Stones. We remember the Manchester Rambler and exchange what we know about the character of Ewan McColl.

The trig point on the top of Higher Shelf Stones is a blob of brilliant white catching the sun, the only tiny spot not sporting the moorland's regimental colours. The path to it appears and disappears but the ground is springy and a joy to walk on.

We crest a slight ridge and from nowhere appears the widely scattered wreckage of the B-29 Fortress that came down here in 1948 with the loss of a full crew of thirteen. Some of the metal is still twisted in murderous fashion, other rusting components look far too heavy to have ever been airborne.

I have seen this devastation a couple times before but came once years ago, with the exact map reference (but no GPS), and still failed to find it. On another occasion, late in the day and without a compass, a little bit lost, and facing a night out, I stumbled across the scene by accident. It was a heart-pounding moment.

Today, we cross Higher Shelf Stones and gaze down into the stunning sweep of Doctor's Gate, a path that freewheels down the side of a steep-sided, winding valley, more Lakeland than Peak in aspect and scale. A dramatic deep dive after all the flat land.

The heat is building into its stride, consolidating, but we are back at the car by 11 and then careering joyously down the Snake Road into Glossop.

Ethels Day 52 – 27th July

Corbar Hill, Combs Head & Black Edge (Combs Moss)

Starting in rain with full waterproofs. Expecting worse. In character for terrain like this.

Up through Corbar Woods with a fine spray filtering through elegantly spaced trees.

Today the pace is determined and I am aware of my breathing. On open hillside, we climb a small buttress. All the holds are there, and my wet bendy boots stay in place. At the top, is Corbar Cross, twenty feet in height. Another Ethel walker told me recently that he had been challenged up here by a farmer with a gun and told he was on private land. We follow a path not marked on the map into access land, keeping well to the side of the farm buildings ahead. Here the wind picks up, the rain increases, first from this side and then from that, reminding us of our place in the natural order of things. It hoods up, heads down. The buffeting. The chuckling.

Along an edge that is new to me. The squall subsides and beneath a dark and brooding sky we can pick out other Ethels to the south. Other distant bumps and hills though, pyramids and peaks shifting in and out of mist and rain, remain unidentifiable.

The location of Combs Head's highest point is mainly a matter of guesswork and consensus, so I stand in a few places to make sure before we turn to retrace our steps. The huge moor of Combs Moss lies between us and our destination and going straight across could be remarkably arduous. So, we skirt the plateau's rim and eat our lunch in a little clough where a greater variety of vegetation, small trees even, attempt to push upwards and enliven the uniformity above. We hear about the uneasy negotiations between local bodies, one that wants to extend the diversity of species and viable habitats and the other that wants to glory in slaughter.

Then along sombre Black Edge. I have walked this two or three times over the decades but it was so long ago now that nothing feels familiar. Below us and to the east, the land is spread out, a substantial new water bottling plant and the much older quarries gouging out the limestone. We are sandwiched between cruelty and commerce.

And the sky is leaden.

Ethels Day 53 – 18th August

Shutlingsloe

'A cloud was on the mind of men
And wailing went the weather'

Juggling extreme heat with electrical storms, trying to spot the gaps in the forecasts and fit in with friends. In the end, the morning looked cooler and the atmospheric onslaught was not expected until mid-afternoon.

Acting on a tip, I park high above Macclesfield Forest and follow a track and path up onto Buxtors Hill. All around the hills assert their presence, Shining Tor and the ridge along to Cats Tor to the north, Whetstone Ridge and the Axe Edge high ground to the east and over in Cheshire to the west, the Quatermass tower of Croker Hill. But right in front, drawing the eye, unavoidable, the beautifully symmetrical peak of Shutlingsloe. The references to this hill as the local Matterhorn or whatever become trite with repetition, but these proportions, this balanced perspective, this poise, does deserve recognition, some special mention in the listing.

From Buxtors Hill the ridge heads south while the land drops away to the west into the forest with its two prominent reservoirs. Darkening clouds beat about the sky, but I judge I have time to complete my peak while Temperature, Pressure and Volume slug it out in the celestial laboratory.

I meet two men on a five-day trip along the Boundary Walk and one stops to tell me of the turbulence and thwarted plans of his last few years – his wife dying of lung cancer, his own two TIAs, his fear of walking alone in remote places. I am reminded once again of that dark cloud on the minds of men, the individuals and the nation, and reprimand myself for not savouring any and every moment.

Nearing the summit, perspective finally drops its pretence. This is not some lofty and inaccessible Alpine jewel after all. It is a lower, magnificent Peak District hill of charming character. The final few minutes of rocky scrambling are deeply satisfying, and at the summit brief blasts of cooler air dispel some of the stickiness. I sweep the far horizons in all directions and then quicken my returning steps.

The wailing weather, after a week or more, is still building and building and the sky is about to collapse, letting loose such ferocious force.

Ethels Day 54 – 24th August

Mill Hill & Featherbed Top

Watching the forecasts, I spend days juggling plans for this, my penultimate outing. As options reduce, I decide that it has to be today. I pack full waterproofs and warm winter gear, fully expecting cold, wet hours alone. And, from the top of the Snake Pass, this prospect looks highly likely.

Through the gate and straight onto the Pennine Way. The slabs are wonderful to walk on and while the rain holds off it is possible to make swaggeringly good progress. The path twists and turns playfully, dips and rises, but maintains a steady overall direction, rising very gently towards Mill Hill two or three miles away. There is no erosion on either side and pockets of vegetation surround small pools of black water that sit among the peat. The sprouting heather is not as vibrant as it has been up here some years, presumably because of the drought, but the constant succession of pink and purple mounds is still a joy to be among.

The weather has not deteriorated, and I need to take off layers to cope with the stickiness of the atmosphere. Away to the left, the north edge of Kinder Scout is revealing itself from out of the cloud, like an impregnable fortress defending miles of territory against some breach.

I meet a chap of my age or more who had set off from Edale this morning. He is irrepressibly enthusiastic about the ease of walking on the slabs.

'.. in all my years of walking …'

I almost match his zeal in response.

'Where are you making for?'

'Oh, uh …'

He waves to the north.

'Begins with 'C' …'
'Crowden?'
'Yes, that's it. Crowden. Then I'll do a couple more days sweeping back that way,' he adds, including most of the Dark Peak within the gesturing embrace of his arm.

I am at the top of Mill Hill within an hour of leaving the car and eat only an apple for lunch beside the eccentrically balanced stones on the cairn. Another walker insists on showing me an app on his phone that can monitor the recent progression of storms from off the coast of Greenland. A large party then arrives from the west – but without that Atlantic rain.

Back along the way I have come, lengthening my stride even, tiny features in the slabs being strangely, almost comfortingly, familiar. I break from the track before the road to head up east on rougher ground to the rounded, ill-defined Featherbed Top, aware that this is my last Ethel apart from a forthcoming local jamboree next week.

It is an understated top. Quiet, unsensational ground. No distractions. Just the sun appearing, a slight ruffling of the grass, a gentle downhill to the car, the body still working, still greeting each new morning. And deeply grateful for the opportunity.

THE 1990s – AND BEYOND

1990. Dovedale

'It'll be heaving down at the Stepping Stones,' said Irwin. 'I know a way in that can avoid all them crowds'. So, before putting down the phone, he gave me a map reference, described the little lane and the layby, and agreed a meeting time. As we hacked our way through brambles and waist high ferns later, I would readily have traded our bloody-minded independence, our high-minded freedom to roam, for the roars and the shrieks and the splashings of the gleeful multitudes further down the valley.

But we were where we were – at the bottom of a solid stub of limestone called The Church, some hundred feet high and plugged into the hillside that formed the western bank of the River Dove. And up through its centre, remorselessly straight and undeviating, unencumbered by any obvious resting places, was a crack leading all the way to the top.

'Snakes Alive, youth', said Irwin. 'VS, 4c, one of the finest in Dovedale. You haven't done it, so d'you want to lead it?'

I was climbing regularly, feeling fit and reasonably bold. But this was at the top of my leading grade and the unrelenting angle told me that if my nerve began to faulter halfway up then it would rapidly drain away and desert me.

'Probably best if you do it,' I said. 'Maybe a bit too much for a sight lead'.

He agreed and we began the preparatory rituals, silently and absorbed. The rope was uncoiled and laid out in a way to minimise tangles later. Harnesses were tightened and adjusted. The rack of protection on his belt was arranged in his preferred order with a check that specific items could be located rapidly by touch alone and unclipped in one smooth, automatic manoeuvre.

The climb was then a disciplined and unhurried operation, efficient and careful. We kept our exchanges to a minimum, the better to aid his concentration. Just an occasional 'Well done' or 'Looking good' from me, just a 'Watch us here a bit, youth' from him.

His progress was steady and assured until he was at the top and shouting 'Safe!'

With the security of the rope above me, I was able to savour the joy of moving, each limb in lockstep with my body's automatic problem-solving. Patient, instinctual and to the side of consciousness. My internal commentary was relaxed and encouraging, I was even able to contemplate the probable differences between this ascent and being on the sharp end of the rope. I enjoyed the paradox of pushing on towards the security of solid, level ground at the same time as wanting the euphoric flood of achievement and calm control to last for as long as possible.

Pumped up with bravado from our success on the climb, we were in no mood to hack our way back the way we had come. We decided on the river crossing, took off our boots and socks and hurled them across to the other side. A shortfall here would be a disaster, so we threw with such force that they landed well into the scrub on the opposite bank.

'Better take yer kecks off and tie 'em round yer neck,' advised Irwin. 'We'll wade across in our subkecks'.

So, with no one in sight and suitably divested of our trousers, we stepped into the river. The rocks underfoot were smooth and slippery, worn down by centuries and the endless hurrying of water, and extreme care was needed to maintain our footing and avoid a painful tumble and soaking. Our measured movements on the crag were being extended into the domain of the trout and dipper.

Suddenly there were excited voices and then two small children appeared from around the bend in the track opposite. Wobbling and in midstream with my trousers round my neck, I tried frantically to find a form of words - something reassuring, explanatory, casually ordinary.
Then their parents came into view.
Snakes alive!
It was my mature student, Keith, whom I had been teaching only twenty-four hours earlier.
'I – eh –'
'I know that this – erm –'
'Actually – '
My mature student, Keith, with whom I would be in a one-to-one tutorial on Monday morning.
'Ah, so, this must be your lovely lady wife – '
'And what adorable children – '

1990. Mount Whitney

'Ay'up, youth. Is bog fixed?'
'Pardon me?'
I saw him stiffen as if sensing danger.
'The bog, is it fixed?'
I couldn't stand it, the tension. Even though, thank goodness, he no longer had his gun with him.
'The toilet. He's asking if it's been mended. It was closed off last night when we got here'.
'Where you boys from?' he asked.
'Heh, heh', he chuckled when we told him.
He seemed to be adjusting some sort of prosthetic device beneath his clothes with the back of his forearm.
'England, heh? You in Inyo County now'.
He laughed to himself again.
'Could fit the whole of England into Inyo County'.
Unsure of how to reply and still groggy from the travelling, we nodded and tried our best to look impressed or cowed or whatever it was he was looking for as a response.
We had arrived around three in the morning after queuing at the Los Angeles Immigration desk until nearly midnight from a flight that was itself delayed taking off for many hours at Heathrow. Even at that small hour, the owner, his wife and a ragged looking old dog were cruising the site in a pick-up truck. With a rifle laid across his lap. He pointed out a tiny patch of grass right alongside the roadway and under a streetlamp of clinical intensity, where we could just squeeze our two tents and try to sleep with brains still in tumult, still swirling in a maelstrom of queues, oceans and continents.
The fine combination of absurdity and deadly seriousness had begun straight away on our arrival at Heathrow. At the check-in desk, our ropes, harnesses,

even all the ironmongery, raised no concerns but Security's whole demeanour ratcheted up a cog or two as soon as Irwin's bag passed through the scanner.

'Sir, can you explain what this is?' said the official pointing to the X-ray skeleton of the bag's contents.

Among all the usual holiday paraphernalia and laid out through the middle, was the menacing outline of a bandolier filled in each segment with rifle bullets or some similar form of ammunition.

'It's me paints, duck. Oil paints', he explained before being asked to unpack the item for close-up inspection.

Irwin had spotted this piece of equipment in an army surplus store and thought it ideal for transporting his tubes of oil paint. And so it proved to be. Ideal for that purpose and enough to set alarm bells ringing across the airline industry.

When safely airside, Terry delivered Irwin a blunt and direct reprimand, in a stylised manner that had been fashioned over a long and close climbing partnership and friendship. It was the first instance of the banter, humour and playful insult between these two that was to pepper our trip and keep us chuckling at its inventiveness and its rough-bodied affection.

On the local radio, we heard news of Yosemite Park being on fire and ten thousand tourists having to be evacuated. At a tourist information office in the middle of nowhere we were told that just about everywhere was closed because of fires but that the Mount Whitney area in the High Sierras, the highest peak in the United States outside of Alaska, was still open. This had originally been our first objective but we had abandoned it in case the long descent ruined Terry's knees early in our trip. And so, after driving across the tops of the Mojave Desert and Death Valley, we came to Lone Pine, Inyo County.

Thunder rumbled past us on the other side of the lake that night and lightning flashes paraded all about. We tied everything down and sat bare-chested as a hot, black wind, as if from a furnace, blew across us. Up the next morning just after six and Derek drove into Lone Pine to get one of the limited permits that would allow us to spend two nights up high below Mount Whitney. To get theirs, others had camped the night on the veranda.

The long slog up from Whitney Portal to Iceberg Lake began with a fight through closely-planted, small alder trees followed by a stop for lunch and skinny dipping at Clyde Meadows. The rest of the hike took us up white scree where the altitude began to take its toll on me. We were at Iceberg Lake and putting up a dome tent flysheet just after four-thirty with the spectacular teeth and needles of Whitney rising straight above us and a switchback of pinnacle ridges soaring all around like a fairground attraction.

Aware that we needed an early start the next morning, we prepared our food and were in sleeping bags as quickly as possible, our only indulgence being a nip of brandy each from a small bottle we had carried up. Tiredness from the day's trek and the thinner air conspired to muffle our chuckles and banter and, despite any apprehensions about what awaited us in the morning, we soon tumbled into sleep.

*

We were up for jam and coffee early the next day with the sun just on the East face and picking out all the details. Irwin and Terry began trudging up the scree before us and we four met again after about five hundred feet at the first col, where we could begin to sense the exposure. We roped up here at eight o'clock, in shorts and tee shirts, with the sun already beginning to burn.

The first pitch proper, involving a traverse straight away above a big drop, felt quite intimidating with a large sac on my back. I was also having to suppress the knowledge that one thousand feet or so of rock climbing lay ahead. However, once committed, having to make decisions about holds and individual moves, my focus narrowed to the immediate tasks at hand and my wandering imagination, and its extraneous worries, were brought to order by the stern control that a cultivated sense of survival will exert.

Once attuned to the mountain arena all around us, to being tiny specks of life inching our way up through huge amphitheatres of rock, it was possible to relax into our position and to savour the body's stretches, balance and control. The satisfaction of exertions successfully resolved, the muscles singing silently to themselves. Derek and I alternated the leading and progressed pleasantly up sections with named features such as The Washboard and the Big Notch until we arrived at the focus of the guidebook description – The Fresh Air Traverse. It was my pitch to lead.

I paused and centred, muttered quiet reassurances to myself, and then launched out across the emptiness with a confidence that had arrived at just the right moment from somewhere. This, the apparent crux of the climb, proved to be a very fine pitch but not as hard or as exposed as I had been expecting after all the anticipation back in England and since arriving in California.

As I neared the stance, blobs of white were floating down and I assumed that Irwin above me was knocking down bits of chalk. Highly unlikely though this might be it still seemed more probable than the truth.

The truth that these were hailstones.

We climbed on up a strenuous chimney as the first crack of thunder arrived. Three interesting pitches up the Giant's Staircase came next and we were realising by the minute that we needed to somehow get into warm and waterproof clothing as quickly as possible. So, on a tiny ledge, Derek belayed me while, still roped up and in my harness, I struggled with the task of substituting my shorts for a substantial pair of long trousers and then adding a fleece to my top. In turn, I belayed Derek while he too performed a similar operation, the seriousness of our situation somehow battling with its ridiculousness.

At the top of the Staircase was a tight chimney, probably a more demanding pitch than the Fresh Air Traverse, especially in these deteriorating conditions, and Irwin lowered a rope to help us by hauling up our sacs. We struggled up this inelegantly and the situation became rapidly more serious still as the hailstones turned to snow with a strong wind behind them. For the last three pitches, even after managing to put on my anorak, I was shivering with comically chattering teeth.

On the penultimate stance, with the others out of sight above me, I heard Derek give what sounded like a low moan and then a shout from somewhere of 'Below!' followed by the sound of a massive rock breaking somewhere far beneath. I wondered whether somebody had fallen and, as my imagination was gearing up to run, I was mightily relieved when the rope above me began to be taken in. Terry had dropped Derek a top rope as our holds began to ice up making climbing harder still but eventually, by fair means and foul, we came out more than fourteen thousand feet above sea level at the summit, right by a little Stars and Stripes flag. And the refuge hut.

Two American climbers joined us inside and although we were cold and wet, we were deeply pleased to be out of the wind. We shared the last disintegrated tuna sandwich and some currants and sat hollow-eyed in the gloom.

We dared not procrastinate and the Americans showed us the way to the descent gully. The going here was straightforward although just tripping on the boulders out of exhaustion could still deliver a nasty blow. At the bottom of our descent route, I could see three lakes and I was so tired that I could not worry about it although I knew there should be only the one. We then turned into a subsidiary gully further down and could see our tent.

I was feeling exhausted and sick, dropping further and further behind the others, and when I did eventually get down, I crawled straight into my bag and took two aspirin. I perked up later and we retired early with a great sense of accomplishment, perhaps more so than on any other of my mountain adventures.

We finished off the bottle of brandy.

It was also a day though in which I was reminded, once again, about the potential savagery of big mountains. I had taken no over-trousers

or woollen shirt and I had paid the price. We speculated that it probably would not have been possible to have spent a night out in those conditions and we had also noted, without saying much about it at the time, the plaque at the refuge which stated that a fortnight earlier one of a sheltering party had been electrocuted by lightning.

1990. Tuolumne Meadows

The torch was shining directly into my eyes.
'Sorry, man'.
He turned the light away.
'No food in the tents is there, boys?' he asked. 'Everything up the tree or safe in the bins, yeah?'
We nodded. We had stored all our provisions, each and every mouthful, in the green, metallic box and secured the catch which, all the signs assured us, the bears were unable to open. We could sleep undisturbed so long as there was no smell of anything edible coming from inside the canvas.
'What about wash bags? Soap? Toothpaste?'
Yes, we had those for a final visit to the toilet block and then morning ablutions.
'In the bins, please, guys. They'd be straight in after any of those'.
What comedian could resist a riff about bears going about their morning toiletries, a wash and brush up, the flyaway hair treatments? The answer was that the four of us could. Despite much merriment and bravado, and not a little ruby deep Californian Merlot, we were stone cold compliant with every regulation. Thoughts of a hungry bear, angry at the obstacles that we might seem to be and ripping its way into our tents, provided the most sobering of correctives.
The campsite at the western end of Tenaya Lake came close to Paradise. Our tents were pitched all alone among trees on a bed of sand and old, dried pine needles. A creek wound its way nearby through the forest to the lake, which was bounded by a thin strip of beach. The water was completely clear and the sandy bottom shelved only very gradually.
This land, we learned, had been taken from Chief Tenaya, who used to bring his tribe up from Yosemite

Valley to these cooler altitudes, a vertical mile higher, when the heat of mid-summer became unbearable lower down.

'Old Chief Tenaya sure knew a good thing', drawled a fat woman whose holiday seemed to consist of sitting with her quarrelsome family in camping chairs at the edge of the lake. Her husband had a grey goatee beard that might have placed him squarely among the city's jazz and poetry circles but whose rudeness to both us and his family challenged my fantasies, carried since adolescence, about the welcome and acceptance that I might experience from the famed bohemian subculture of the place where these people lived - San Francisco, the City by the Bay.

I asked the woman the name of the Chief Tenaya's tribe but she did not know. Nor did she seem to care.

*

From the forest in which we were camped, it was possible to look up the length of Tenaya Lake towards a breath-taking panorama of huge granite domes. These mountains huddled together awkwardly, almost self-consciously, as if uncertain of their place in Nature's spectacular pageant. To dip into that water at the end of an ecstatic day's climbing on cliffs of unblemished rock soaring upwards into the sky, to be confronted by their blunt solidity, was to be as close to a state of bliss as I have ever been.

Stately Pleasure Dome, only a few minutes' walk from our tents, was our nearest cliff. The first pitch of each climb began at the roadside and the routes forced us up into chimneys and cracks and across slabs where perfect friction more than compensated for the lack of large, substantial holds. Below, and growing further away as we climbed, was the lake with its ruffled waters and the cars hugging the road along its edge. In shorts and tee-shirts, we were emboldened by the sunshine, energised by a sweet, unadulterated air. Stretching, reaching, rising in controlled and fluid movements, we left behind the everyday and life's limiting horizons.

Days passed like this. My body, toned and tanned, became a new acquaintance, a being I had never known before. The laughter, the food and wine, the heavy sleeping and the enveloping presence of the forest, all conspired with the sheer, physical efforts of our days, towards this new identity.

*

'The bears have been,' said Derek one morning as he returned from the toilet block. 'In the night'.

The other three of us were straight out of our sleeping bags, pulling on whatever clothes were near at hand, and following him through the trees on tracks we now knew instinctively.

There at the car park, our night visitors, these proud, silent vandals, had left their destruction as if with disdain or contempt. One car door had been peeled back like a sardine can, its metal frame curled as if it had met no resistance, its glass fractured and scattered about the passenger seat and the ground, like a stash of diamonds abandoned in a botched raid. But these artful robbers had no interest in jewels, their prized bounty would have been the remains of a stale sandwich – or a bar of soap!

The power required if limbs were to accomplish this was beyond imagination. The grip to be exercised by claws, the very tips of claws, was equally outside my experience as was confirmed when I tried and failed to insert my own puny finger ends into the tight seal between a locked car door and its chassis.

We stood in silent contemplation. We occupied the same forest as these mighty animals. We co-existed in our separate worlds, parallel and close, but well aside from each other's comings and goings.

We wandered back by a longer route to the tents, as if chastened and contemplative, but feeling relatively safe in the daylight. Birds were busy in their morning routines, flitting and singing among the trees. Sunlight was breaking through the branches where it could, playful and full of levity. And there, exposed to it all on the path of dried pine needles in front of us, with no canvas to cover her, lay an older woman in a sleeping bag.

'Hello. Gosh. Are you – ? What are you – ?'
'Hello you boys', she said. 'Sorry if I'm in your way'.
'No,' I said. 'You're – '
'Have you been sleeping there?' asked Irwin. 'On the path, like that?'
'Oh yeah, I've been here two nights. My husband's up in the mountains', she said, gesturing grandly in the direction of the High Sierras. 'He'll be down in another day or so, when he's had enough'.

Once again, as in significant junctures in my life, I was overwhelmed by the example being set by somebody older than myself. Her long grey hair, tied back with a ribbon, and her weathered features, made her at least fifty in my estimation. She had been sleeping in these woods alone, on a path, and seemingly without fear. But it was the absence of any tent that struck me most forcibly, her exposure to the elements – and to our fellow dwellers in the forest. Aware of the absurdity of the notion I nevertheless valued greatly the sense of sturdy protection from the bears that a thin sheet of canvass still seemed to provide.

We stayed chatting for a while and Margaret, when hearing that we planned to visit San Francisco at the end of our holiday, insisted that we stay at her house in Berkeley the night before we crossed the Oakland Bay Bridge to the city. She taught classical piano, she told us, and her husband crafted large wooden sculptures. We would very welcome to put down our sleeping bags on the floor of her music room. It would be a change from the tents, she said. Hers was a very welcoming community, she added, and her friends would enjoy meeting the bunch of English climbers with whom she had shared the forest floor.

*

While I was becoming fitter with each day's climbing, I felt as though my core, residual strength was also beginning to ebb. My desire to keep climbing was declining as the autumn was beginning. In the large tent where we shopped for provisions, the staff were eyeing the sky and the forecasts. When it comes, the snow, they said, it comes with a force and a suddenness. And sure enough, at the first sign of a drop in temperature, they swung into action, emptying the store of its contents and dismantling the structure. In less than a day, the ground bore no sign of this commercial lifeline. And within another day, the snow had begun.

We quickly packed our tent and belongings and set out to descend into Yosemite Valley, two taking the car and two on foot for a day through woods and then a descent down beside Yosemite Falls and the outrageous, improbable proximity of Lost Arrow Spire. Here, from Sunnyside Camp, we had promised ourselves a twelve hour round trip to climb Snake Dike, the classic route right up the bulging flank, and to the very top, of Half Dome.

And beyond that, we would emerge into the world to engage with the polished sophistication of Berkeley, the Bay and San Francisco.

1992. Grand Combin

There was little conversation. The refuge warden had woken us at 3.15am. Headtorches were focused on the tasks in hand – a peculiar ritual of silent, unhurried movement, everybody dressing and packing in silence. Efficient and well-rehearsed routines as the first climbers stepped out into the dark. We too recognised the need to be moving, to be established on the snow, our bodies, axes and crampons moving in an easy rhythm, before the sun came up.

I take full responsibility for how the day unfolded, for us being on that unstable mountain in the first place and in such a state of ill-preparedness. My companion's drive, his eagerness to make the attempt, had in the main brought us here but I was the more experienced and the near fatality some fifteen hours later was the result of my errors of judgement.

In the weeks before, back at home, we had pored over the guidebook, somehow minimising the sense of risk despite the warnings about this peak being out of favour with British mountaineers, about its propensity for rock and ice falls, and about the long days required for a summit bid. Downplayed too, was my companion's rudimentary knowledge of rope work and the levels of stamina required from both of us for such sustained hard physical work at altitude. And the mental discipline.

Being on the snow well before 5am gave us two hours or so before the sun would touch the snow of the glacier. The front points of our crampons found secure purchase and our ice axes provided a steadying hold. The steep ascent was taxing but straightforward and we managed to gain height in bursts of activity alternating with short rests. The magic of another mountain dawn crept into being all around us. A cold, clear light was renewing its acquaintance with our frozen slope as we bent over our axes to bring our breathing back under control at the top. The route then consisted of a series of short and straightforward rock-climbing pitches interspersed with some ridge scrambling between minor buttresses. Finding the way sometimes required a best guess approach and, as I had often experienced in my Alpine days with Andy back in the early 1970s, there were times when it was necessary to gather in and carry coils of rope to avoid it trailing and snagging. At other times we had to thread between pinnacles to provide some possible security should one of us slip from the ridge.

The sun's heat built through the morning, and we were careful to keep hydrated whilst also maintaining control over a water supply that would have to last us many more hours. I estimated that our progress was holding to the rough schedule in my head and managed to push away thoughts of how we would descend and whether we would require a high-level bivouac at the end of the day. But the minutes lost here and there as decisions were made, the relaxing of the pace as difficulties were encountered, all ate into our endeavours. We found ourselves needing food as the day drifted past its midpoint. We caught glimpses of far higher ground still ahead with the summit seemingly as out of reach as it had been a whole eight hours earlier. My ability to make decisions was slipping way. We needed to rest. Our range of options was slowly narrowing. I needed clarity of thought to weigh realistically the risks associated with each.

There was only one feasible – and safe – course of action.

Climbing back down the rock pitches would be a fairly straightforward business for him. On a tight rope from me, he was able to make the moves swiftly, unencumbered by the fearful consequences of any mistake. For me, it was potentially more dangerous than my earlier ascent. I asked him to place running belays every twenty feet or so to enable him to belay me from below and hopefully arrest any fall of mine that might occur.

But we were tired, the afternoon was weary too, and a storm was building. He made a swift descent of his first pitch - but placed no protection for me. This meant that I had to climb down exceptionally carefully and therefore slowly. When we were together again, I explained in more detail what I was asking him to do. And why it was essential to my survival.

As he climbed down the next pitch, I could see that he was again not placing running belays so I shouted down a reminder.

But nothing changed.

The first rumble of thunder shook the sky and the mountain, a distant growl but one with every intention of seeking us out. I worried that he could not absorb my message, as if panic was blotting out anything not focused on his own immediate circumstances. I shouted louder this time, the calm reassurance that I had been seeking to exude now replaced by a tone with greater urgency.

On he went, seemingly paying no heed. Was it fear driving him on down? Or thought-stopping panic? Or was it a mangled pride, an objection to 'being told'?

The next pitch felt very testing, as I juggled the need for speed with that for tremendous care. Feelings of being ignored, taken for granted, uncared for – playground emotions – boiled up within me, an unwanted additional complication to the already fraught problems of the material, mountain world.

'I'm doing everything I can to save your fucking life!' I yelled when I reached him at about 7 in the evening and at the top of the snow slope. It was anger pouring out from me. It was unlike any I had ever expressed to anybody, coming with a force from deep inside. Standing there on the narrow ledge, face to face. All of it spontaneous. Unconsidered. Uncontrolled.

'And you are doing nothing to save mine!' I yelled again, spontaneously.

Thunder, operatic in its intensity, engulfed our confrontation. Mist was also closing in rapidly. We unroped, still able to maintain a degree of concentration and some semblance of teamwork as we prepared to descend the two-thousand-foot snow slope. I placed my left foot onto the white surface where our crampons and axes had found such firm bite back before dawn. And – WHOOSH!

My feet both shot away from beneath me and, falling onto my back, I was immediately moving very fast. My ice axe was still attached to my wrist with a loop of tape and I remained clear-headed enough to know that the solution lay, literally, in my hands. I managed to roll onto my front and plunged the axe into the snow. Nothing happened. I had expected it to act as a brake and slow my hurtling downhill, just as it always had done when I had practiced such routines decades before on winter days in Snowdonia.

I was talking coherently to myself despite the buffeting my body was taking, fighting against accepting that this was it. Below me I could see a bank of rocks across my path. I braced for the impact but, instead of arresting my fall, I just flipped over and continued careering downhill but headfirst this time. Thank goodness I was still wearing my helmet and my axe was still attached. But neither seemed to be of direct help.

And it was then that I just drifted away. This was the moment, the time and the place, in which I was to die. No more panic, no need for decisive action. Freed at last from problem-solving. No more ever. Instead, a deep stillness and sadness with time slowed right down. Old friends appeared before me. I wanted to shrug, explain to them that if only I had known, I would have made a point of visiting, of saying goodbye properly. I imagined being fondly remembered, saw a fine, gauzy curtain being stirred by a breeze in a room flooded with summer morning light.

Then I hit the second band of rocks, shoulder first. The pain jolted me back into the here and now. I rolled over and continued on downhill, but with my speed temporarily slowed. I was still alive and the next break of rubble was rapidly approaching and seemed more substantial. This might well be my best – and last – opportunity for survival.

A by now familiar jolt through my body with the impact but this time I had stopped. I was no longer hurtling downwards. I lay on the rocks, shaking but surprisingly clear-headed. Out loud, I told myself to do nothing despite the darkness, being miles from the hut, the thunder and now the lightning. When my shaking eventually stopped, I picked my way carefully across the snow to the next band of rock and shale and then across to the next. In the dark I eventually heard my partner shouting somewhere above. Eventually he reached me, and we proceeded together in a wide zig-zag fashion down the shale and snow.

We reached level ground eventually as the mist began to lift but a volley of stones had begun. Like giant bullets, they zipped through the air around us but fortunately – and it was only luck deciding to operate in our favour this time – fortunately, none came close enough for impact. As if standing in a firing range, we seemed doomed whether we moved of stayed put. And then I saw a huge rock above, a boulder the size of a dustbin, spinning in the air like an asteroid. As it bounced against the snow slope each time it took off again at erratic angles making its likely course impossible to predict. We had no option but to surrender to this crazed dynamic, our day, our lives, doomed to end here after all. Or, to walk away unscathed.

Indifferent to our exhausted resignation, it cascaded past at about fifteen feet to our side, lumbering on downwards in its purposeless descent.

We began moving towards the edge of the glacier and gained the rough path without further incident. Then, in effect sleepwalking, we stumbled on towards the hut we had left more than sixteen hours earlier and where the other guests were already asleep. I must have been radiating something of the day's experiences in my face or posture as the warden, without asking and in contravention of the strict mealtime rules posted on the wall, immediately began preparing a dish of hot, calory-heavy reassurance for our bone-weary bodies.

I was alive. I would re-enter the world I loved. And I resolved to never again venture onto mixed snow and rock Alpine routes.

1992. High Tor

Matlock Bath is an inland seaside resort, boasting as densely packed a parade of chip shops and amusement arcades as any of its coastal competitors. At the southern end of the 'promenade', just across the River Derwent, are Wildcat Cliffs, offering a run of enticing limestone routes that stetch and test the middle grade climber while always embodying some sense of security. Since being introduced to this playground by my friend Irwin at the beginning of 1980s, I have been rewarded by many wonderful afternoon and evening climbing sessions here (and only one heart-stopping occasion in 1985!), testing my limits, stretching my capabilities by degrees.

Bookending the resort to the north and just beyond its main, tourist-heavy section, is High Tor, a mighty barrel of a cliff towering above the road and river. To me, it has always been everything that Wildcat is not – austere, forbidding and, not to pussyfoot around, terrifying! Despite a few of High Tor's easiest routes having the same difficulty grade as some on Wildcat, the difference in the 'feel' of the two places remains enormous, at least to me.

I had always assumed that I would never venture onto this cliff, one of the most significant in the Peak District's climbing history. People who could manage those routes were somehow structured differently to me, in both spirit and sinew, and this difference was insurmountable.

But we had been climbing well, I wasn't getting any younger, and technically there were routes on High Tor that should be within my capabilities.

So, one evening in September 1992, having psyched up for the occasion, I stood with Derek in the trees beneath this mighty cliff. Its top was out of sight, lost behind the curve of its wall. Derek began to climb Debauchery, our chosen route, slowly but in full control. As he moved beyond my view, I tried to give my full attention to paying out the rope when I felt him moving and anchoring it securely when he seemed stationary. By concentrating in this fashion, I was also trying to block fears of being unable to work out the moves and ending up in a wretched state swinging on the rope.

On a smooth rock face, you must hold yourself steady with finger ends locked behind a flake or squeezed into a crack. Your feet must seek out miniscule ledges, a sliver of instep here or there, holding you in place. Mind and muscle are under threat from gravity's dispassionate certainty. Some sort of vital discipline is necessary to quell the tremor in your limbs that will otherwise escalate rapidly into uncontrolled juddering and then dislodge you. There is an over-riding prerogative to stay in charge and cool the urgency.

When Derek was eventually safe and belayed on a small stance above, he began to take in the slack, and it was my turn to climb. None of my anxieties came to anything and instead I found myself confidently swinging up technically challenging moves feeling skilled and inspired, emboldened, of course, by the nice tight rope around my waist.

I gained height with a mounting sense of achieving something important, something really important. Of removing a fundamental barrier not just from my climbing but, in a much wider and more profound sense, from how I approached all of life's challenges.

By the time I reached Derek on the belay ledge halfway up the cliff it was obvious that the failing light made pressing on with the second pitch a difficult and foolhardy undertaking. Instead, we decided to abseil back down to the ground and return to complete the route as soon as possible and before night began to tighten its grip on any light lingering for too long on autumn afternoons.

*

We were back exactly one week later, coincidently, on what some newspapers called 'Black Wednesday,' 'the day the British economy went over the edge'. We were going over the edge too, from the very top of High Tor in beautiful evening sunlight and by means of an abseil rope looped around a tree.

Derek set off first, aiming to land back on the belay spot that we had reached the previous week. When I felt the tension in the rope slacken, I knew that he must have reached our tiny eyrie and I prepared to fasten the rope to the descending device at my waist.

I had always retained a particular level of scorn for people who talked light-heartedly about going out for 'a good bit of abseiling'. It is a serious business! A couple of decades earlier Andy Handford and I had been forced to descend many pitches of the North Ridge of the Piz Badile in the Italian Alps, casting our rope out into the void repeatedly. And trusting our anchors to hold each time. We all knew of incidents when these had failed. Similarly, a big, final knot was absolutely essential to jam in one's device, to avoid reaching the end of the rope and just sailing free. Again, we knew of stories such as that of the ferocious Scottish mountaineer, Tom Patey, who lost his life because of such a fundamental oversight. So, stepping over that cliff top remained for me as big an act of faith and commitment as ever.

A slow methodical descent – no histrionics, no leaping and bounding! – brought me to Derek and our familiar ledge where we quickly set about anchoring a belay for me and arranging his rope so that I was able to pay it out smoothly and safely. Once again, failing light would concentrate our efforts.

Despite this imperative, Derek took a long time on the difficult crack after the first bulge, the cool and careful climber that he is. I was wondering whether we might end up trying to get him back to the stance if he failed or if I might be finishing in the dark. But he progressed and his rope continued to run out above me, sometimes pausing when he must have been thinking or summoning up the bottle for a particularly hard move, at other times moving rapidly to cover ground where there was no possibility of lingering.

He succeeded and soon the rope was moving quickly, indicating that he was ready for me to climb. And within a handful of moves, I was completely committed to it. The tight rope disappearing above me could prevent my falling, but Derek would not be able to pull me up the cliff if I failed, and neither was the rope long enough for him to lower me all the way to the ground. I had no option but to make that exhausting sequence of move upon move all the way until I eventually reached the top. And it was on this pitch, just a couple of miles from my home in the centre of that huge, imposing wall of limestone, that I had an intense feeling of being as alone and insignificant, or more so, as in any mountain landscape or desert vastness. I could see cars below on their smooth and silent glide through Matlock Bath, hear the odd shout from a holidaymaker carried way up into my isolation. The walls to either side curved away into the encroaching night. Each and every hold might be improbably small and cunningly hidden. I was supremely alone, beyond being saved by anybody else, in need of giving myself the firmest of talkings-to and reliant totally on whoever I was at core and on whatever it was I might have accumulated over two or three decades on the rock.

'You go, you commit yourself, and it's the big effort that counts,' Joe Brown, the Manchester-based climbing legend, once said.

And somehow that night, I did go, focused down onto every move and nothing else.

And thankfully, gloriously, the big effort did count.

1997. Dinas Mot

'Come on! Climb when you're ready!'
There was no reply, no sense of movement at the other end of the rope.
'Irwin, climb when you're ready!'
The light was slipping away. We had one more pitch ahead of us and having to descend in the dark would add to the risk of an accident.
We had been climbing efficiently and well within our capabilities all afternoon. So, why was he hesitating, slowing our pace just when we needed to be at the top of our game? And at the top of this crag.
We had been alternating the lead on this classic Hard Severe, The Cracks, up the left-hand flank of Dinas Mot's mighty open book of a cliff. Five pitches in total, this had been an interesting choice. Early in the season in terms of our climbing fitness, but late in a winter still reluctant to be gone from the deep, dark defile of the Llanberis Pass. High up on the southern side of the valley, this cliff would catch any turn in the weather and rapidly surrender to the night or any wandering storm. Not a place to be hanging around.
I could feel no activity on the rope, no sense of thoughts and intentions that climbers can often read somehow through one hundred and fifty feet of nylon rope dragging against the friction of a cliff face. He could probably hear me and if not, then at least feel my urgent tugs, designed both to reassure him that he was being safely held and at the same time demand that we keep ahead in the race against the afternoon's demise.
By stretching against my belay, I could lean out and look down from my ledge. Irwin was still visible below, a small figure in the dwindling light, but his attention seemed to be fixed on something to his side, some distraction beyond my view. He seemed to be talking to

someone or something over in the very centre of the cliff. Over in areas of the greatest severity.

'Just give us a minute,' he finally shouted up with all his usual levity missing. 'I'm just waiting on here for a minute'.

Below him a raptor, its species unidentifiable in the gathering gloom, was making one final proprietorial sweep of the hillside. I was beginning to feel the chill in the air.

I could hear Irwin talking but his words lacked definition in the hugeness of our surroundings. And it was then that I realised that we had not been alone in our mountain vastness.

'Give us a bit of slack', he shouted up. 'I'm giving this lad a hand'.

From his position belayed on his own small ledge, Irwin was attempting to cast a loop of rope to his side, and all I could do was sternly direct myself to keep my impatience in check.

Slowly, another climber, assisted by a loop of rope from Irwin, came into view and eventually joined him on the ledge. Their attention then appeared to turn to bringing in the rope behind this person. Obviously, he too had a second below him who needed help in traversing across onto our climb but by now they had been swallowed by darkness and I had no option but to wait for shouted instructions.

These moments, of being alone and not in control of developments, of being an insignificant dot against a great, impersonal backdrop, have a rare and delicate quality. The child in me says this is a magnificent adventure, requiring a composure almost beyond my abilities. The adult replies that this is all that you are, you have arrived at your destination. This is the point at which you stand alone drawing solely on resources gathered from life along the way. The sky, the air, echo this completeness. Every pulse beat confirms the message.

'Okay, take in!'

The shout shatters my reverie. It is focused and precise with a managed urgency. I have work to do, a task requiring full concentration, perfect coordination of mind and body. The here and now takes complete control, the metaphysical dissolves instantly in the slightest stirrings of a breeze.

He's climbing now, the rope is coming in at a steady pace. I am wondering whether the situation, whatever it involved, is now resolved or whether this is merely the opening stages of some emergency.

Irwin's head appears above my ledge. His expression is serious but is this just a business-like concentration or a demeanour born at the edge of panic – or tragedy?

I bring the rope in for the final few feet and then Irwin is on the ledge and tying himself to my belay points.

'Those lads got into difficulty, and I had to get them across to our route. They'd bitten off more than they could chew. Everything was getting a bit desperate. I'll bring them up after me, but you get on to the top first'.

We needed to be off this mountain. To allow the accumulated emotions to dissipate – raucously or silently. But first we needed to be safe.

The last pitch then – and in the dark. Some highly competent, efficient and silent character had occupied my being and was moving with great fluency up the final fifty feet of rock. My hands found the holds, my feet automatically landed where they needed to. Progress was smooth and mechanical, organised and administered from somewhere beyond my being. Some reassuring voice, some steady calm, talked me up the final stretch and I was at the top arranging a belay and preparing to bring our extended party up out from their vertical world.

When we were finally assembled, I could appreciate how young the two lads were. Probably not out of their teens and fulsomely grateful. And apologetic.

'We can usually climb this grade, no problem,' said one of them.

'Stick with us,' said Irwin. 'We'll need to be a bit careful getting down from here in the dark'.

'Can you take this for a drink?' said the other, trying to press a five-pound note into my hand.

It felt ridiculous. Here we were, the four of us on top of a cliff and we were stumbling over courtesies. Does one tip one's rescuers? What is the going rate for a life? A fiver? Where were the protocols?

Climbers look after each other when the chips are down. It's unwritten and unquestioned.

'We can usually do 5b at home', the first one said. 'So, there shouldn't have been a problem'.

'Where d'you usually climb then?'

'On a wall, in the sports centre'.

A sports centre! Not the hall of some mountain king, not the domain of the buzzard and the peregrine. Not high on a Welsh valley hillside with night tightening its grip.

'And where's this sports centre then?'

Rain began.

'Norfolk', he said.

2000. Tour de Monte Rosa

Not the glacier.
The one hundred odd miles, the forty thousand feet or so of ascent – we were on board for all of it. I was also prepared for a week or more's tough walking and the possibility of an emergency bivouac or two.
But not the glacier.
Rob would make a judgement about crossing it when we arrived there on the last day, but Jane and I were adamant. She and I would follow the tracks of the skiers' snowmobile down the mountain even though it would involve a lengthy addition to an already long day. We might even fork out a fortune for a ride on it if we were flagging and so desperate that we were prepared to destroy the purity of our otherwise 'unaided' expedition. But we would not be crossing the Theodul glacier. Period.
And on that understanding, we set out from Zermatt on the classic but relatively underpopulated circuit of the Monte Rosa, the huge mountain massif that forms part of the boundary between Switzerland and Italy. I could almost forget about disappearing through crevasses into a cavernous emptiness beneath the ice as we wandered lonely valleys and hiked up punishingly steep banks of scree. There was enough to occupy my mind as we teetered along precipitously situated tracks or swam in torrents of glacier melt. Fear could slip away into the drowsy air as we napped and read at lunchtimes deep among the grasses and the flowers of Alpine meadows. And a night in a small cuckoo clock hotel constructed from a whole forest's worth of timber, lulled me into an ever-deepening sense of security.
But the knowledge of what awaited on the final day was never completely extinguished.

The plan had been to reach the high Theodulpass the night before, so that any glacier crossing that Rob contemplated could be carried out in the very early morning when the surface would be at its most frozen – and hence most solid.

However, the absence of any streams or springs from which to replenish our water bottles and the extensive areas of devastation caused by the skiing industry, all brought about an extreme weariness in Jane and myself on our penultimate day and forced us to stop long before the pass. Among hillsides blasted and broken by heavy machinery, nothing grew. The land had been destroyed and Nature expelled by the rapacious demand for more playgrounds, more profits. In winter months none of this would be apparent. Minds could easily be softened by illusions of Paradise. Guilt and responsibility could be buried beneath the carpet of snow.

Among this Mad Max wasteland, we came upon an abandoned ski lift station, rusting and rotting in lifeless isolation. Rob climbed a short ladder and managed to access a platform sheltered by patchy roofing that appeared still capable of providing cover from any rain or snow that might fall in the night. While Jane and I laid out sleeping bags on the open-sided platform and searched our rucksacks for any remaining food, Rob scoured the hillside further up for water. To keep the weight of our packs to an absolute minimum we had strictly limited the amount of food we carried. At one stage we had had to resort to four-day old bread and little else! As we prepared a meagre meal, Rob returned with a bottle of fizzy water that he had 'borrowed' from an unlocked workmen's hut and, although he had been unable to find any obviously uncontaminated spring or stream, he did also bring back some snow melt that appeared to be clean.

We slept fitfully because of a loose wall panel of corrugated iron that flapped and banged all night in the wind and were awake early the next morning to resume our plod upwards like tiny insects beneath the stern but hugely indifferent Matterhorn. We climbed and there was a shift in the weather's demeanour. No longer companionable, the temperature was dropping and a wind was picking up. And when we were at last able to finally leave Italy and look down into Switzerland all we could see were hillsides rapidly clearing of skiers with their vehicles. Alone on the saddle of the pass, the snow eddied around with an increasing intensity and we became locked within a lost visibility, within the weight of an alien atmosphere swirling unleashed and callous.

Muffled within our cagoules, we made shouted decisions and agreed to descend to lower ground as quickly as we could. We were fortunate that the confidence-sapping storm abated as quickly as it had arrived and our descent route soon became more discernible.

And as the view cleared, there was a line of footprints, presumably the most feasible crossing, leading out across the ice to the opposite bank of the glacier. Rob was confident in his appraisal that he could safely traverse it – a judgement honed by a lifetime of tough mountaineering endeavours. Undaunted in his younger years, for example, by having to retreat after a day and night on the North Face of the Eiger because of a companion's loss of resolve, Rob had nevertheless returned and succeeded on this most notorious of Alpine testing grounds.

Jane and I were of characters forged less by such extreme environments but the plan that had sustained the journey for us had been scuppered by the sudden storm and the consequent disappearance of the snowmobile. Now we were faced with a punishingly long diversion on foot – or with risking the crossing along with Rob.

His confidence was extremely reassuring and so we set off, without a rope and extremely gingerly.

'*Touching The Void*'. Was there ever a more chilling title for a book, a more terrifying three words?

Rob stepped out onto the ice with Jane fitting quickly into his footsteps and me tucked equally close behind her. As if we were some kind of unit, some mutually supportive tight knot, capable of exerting mutual protection and security. The reality was that if any one of us were suddenly to vanish through a thin covering of snow, disappearing through a hidden crack in the roof of some vast, icy, cathedral dome, the other two would be powerless to offer any kind of help.

It was not reality, however, but fantasy provided by human proximity, that kept Jane and myself making each step behind Rob and further out onto the ice.

Each time I crossed a crack or a slightly wider gap ringed with a deep aquatic green that fused into the darkness beneath, I tried not to imagine this as my last moment. When Jane stopped to consider a crossing, I silently urged her to keep moving lest she was standing on some thin, weakening crust. Every time she went to move, I wanted her to stop, to not relinquish some seemingly safe standing for who knew what?

And so it was, in the highest sustained state of alert I have ever known, I endured one after another of the potential last moments of my life. One more. Then the next. Then another. Still alive, for one more, then the next, then another.

Rock at the glacier's edge came into view. A secure anchor to life, to everyday solidity. But there could be no hurrying. Only one excruciatingly slow, careful step after another. No end to it yet. Every inch of potentially vicious intent.

And so to the rock. To permanence. To structure and stability. To immense relief flooding through my body.

291

At the refuge, we were the sole customers. The storm had cleared the mountainside. Just us, the proprietor, and the coffee machine.

Jane and Rob sipped theirs while I gulped and then scrabbled around in the bottom of my sac for coins with which to buy more coffees. And another and then another again, each caffeine hit doing battle with the adrenaline arousal still coursing through my body.

Coins, caffeine, hit, thud, repeat.

2012. Tall Ship

(Between 2000 and 2017, the SS Stavros was owned by the Tall Ships Youth Trust, a charity providing 'character-building', adventure holidays for deserving youth parties. To supplement income, occasional trips were also run for older, paying 'voyage crew')

The gentle, undulating, to and fro movement was certainly disconcerting, even though the angle was not as steep as on many climbs. Unstable rock, loose or liable to avalanche, is avoided at all costs. Solidity and stability are highly valued. And a rope is essential. So, even though the holds here were perfect, this was still a strange and unsettling undertaking.

I had put my hand up when the first mate asked about prior experience even though I had never been up any actual rigging.

'Not exactly,' I quickly added. 'Not on a ship. But I've done quite a bit of rock climbing'.

'That'll do', he said. 'You're out on the first yard. On that end'.

I looked up at the spar, some fifty feet above the deck, and its extremity extending out over the sea.

'Okay,' I said. Tentatively.

I was reassured by having a full harness with its two karabiners fixed to tapes. Familiar gear. Confidence inspiring. But being above a moving sea without a rope, whatever the gradient, seemed a far cry from climbing at Cornwall or Portland. I talked quietly to myself as oft times before – 'nice and steady', 'no rush', 'three points of contact'. But as the first triangle of rigging narrowed near its top and the rope footholds became tighter, I needed to concentrate more on forcing my toes into the gaps. And, as I approached a short but vertical ladder, I had to contemplate letting go with one of my hands to reach out and clip into its accompanying security line.

Rock faces from my past – Derbyshire, Snowdonia, Colorado, California – came rushing back into consciousness. I felt my sinews stiffen, my ambition rise to the occasion. Full concentration now. The real thing.

From the top of the ladder another stretch to clip into the wire that was fixed firmly to the huge round horizontal spar. Then a step across space to place a foot on the wire that looped below the beam to provide the footholds. Spreadeagled temporarily with one hand and foot on the spar and the others still on the ladder, everything focused down onto my sequence of movements. Just as at the crux of a climbing pitch. The apprehension, the racing imagination, unwanted and unhelpful thoughts, all somehow automatically supressed. In their place, that rare, delectable surge of delight in my power, my conquering of fear. Concentration in its purest form.

With both feet on the wire beneath the yard, I could move slowly out to its end. The line to which I was attached was secured to the beam at regular intervals and the drill was to unclip and move one karabiner onto its new section before transferring the second. Like on a Via Ferrata. We had been given the warning at our briefing to always adhere rigidly and unwaveringly to this procedure and, to ram home this injunction, we were told of the person who unclipped both at the same time to pass around another shipmate on the wire. She had fallen to the deck below and to her death.

Out on the end of the yard, I tried not to dwell too much on the murmuring sea below. I tried also to loosen my grip on the beautifully rounded, wooden spar. Clinging to it served no purpose. My position might look and feel precarious and balancing on the swaying wire demanded some of my attention, but I was fixed securely by my karabiners.

Both of my grandfathers had been sailors and it is very likely that others further back in my hazy genealogy were as well. They came to join me up there on that yard, shadowy and silent presences. In gale, in lurching sea, unattached, they had been secured only by ingenuity, determination to survive and physical strength.

On the yard with me that day were two other men from my watch, spaced out along the line at equal intervals. Our task was to raise the enormous sail beneath us by grabbing and hauling up handfuls of the rough and weathered canvass. Although I pulled with everything I had, my legs braced against the wire, my efforts had little effect. Les, my elder by a decade or so, witnessed my struggles and inched his way along the yard to help me. He seemed possessed of strength of a different order to mine and after some grunting and oaths, and with our stances adjusting to the rolling of the ship, we completed the task and were able to lash the bulky sail to the yard with 'slippery hitches'.

With duties complete, there was time to chat and get to know Les and the others a little better. He and his mate, Dave, were regulars on these trips and he told me that the sailing charity's policy had originally set seventy as the upper age limit for crew members. Following lobbying from them both this had been raised to seventy-five, with the stipulation that this would be the final amendment.

'And how old are you now, if may I ask?'

'Seventy-five. We both are. It's our final voyage'.

My deep respect for these tough, softly spoken characters must have been obvious. They displayed qualities that I had also seen among the best in the climbing world, the best in terms of their quiet strength, skill and dependability.

'My missus said I could only keep coming after I turned seventy if I stayed on the deck'.

'But you're up the rigging!'

'Yes, but she's not here'.

*

We were aboard the magnificent SS Stavros in January and about to leave Tenerife for a week of sailing around the Canary Islands. There were six on my watch, all of us of an age, and we were squashed below decks in a tiny room with six hammocks fitted into bunk bed frames. We were on duty for stretches of four hours at a time and also required, whether resting or sleeping, to answer the call of 'All hands on deck!' as and when the senior officer required extra bodies to haul on ropes in order to raise or lower the sails.

On our first night, we were responsible for the eight until midnight watch. We were assigned to a rota of duties up on the quarter deck where unobtrusive oversight by the captain allowed us to feel completely – and frighteningly – in charge of the ship's progress. At first, I was stationed where I could scan the black, silent sea to starboard, on lookout for potential obstacles. Then, it was the ship's wheel, braced in a film star pose, with the awful weight of lives and tonnage dependent upon my actions. Such power and such responsibility. Beyond anything I had ever encountered on any mountain. Beyond nightmares.

However, beneath our very feet, the real decisions about the ship's course were being made by the captain in his cabin with his radar equipment. Under the stars though, with the ship creaking and listing, this knowledge easily pushed itself to the back of my consciousness.

'Two hundred and eighty degrees' came his command through the speaker.

'Two hundred and eighty degrees', I acknowledged before beginning to adjust the wheel.

And then, as I stared at the bearing on the illuminated dial in front of me, I realised that my glasses were three floors below me in my bunk. The numbers swirled past and I turned the wheel. Was that 280 or 230? Was that a

2 at all, or perhaps a 3? I could not abandon my post by letting go of the wheel, and my pride stopped me from calling one of my new ship mates from his duties. I blinked and squinted, aware that the captain was monitoring my panic with his instruments. I felt completely wretched.

'Two hundred and eighty degrees,' I confirmed, hoping against hope and steadying myself ready for excoriating censure.

But nothing came up from below deck and we sailed on into the night without incident. When Les came close enough later, I told him of my plight and he took the wheel temporarily while I scrabbled down ladders to my bunk to retrieve my crucial aids to vision.

*

At sea, the distinction between day and night dissolved. Instead, our new units of duration were those on-watch and those off. The work was exhausting – the physical toil of hauling ropes, raising huge weights, coaxing beams and spars through creaking angles. We ate every scrap of food available, packed in snacks between substantial meals, sat summoning the strength to speak or grabbing periods of sleep as the ship careered on, treading the dawn.

There were few idle moments but during one I happened to look down from the very front of the ship to see a group of dolphins. There, criss-crossing inches from the prow and risking being sliced as we cut through the waves, they formed a herring bone mesh, dare-devilling each other, keeping up their perfect symmetry, ever closer to the ship, ever joyous in their escapade. On another occasion, with a wind carrying us to the west and a magnificent sun dominating the day, I looked out to starboard and there accompanying us, matching our speed, the arcing, dark blue backs of pilot whales.

On our final night at sea, we returned along the coast to Tenerife. I was stationed up the mast in the dark with the sea rolling a little beneath me. The line of lights along the shore seemed to dip and rise of its own accord while I was braced full square and steady up on my stance. Then the hundreds of stars in their constellations turned and turned again as if all part of some crazy, malfunctioning astrolabe.

It was the perfect ending to our journey, all land locked logic abandoned, the obvious and everyday surrendering to the inevitable forces of tide and time.

2012. 'Over The Moors'

In the late 1980s I published a booklet of ten poems and essays called '*Hanging in the Balance*', which examined both the world of rock climbing, with its dangers and delights, and personal matters around the ending of my marriage.

It felt like a risky undertaking. The climbing material because, in the fiercely competitive (and very male) culture of that period, an at-best-average-climber should not intrude into the preserve of the elite and might expect a contemptuous response if he dared to do so. And the personal stuff because, well, we all know how indulgent or unethical, such writing can easily become.

But I took the risk – I was writing about risk after all! – and published. And I was stunned when two leading writers, Ed Drummond and Terry Gifford, gave it highly complimentary reviews in the main climbing magazines of the time. I was even invited by Terry to give a presentation at the Festival of Mountaineering Literature which he organised.

In terror, I courteously but hastily declined.

The hoo-ha around the book died down of course and it went out of print. Decades passed.

Then, out of the blue, I received an email from Martin Kocsis of the British Mountaineering Council, who had tracked me down via a long trail of emails. He was seeking my permission to use quotes from '*Hanging in the Balance*' in a forthcoming climbing guidebook for the northern areas of the Peak District. This time I readily agreed, desperately curious to know which piece or pieces he felt warranted inclusion in '*Over The Moors*'.

It was some years again before the BMC book saw publication and my wife and I were invited one summer evening to the launch in the upstairs room of a pub in

Glossop. It was a wonderful evening and, although all strangers, it was company in which I felt immediately at home. While I have spent my years in the worlds of psychology, prose, poetry and politics, there has also always been this other one where I could be a very different sort of me – a somehow younger, freer me.

The guidebook was a lavish affair and over six hundred pages in length. As various speakers said their piece, I tried, with the book in my lap beneath the table, to flip through the pages past one spectacular colour photo after another, looking for my citation. It was an impossible task and one that threatened to remove me from the room's flow of enthusiasm and goodwill. So, I surmounted my burning curiosity, closed the book and re-entered the vibe – back to Kinder, Bleaklow, the Chew Valley and all the rest.

It felt – it feels – deeply rewarding and I am so proud to be included, rooted somehow, in this formidable and staggeringly beautiful area.

2016. Visited upon the Sons

'You need a proper hat because one third of your body heat – '
'Ow!'
'Don't throw snow – if you get wet then – '
'But he – '
'I know, I know. But it's important to keep your body heat – '
'Wee – ay!'
'No! Don't dive in it'.
'Yay. Look!'
'Don't you do it too!'

We were on the track under Burbage Edge in the snow, my two young sons and me. It was 1978 and I had judged the time to be right to share some of the lessons I had learned in the mountains, to tap into their boyish hunger for adventure. Back into mine too, I suppose.

And I had miscalculated terribly.

'Andy Handford and me, before you were born, we once – No, stop it, you'll get soaked!'

Winter wilderness survival techniques had failed to seize their imaginations. Three and five was obviously far too young to be interested in snow holes, bivouac routines and the essential conservation of body heat.

Son Number One flung himself with glee into the bank of snow, copying the sense of abandon shown an instant before by Son Number Two. My experiences, the toying with danger and the dance between risk and resilience, were way outside their nursery worlds. As well I should have known.

*

Back when my sons were children, I suggested that soon after each of their seventh birthdays, we should make an ascent up Grindsbrook to the top of the Kinder Scout plateau. And so, in their time, we completed this challenge, companionably and with little mishap or complaint. I had intended this to be an adventure, something to be looked forward to in excited anticipation and completed with a memorable sense of satisfaction.

And I assumed that that was what we had achieved until I overheard one of the older ones telling Son Number Three who was still only two at the time –

'When you're seven you have to go up Kinder with him'.

It was that 'have to'.

It was said in a matter-of-fact tone of voice, this initiation, and perhaps I was the only one who heard in it a feint, chilling echo of Abraham and Isaac.

*

During their teenage years, we sometimes took a Saturday walk, pushing up into the wilder wastes of the Dark Peak.

'But I'm going out tonight, Dad. So, only if we will be back in good time'.

And sometimes, the miles seemed to stretch and dusk would be descending while we still had considerable ground to cover, before we could drop back down to our car.

'It's typical! He always does this! It always takes loads longer!'

*

Risk. It was always a consideration but, before the Cairngorm tragedy and with the airy arrogance of youth, any serious consequences of rock climbing and mountaineering always seemed unlikely. They happened to distant figures, different in type and ambition from my friends and me. Before I had children, I used to quote statistics for climbing-related deaths that I had gathered from somewhere: 1 in 1,000 for the UK, 1 in 100 for the Alps and 1 in 10 for the Himalayas. Trusting that these were relatively reliable, and confident that my Alpine forays were behind me, I argued, when challenged, that motorways were widely used yet dangerous arenas. In defending my desire to continue climbing if possible, I asserted that few of the people who might judge me adversely also advocated banning or even avoiding the use of motorways. I added that local crags, carefully approached, might be only equally or just a little more hazardous.

But with the responsibilities of becoming a father and to reassure myself and others, I enquired about life insurance and the implications of occasional outings on the crags.

'Do you use ropes and other specialist equipment?' the firm enquired.

'Oh yes', I replied, eager to display a responsible attitude towards safety.

'Hmm', they must have thought, 'it's serious then', and whacked up the premium.

*

None of my three sons became hooked on rock climbing and, apart from playing around with ropes on a few boulders when they were young, I was very happy not to encourage them. But we did enjoy outdoor adventures over the years, the highlights of which were probably:

Son Number One – We had mooted the idea of a long walk through the Dark Peak for some time and, during his student years, finally set off on a three-day expedition. The plan was for consecutive days each comprising nigh on twenty-five miles over demanding terrain. Was this a grand ambition or a delusion of potentially disastrous proportion?

On the first day, we keyed straight into the wondrous world of gritstone uplands, walking from Buxton over Black Edge and then Rushup Edge. It seemed like a long day and we were reaching Kinder Downfall by late afternoon and, later still, Fairbrook Naize where we descended for an overnight stay at the Snake Inn.

The second day took us over Bleaklow to Grains in the Water, Grinah Stones, Barrow Stones, lonely, empty places all. Coming down from these high wastes, we could follow the track all the way down the eastern banks of Howden, Derwent and Ladybower Reservoirs. We stayed that night in the Yorkshire Bridge Inn where we ate among the many tables of cheery diners out from Sheffield for the evening. The miles were taking their toll and I sat dazed and zombie-like through much of the meal, concentrating on raising each mouthful on my fork and accurately locating its intended destination.

Our third day started with a long, unrelenting and punishing uphill that brought us beneath Stanage Edge. Four miles along the top of that mighty crag and then beneath Burbage Edge to the Longshaw Estate. We stopped to eat lunch on the top of Frogatt Edge and, when I tried to stand afterwards, my legs had seized up like a rusted engine and would not function. We were halfway or so to our intended finishing spot, Matlock, and I had to be helped down into Baslow where we devoured hefty portions of sweet cake and tea.

We savoured our achievement, a grand folly almost fully realised.

But folly and disappointment were to nothing compared with what was to come.

I was preparing to introduce him, right on our home territory, to the grotesque and embarrassing 1960s pastime of hitch hiking.

*

Son Number 2 – In the summer between his sixth form years, we made a week-long, high-level traverse across Austria's Zillertal Alps, although the trip almost ended after day one.

That morning, we had left the village of Vipiteno in the Brenner Pass and slogged upwards to our first refuge through a thick wet mist. Route finding for a week in such conditions would be extremely difficult and the level of detail on our map seemed pitifully inadequate. It would take sustained and pleasure-wrecking concentration to navigate our whole route with the continual risk of fatal errors. But we did manage to locate the hut, looming into visibility like some filmic cliché. Settling to sleep that night though proved very difficult. The bunk room was stuffy and stiflingly hot and we were wedged tight along the mattress like sardines between a crowd of restless, young Belgian lads. As I lay awake in the small hours, the logistics, expense and potential humiliation of a failed mission and returning home after only one day pulled my thoughts in all directions, in that room alive with whistles, snores and farts.

The mountains, however, are unpredictable. They can delight every bit as much as dash all hope. And delight they did as the next day dawned in splendour - pristine and clear!

Thereafter, for the rest of our week, each day intensified the experience. We slogged up switchback paths and crested ridges at altitudes of up to ten thousand feet, surrounded in all directions by a sea of snow-capped peaks. Sometimes we benefitted from fixed cables and even ladders on steep, exposed sections. We ploughed on across rugged upland plateaux and skirted gorges and glaciers, descending through scattered dwarf pines and into lush forests.

We grew fitter, lungs filled with clean, clear air. Food tasted delicious. We became tanned under the sun's calm and benign authority. Even our sleeping arrangements improved dramatically with silent, settled dormitories and, once, a cabin to ourselves.

A week passed like this, sixty or so miles, twenty thousand feet or thereabouts of ascent and descent, and when we eventually dropped back down into the everyday world, we were changed.
Even if we did not at the time realise it.

*

Son Number 3 – In his mid-teens, we dipped the front wheels of our bikes into the Irish Sea at Whitehaven and then set off to cross the Lake District, Pennines and shattered industrial landscape of the North East, to dip them again in the North Sea at Sunderland six days later. We had been encouraged to feel up to this demanding outing after completing a ten-day, two-hundred-mile cycle trip the previous year from Rotterdam up and back along the Dutch North Sea coast. Purpose-built and immaculately maintained cycle tracks, junctions where bikes have right of way over monstrous lorries, courteous and helpful people, beaches for lunchtime swims, clean comfortable accommodation – Holland had all the components of a perfect cycling trip.
And, the most perfect ingredient of all – it was flat!
But the Sustrans 'Sea To Sea' route (or 'C2C') the following year, proved to be a far more demanding undertaking with the going particularly tough in places. I had to push my heavily laden bike up a stony track outside Keswick on the second day and again, on the fourth, up steep hillsides to surmount the watershed between the Irish and North Seas. We savoured the short section along the spine of England, the deserted lead mines and the freewheeling splendour as we swept down through moorland that extended all the way to heat haze horizons.
We laboured with a hidden double puncture under an unrelenting midday sun up on the Durham Moors, using all of our precious drinking water in identifying the hole(s). At the rundown farmhouse where we stopped in

the hope of refilling our bottles, we were ushered by a wild looking man into his dismal hovel where he insisted that we also took a drink of 'this new banana cordial'.

Unscathed, we carried on along tow paths and cycle tracks, until eventually crossing the iconic Wearmouth Bridge in Sunderland on match day an hour or so before kick-off. How strange, how delightfully bizarre to be wheeling our bikes – there was no possibility of riding them – deep among such a raucous army roused and ready for battle. Feigning fellow feeling we marched in their terrifying but jovial company, sensing a sort of a welcome, after our rarefied and solitary exertions, a welcome back to the country called home, land of loyalties.

*

The decades passed and in due course and in an unfolding tradition, Grandson Number One made the journey with me and his Dad up Grindsbrook to the top of the Kinder Plateau. We were a little later than his seventh birthday mainly because of my lack of organisation.

And in due course too, the following conversation took place –

'A long time ago, when your daddy was seven, he walked up the mountain with me. And when both of your uncles were seven they walked up the same mountain with me. And your cousin is going to as well. So, when you are seven, would you like to walk up the mountain with me too?'

Granddaughter Number One – 'No!'

There is always time.

FINISHING STRETCH

2016. Refresher Session

It was well meant. And probably necessary. A one-hour refresher session at the local climbing wall – a fitting seventieth birthday present from my wife for someone who was now getting out onto the rock once a year at best. And who was forgetting much of what was once automatic and routine.

Not too old to learn something new. Not so experienced that I had seen it all.

I would approach with humility.

Early twenties I put him at, my instructor. A lanky lad who may have already had a long day and was now having to entertain some ancient wannabe.

'So, have you done much climbing?'

'Oh yes . Over the years I have,' I said dragging my old rock boots from my sac.

'Blimey, they've seen a bit of use'.

'Yeah, I've had them twenty-five years or so,' I said, 'They belonged to a mate who died in the Alps. We auctioned his gear off afterwards'.

I wasn't being deliberately melodramatic. I just wanted him to know that the shoes had a special meaning for me. The fraying stitching wasn't just me being casual or cheapskate about my gear.

'God! How old is that harness?'

Ok. He had me here.

'Mmm. I suppose it must be the best part of twenty years. But I don't use it that regularly. Once a year perhaps, if that, over the past ten years.

'You should renew a harness every five years. More frequently if it's getting a lot of use'.

'Five years, is it? I know...um...I know that...um...I just...'

The sweaty gymnasium smell of my school days seemed to be intensifying.

'Hang on, is that an old Wild Country harness? You don't see that model around anymore'.
'It is, yes'. I bought it from Mark Vallance. Wild Country was his firm'.
'He's the Friends guy, isn't he?'
'He is, yes. He manufactured them. A guy called Ray Jardine actually invented them. Ray was a NASA engineer who dropped out so that he could do more climbing. Mark met him in the States on his way back from Antarctica. Ray agreed to sell him the licence and Mark then set up Wild Country to manufacture them'.
I was slipping into lecturing mode. Name dropping! Trying to gain some credibility with my interrogator. To recover my sense of being an experienced climber, albeit a somewhat rusty one. Not a halfwit who was unsafe to be on a climbing wall, let alone out on the crags.
'You seem very well informed'.
'Yeah. I've known Mark for years. Fifty or so, it must be. We've climbed together on and off since way back'.
'You climbed with Mark Vallance?'
I had fallen into trading on the reputations of friends. Pathetic. It had just somehow happened. That deeply ingrained competitive nature within the world of rock climbing, wrapped up inside all the genuine camaraderie, was surfacing in me. The hunger for credibility, the need to have one's place in the pecking order recognised.
Pride. It comes before a ...
'I was with him one night when he swore me to silence then showed me a prototype for the Friend. He had it locked up in his shed'.
'Wait a minute. Are you alright with that buckle?'
Of course I was alright with it. Except that I was not now so completely sure. And about knots too, if I was being honest. I was having to go right back. In my head the rabbit was coming up out of the hole, round the back of

the tree, and then back down the hole. Finishing off with a half hitch.

'Yes, just making sure. Always like to double check', I mumbled. Unconvincingly.

'So, is that how you started? Climbing in Derbyshire with Mark Vallance?'

'Oh no. I first started on the Dorset coast when I was still at school. Back in the early, mid sixties'.

'Swanage?'

'No, we were at Lulworth and, mainly, Portland'.

'But those routes on Portland aren't that old are they? I've never been but they're all sports climbs, aren't they? Just watch that buckle, you need the belt a bit more snug'.

'Yes, I know, thanks. I was climbing on Portland with a guy called Bob Shepton. Have you heard of him? They used to call him the climbing vicar'.

'I don't think I have, no'.

'He was developing the island's climbs and writing the guidebook. So, we were often doing new routes of an evening after school. I thought that was what everybody did, first ascents'.

'What happened to him? Did you keep in touch?

'Oh yes. He moved to London and then to North Wales. But he diversified into sailing. He's still going, must be in his mid-eighties now. I saw a photo of his ship recently, taken through an arch in some massive iceberg. To the north of Greenland, I think'.

'Hey, that's good going. So, you're still climbing a bit then? Do you get on this wall much?'

'Not this one, no. I used to go to one in Nottingham that was opened by two guys I knew and to The Foundry in Sheffield sometimes. That was Mark again, opened that. First purpose-built wall in the country'.

'Oh yeah. We all know the Foundry'.

'I had my fiftieth birthday there!"

'Ha! So, you've had quite a bit of experience on walls after all?'

How could I tell him that they were for me a very poor substitute? Just about acceptable for a winter evening, perhaps. Or for getting fit quickly at the beginning of the season. But compared to the feel of real rock – the rough graze of grit, the shine of limestone or the angled bite of quartz and sea cliff granite – compared to such geology, to the solid force of Nature, this place seemed not only trivial, but silly. Holds made from strange lumps of artificial material splattered across vertical boards. And this was supposed to somehow equate to a mountain environment?

Somewhere, in another part of the building, the shouts and groans from a raucous football team could be heard celebrating a goal or a near miss. Not the eerie cry of a peregrine echoing in a cwm beneath a crag. Not the first ominous crack of distant thunder necessitating a change of pace and priorities.

'What about round here? You've presumably done a bit outdoors too? There's some good quarries round here.'

Quarries? Outdoor climbing walls really, bolted up to high heaven. Ugly environments usually, routes of a very high technical difficulty rendered safe and risk free by artificial means.

We had delighted in climbs reasonably close to the roads, of course we had. We had learned technique, history and the culture from older, more experienced hands on the Derbyshire Edges and in the Llanberis Pass. But we had always valued remote landscapes, terrain that forced a reckoning with one's own resources, away from the helping hand and the safety net. Andy Handford and I had trekked across Dartmoor at New Year in 1968, navigating through mist and rain in limited visibility over three days, enjoying the challenge of managing our clothing, tent and sleeping bags, preserving our last layers of protection from the damp and cold. With my friend Trevor, in the early '70s, we sought out less accessible cliffs; first, climbs high on Tryfan's imposing east face, climbs iced up and dripping with history. Then, even further from habitation, a determined trudge up into the Carneddau range to Crag-Y-Isfa and the challenge of its Pinnacle Wall. With a mighty swell of accomplishment afterwards, we noted the location of the formidable Mur Y Niwl – Wall of Mist – for a later date. It was one of those routes, like Dream of White Horses, that was to drift in and out of my own dreams for a further twenty-five long years.

But I was here for a refresher course, not climbing chat, and my hour must be more than half gone. He was obviously sensing the same.

'OK. Let's start with belaying. I'll climb a few feet and I want to see what your technique's like. Just pay out the rope through your device as you normally would'.

He eased himself up onto the blocks with quick, dynamic movements, flexible in a way that I had once been and probably was no longer. He was looking back down at the rope in my hands.

'Right', he said as joined me on the mat again. 'You need move this left hand up with the rope as you pay it out, then hold both with the right as you slide the left back again. You're a bit slack on that'.

OK, a point well made. But how many times had I belayed somebody when it really mattered? Hundreds. Thousands more like. On short, brutal Peak District classics. On Snowdonia's traditional test pieces. On Cornwall's Atlantic fortresses. On Lake District crags drenched in mountaineering lore. Over the seas to Zermatt, to the Piz Badile, to the Colorado Rockies and California's High Sierra. My belaying had never been a problem but neither had I ever had to arrest a major leader fall.

Be humble. Accept this guidance. It could have saved a life. Might do still.

'Right, let's get you onto this wall,' he said, aware that our hour was slipping away like a rope running freely through a belay plate.

Ethels Day 55 – 31st August

Bolehill (Cromford Moor)

Very strange to think that this is Ethel number 95, the final one, and that I have visited so many Peak District hills within a one-year period. Sometimes I try to remember them all to allow them to flit through my recollection like a private lantern show.

Today, a group of five of us walk directly from our homes up around this top, which is known by various names – Black Rocks, Barrel Edge, Bolehill and Cromford Moor.

On these familiar paths, my thoughts wander to other, far more extensive expeditions, undertakings that seem to belong to my past and requiring more than I am now physically and, perhaps, psychologically capable of.

*

Two decades, a long weekend each year, climbing the Munros with my friend Simon as he worked his way towards completing all 282 tops. The views of wave upon wave of hills rippling into the distance, occasional glimpses of the sea and the magical 'Islands', the long days – and the occasional but excruciating agony of arthritis.

The four-day walk down the Northumberland coast in 1996 where my long-held beliefs about 'wilderness' were shattered. Each day brought long empty beaches and very few other people. Fortresses, sandbars and reefs. In the evenings we found lodgings in quiet villages or harbour towns. Returning a year or so later by car, eager to once again fill my being with the experience of extended, unsullied spaces, I discovered that behind the sand dunes that had bordered our whole walk, was a busy road! I was shocked at my naivety and disappointed until the realisation grew that 'wilderness' is not solely, or even primarily, a matter of geography. It is also an aspect of the soul, an awareness of the here and now, of existing beyond unnecessary distractions.

Long distance projects became more and more attractive as I grew older. A solo cycle trip from Nottingham to Edinburgh, split into two legs a year apart, took me on Sustrans paths and trails and a meandering route for about five hundred miles. Forests, hills, moors, the coast, post-industrial wastes, the back streets of tough towns, early morning ferries, shuttered workshops and factories, high, wonderful country lanes and the entry into a bustling city in early morning light. Travelling alone I was able to savour each fully but also enjoy greatly occasional conversations with strangers encountered along the way. People, as well as landscapes, become increasingly more rewarding and interesting in proportion to the work and effort expended in reaching them.

By far the biggest project, sweetened for me by its air of ridiculous and unattainable proportions, was the South West Coast Path. On a dark and dismal day in early January 2004, I had set myself the challenge of completing this 630-mile hike around the whole of the English south western peninsula. Having estimated that it would take about 8 weeks over 4 years, I wrote to friends and family outlining the project saying that I would notify them about each leg in advance and welcome their company if they cared to join me.

The four years became eight and there was barely a handful of the 630 miles that did not delight. Revitalising weeks in Spring were highlights of the year, as were autumnal wanderings with late summers stretched out along those far coasts. There was time to walk and talk with friends, with one of my sons, and with the woman who became my wife. There was also time to relish being solitary, to drink in the splendour and to jog along in the company of ghosts and memories.

Truly, to me, these 630 miles, every inch of them, form a Wonder of the World.

*

Today, we walk past the National Stone Centre, along the High Peak Trail and scramble up the scree slope alongside Black Rocks. Flooding back come memories of rock climbs here, a testing ground for technique, strength and boldness. Glorious afternoons and evenings with Irwin, Derek, Rob and others down the years.

We reach the high woods and pick our way up and out onto Cromford Moor. It is only a short hop now to the trig point marking my final Ethel. I had contemplated having some sort of ceremony but, on a familiar stroll from home it would seem rather ridiculous. So, instead we take a few group photos, make half-hearted attempts at profundity, and then set off back towards home, chuckling and content.

Over the past year, I have walked half or so of these 95 Ethels on my own, about a third with Alastair and Suzanne, and the rest with various friends and family.

Companions all, thank you!

*

So, do these Ethels form the quintessential list of Peak District high spots? A bucket list of the 95 hill tops one must visit? The Munros of the Peak District?

Not at all. The Munros, for one thing, have a very precise 'mathematical' definition. They are all big and require considerable effort.

The Ethels, by contrast, have been selected from a wider set of criteria. The highest points of the Peak District are included, of course, and there are a few interestingly long days out. But there are also some tops that are little more than ten minutes from a car parking spot, chosen presumably to give a wider geographical spread.

One of their common features is the magnificence of the viewpoints they offer. Offer not give. They are under no obligation. One of the greatest pleasures of being out, now as ever, is to be reminded that I am not in charge, that my species does not control mighty Nature's moods. I've relished the mists and the downpours every bit as, or more than, those beautiful clear, blue skies and the distant views that stretch our vision and our hopes.

Well done the Council for the Protection of Rural England and well done Ethel Haythornthwaite! Thank you.

ADDENDUM

Francis (Andy) Handford (1946 – 2017)

A week ago my long-time friend, Andy Handford, died. We met almost fifty years ago to the day in the freezing conditions of Williams' Barn in the Ogwen Valley and went on to complete many climbs in the UK and abroad. He had a strong sense of loyalty to family and friends and a bubbling sense of fun and of the absurd.

Our adventures on some of the bigger peaks of the Alps in 1971 and 1972 included bivouacs on the edges of glaciers, lying directly on the rocks. Or sheltering from electrical storms in hastily hollowed-out caves after throwing away all our ironmongery. He once walked alone through the night from the centre out to the edge of New York to begin hitch-hiking at first light. Similarly, he walked at night from central London out to our flat in East Dulwich once, climbed a drainpipe and managed to squeeze through a skylight to be sitting grinning at our kitchen table when we arrived home even later.

Andy was best man at my wedding in 1969 and subsequently travelled considerable distances to see each of my three sons within days of their birth. The first of these occasions, for example, involved his hitchhiking from Edinburgh to Doncaster – again as an unannounced surprise!

*

We kept in touch when he moved to Colorado in the late 1970s even though the price of transatlantic phone calls was prohibitively high for both of us and we only spoke to each other for two or three minutes each Christmas Eve, alternating who phoned whom each year to spread the cost. We met up occasionally on his return trips with Lynn to his family here and I made only my second ever flight anywhere to see them and attempt to settle myself when my life seemed *in extremis* in 1987.

It became possible economically in the last fifteen or so years of his life for Andy and Lynn to visit more often. He was at my side when I married again in 2008, crossing the ocean to be with us. In his final years, he was the willing recipient of various experimental new treatments for his cancer and refused to let the illness stop his adventuring with Lynn or his visits to friends and family here. On one occasion I met them at our local railway station as they arrived from Edinburgh with rucksacks and bags and a huge painting they had purchased and covered in bubble wrap. As I watched my old friends, my dear friends, negotiating the lift from the platform, I thought that there comes an age at which one must stop trying to do such things. And then immediately I thought that there must never come age at which one stops trying to do such things!

Andy expressed a desire to go and look at 'an Edge' during that visit so we drove out to Frogatt. Standing beneath the main climbing area we tried to pick out the lines where we had first cut our teeth – and shredded our hands – on lines up these classic gritstone routes. We could have been twenty years old again, looking up a cliff face, silently considering the options for our way forward. Instead, we were fifty years older, silently considering the way we had already come, the tick of time and the essential, transient beauty of life.

Back in 1967, a friend from the climbing club had wanted to take our photo on the back field at Goldsmiths. Andy immediately suggested a ridiculous pose which I think came from some Victorian hunting party or group of mountaineers or whatever. It consisted of grasping one's forearm with the opposite hand, raising one knee slightly and out to the side and fixing a haughty and arrogant expression to one's face. Down the decades we attempted to replicate this if we remembered on those occasions when we met up.

In his last few weeks, Lynn asked that we sent cards and messages, and I put together a montage of four of these photos made into a card. Lynn said that all his visitors to their home in Colorado burst out laughing when they saw it by his bed.

I like to think of Andy and his visitors all laughing together. And then the terrible loss and sadness fills me up.

And then I start laughing again too.

Mark Vallance (1944 – 2018)

(a version of the piece read at Mark's Memorial Service)

My long-time friend, Mark Vallance, died the week before last, aged 72, and obituaries are appearing in the mountaineering world. I would like to add my own recollections of the man I have known for over 50 years. We met in 1966 at Goldsmith's College, London, where we both lived in the same men's hall of residence. Although only two years older than me, Mark was already well-connected in British climbing circles, had an impressive list of rock climbing and mountaineering ascents to his name and had lived and worked in India for a year.

From the outset I found Mark to be forthright, determined and generous with his time. He introduced me to the major climbing areas of the Peak District, Snowdonia and Cornwall, encouraged me to attempt climbs that he judged suitable for me and dragged me up a few that, with a less experienced and/or patient companion, would have been way beyond my capabilities. (The only quid pro quo in this climbing relationship, but one that still pleases me, is my introducing him in 1968 to my old stomping ground, Portland – now a major English site but then home to only a handful of routes).

I remember Mark buying 'Sgt Pepper' in 1967 on the day it was released and listening to it that evening with him in his room in silence and shared admiration. I also remember introducing him to Jack Kerouac's 'The Dharma Bums' which I thought he might find far too debauched and undisciplined but, with its strong Buddhist influences, appealed to him greatly. He told me that he had read it bivouacking on Chesil Beach and watching the sun set over West Bay the night before visiting me in Dorset in 1968.

Mark lived a full life and accomplished much. I loved receiving the occasional letter from him in Antarctica when I was settled into my first teaching job on a dreary winter's morning in the Home Counties. When he returned a few years later, now married to my friend Jan, we kept in touch and met up every now and then. In 1977, over dinner at their Peak District cottage, Mark revealed that he was going to re-mortgage his house, give up his job and sink all he had into manufacturing a revolutionary piece of climbing equipment. He would not be drawn into saying more but then, at the end of the evening, and swearing my then wife and myself to absolute secrecy, he went out to his shed and returned with an object covered by an oily rag. He unwrapped it to reveal the 'Friend', a sophisticated piece of machinery – camshafts, cables and moving parts. It almost seemed to require two hands to hold and operate it and I could not imagine anything so heavy and cumbersome (and potentially expensive) hanging from a climber's harness. On the drive home afterwards, I feared that Mark had made a terrible, disastrous misjudgement.

Mark's 'Friends' quickly became a worldwide sensation and a vital piece of every climber's equipment! They were soon hanging from my belt as well and enabling me, in middle age, to push up my standard way beyond a level I had ever expected.

We met up every few years for an afternoon's climbing, a walk or just a meal and a drink. In the 1970's we debated politics and industrial relations (Mark was the only entrepreneurial businessman I knew). In the 1980s he donated some of his rapidly expanding firm's new line in tents and sleeping bags to the Greenham Women via the Buxton Campaign for Nuclear Disarmament, of which I was the Chair.

Around the end of the millennium, he told me of his Parkinson's diagnosis and his plans to remain as superfit as he could for as long as possible. In grim weather on Boxing Day 2002, as we took a 15-mile walk through the Peak District (down from his customary 30-milers), he told me of his plans for the British Mountaineering Council as he prepared to become its President ("my last mountain"). And I was delighted when he came to my 70th birthday eighteen months ago and presented me with a copy of his newly published autobiography, 'Wild Country. The man who made Friends'.

I last saw Mark a month ago in a care home on the western edge of Sheffield. He looked so out of place among the high-backed chairs, in the padded silence of an over-heated day room. With Jan, we reminisced for an hour or more about moments across the decades, hopping from Goldsmiths and the 1960s to his current predicament with Parkinson's and with many favourite diversions in between.

I realised that I had not seen enough of him in the recent years and as I was leaving, I placed my hand on his shoulder and said

'I'll try to come and see you a bit more often, Mark'.

'You won't,' he replied in a quiet but steady voice. 'This is 'goodbye'.

Only, he said the word with a capital 'G' and my words froze in my mouth.

Jan and I had lunch afterwards and talked some more while one of the very first days of Spring attacked the remains of winter in the fields and hedgerows with a savage vitality. It was only then that the penny dropped and I learned that he was well advanced in his plans to visit a Swiss clinic within the coming weeks.

Mark was a significant figure in my life and in the lives of many people. He often surprised me, sometimes amazed me, with his creativity and ambition, drew me into lengthy conversations on weighty matters as we travelled on through life and amused me with his dry wit. Thank you for all these memories, Mark. Thank you so much.

A YEAR ON THE ETHELS
INDEX

Aleck Low, 129
Alphin Pike, 237
Alport Moor, 244
Ashway Moss, 239
Axe Edge Moor, 102
Back Tor, 178
Black Edge (Combs Moss), 251
Black Hill, 9
Black Hill (Whaley Moor), 168
Blakelow Hill, 101
Bleaklow Head, 249
Black Chew Head, 237
Bole Hill (Burton Moor), 163
Bolehill (Cromford Moor), 317
Bradwell Moor, 167
Brown Knoll, 172
Britland Edge End, 240
Burbage Edge, 170
Carder Low, 44
Cats Tor, 134
Cheeks Hill, 102
Chelmorton Low, 113
Chinley Churn, 121
Chrome Hill, 127
Corbar Hill, 251
Combs Head, 251
Cown Edge, 118
Croker Hill, 26
Crook Hill, 176
Dead Edge End, 240
Durham Edge, 132
Eccles Pike, 121

Ecton Hill, 108
Eldon Hill, 123
Featherbed Moss, 237
Featherbed Top, 255
Fin Cop, 165
Foxlow Edge, 134
Gautries Hill, 123
Grin Low, 117
Grindslow Knoll, 41
Gun, 26
Harborough Rocks, 39
Harland Edge, 46
Hen Cloud, 19
Harthill Moor, 120
Higgar Tor, 51
High Edge, 166
High Neb, 51
High Stones, 242
High Wheeldon, 116
Higher Shelf Stones, 249
Hollins Hill, 166
Kinder Scout, 103, 174
Lantern Pike, 118
Lees Moor, 115
Longstone Moor, 106
Lord's Seat, 125
Lose Hill, 125
Lost Lad, 178
Mam Tor, 125
Margery Hill, 242
Merryton Low, 133
Mill Hill, 255

Minninglow, 43
Mount Famine, 247
Musden Low, 48
Oliver Hill, 102
Parkhouse Hill, 127
Pilsbury Hill, 44
Ramshaw Rocks, 19
Revidge, 133
Shutlingsloe, 253
Shatton Moor, 132
Shining Tor, 134
Sir William Hill, 51
Slitherstone Hill, 123
Snailsden Pike End, 240
Sough Top, 113
South Head, 247
Sponds Hill, 168
Stanedge Pole, 51
Stanton Moor, 130
The Cloud, 26
The Roaches, 19
Thorpe Cloud, 171
Tissington Hill, 171
Wardlow Hay Cop, 111
West Nab, 9
Wetton Hill, 108
Whetstone Ridge, 49
White Low, 9
White Path Moss, 51
Win Hill, 177
Wolfescote Hill, 110

ACKNOWLEDGEMENTS

My initial plan to walk the Ethels within a one-year period was greeted enthusiastically by my friends Alastair and Suzanne Clark, who then accompanied me on a good number of the subsequent outings. Others whom I have climbed and wandered with over many decades crop up and are named in these pages, and to all of them I owe a great debt. I am fortunate to have such friends, who have regularly reminded me of what is important in attempting to live a full and rewarding life – and of what is distracting and irrelevant. Both in their company as well as in splendid isolation, the Life Force has often held me its mighty grip.

Writing, as ever, has proved both a compulsive struggle requiring discipline and a great joy. I am very grateful in this endeavour to Vally Miller for her ongoing support, to Luke Miller for his technical wizardry, and to Jenn Morgan for her expertise and guidance through the tough old world of publishing.

WHILE GIANTS SLEEP

Andy Christopher Miller

Andy Miller's prose and poetry has won a range of awards and commendations. Daisy Goodwin, the judge for the 2011 international Yeovil Literary Prize, described him as having '. . . *a distinctive voice. . .*' and his prize-winning poem 'Attempting to Interfere' as being '. . . *mysterious but repaying a close reading'*. His long out-of-print booklet 'Hanging in the Balance' also attracted critical acclaim and is reprinted here in full. This new anthology displays a twin focus on mountaineering, rock climbing and outdoor adventure and on relationships across the adult life span.

'This collection pulses with life and energy ... Previously published and unpublished work spanning forty-two years is combined in this book, providing an intimate overview of a life lived on the edge in the most literal sense ... Miller's writing is sometimes humorous, deeply personal, and full of richly detailed observations, part of a continually developing tradition of walking and climbing literature'

Aly Stoneman, *Left Lion*, Nottingham

Independently Published (2nd Edition 2015)

THE RAGGED WEAVE OF YESTERDAY

Andy Christopher Miller

When an old mountaineering friend fell gravely ill, Andy Miller found himself looking for solace in the oldest of a set of personal diaries that he had faithfully maintained for fifty years. Would their youthful adventures be recorded? What shared memories had he forgotten? Was there an anecdote or two that might help lift his stricken friend?

So began a journey not only into his own life story but into the role of diaries in our lives and, ultimately, into the very nature of human memory and the sense of the self.

"...an intimate and immensely readable book"
Dr Phil Stringer, Dept. of Psychology, University College London
"... likeably self-deprecating ... accepts that to identify the real threads of a life is not as simple as it might seem"
Judy Brown, 2013 Poet in Residence at the Wordsworth Trust at Dove Cottage

"...as well as being an entertaining read, this book is also a fascinating journey into the nature of memory"
Paul Anderson, Nottingham Writers Studio

Independently Published (2017)

THE NAPLES OF ENGLAND

Andy Christopher Miller

The War is over and a generation returns home to build peace, determined to create a new society, protected from cradle to grave.

On the beautiful Dorset coast, baby boomer, Andy Miller, grows up surrounded by the security and nurture of the 1950s welfare state that will propel him from council estate to university. In a series of vignettes and stories, some humorous and some poignant, the author describes growing up in this vanished post-War world.
What happens then when one day, decades later, he discovers that everything he thought was true is not?
This is a memoir of family, truth and secrets and what it was like to grow up in Britain in the years following the Second World War.

> *'... a wonderful book ... anyone yet to read it has a real treat in store'*
> John Lindley, Cheshire Poet Laureate
> & Manchester Cathedral Poet

Independently Published (2015)

NEVER: A WORD

Andy Christopher Miller

In 1927, on a beautiful stretch of the Dorset coast, a mother of three walks into the sea and drowns. Fifty-five years later, Sue Roberts hears about the manner of her grandmother's death for the first time. As she delicately prises further information from her unstable mother, Sue learns that her kind-hearted father has forbidden all discussion of the tragedy. He has never even allowed his mother's name to be known!
But 'never' is a word Sue cannot accept.
How and why have her parents kept this shocking secret from her?
What has blunted her own curiosity so effectively and for so long?
Will Sue's life and family break apart as she seeks the truth?

"Impressive ... raises issues of identity and family relationships that are likely to resonate widely ... they certainly struck chords with me"
Graham Sellors, Playwright

Independently Published (2021)

WAY TO THE WEST

Andy and Vally Miller

A glorious collection resulting from a collaboration between disciplines of art. Featuring twenty-five beautiful full-page watercolours alongside accompanying poems, its focus is on the western tip of Cornwall. For Andy and Vally Cornwall's geographical remoteness, its abiding attraction as a holiday location, its proud mining and fishing history and the varying and often dramatic moods of its weather and sea are an inspiration and a cause for celebration.

The profound emotional and psychological effects on visitors to Cornwall is not lost on the authors, who have a long association with the area.

Way to the West is a celebration of the natural world and the home, the past and the present, and of the fierce interconnectedness of people with their landscape.

Renard Press (2023)

Printed in Dunstable, United Kingdom